Public Confessions The Religious Conversions That Changed American Politics

REBECCA L. DAVIS

THE UNIVERSITY OF

NORTH CAROLINA PRESS

Chapel Hill

Set in Miller and Walbaum types by Tseng Information Systems, Inc.
Manufactured in the United States of America

The University of North Carolina Press has been a member
of the Green Press Initiative since 2003.

Jacket photographs: (left to right) White House Special Counsel Chuck Colson,
ca. 1969. Courtesy Wikimedia Commons; Claire Boothe Luce speaking at
Republican National Convention, 1944. Courtesy Library of Congress, Prints
and Photographs Division, NYWT&S Collection; and Muhammad Ali at a
National Islam meeting, 1966. Photo © Roger Malloch / Magnum Photos.

Library of Congress Cataloging-in-Publication Data
Names: Davis, Rebecca L. (Rebecca Louise), 1975– author.
Title: Public confessions : the religious conversions that changed
American politics / Rebecca L. Davis.
Description: Chapel Hill : The University of North Carolina Press, [2021] |
Includes bibliographical references and index.
Identifiers: LCCN 2021010003 | ISBN 9781469664873 (cloth) |
ISBN 9781469664880 (ebook)
Subjects: LCSH: Conversion—History—20th century. | Religion and
politics—United States—History—20th century. | United States—
Politics and government—20th century.
Classification: LCC BL2525 .D4235 2021 | DDC 322/.10973—dc23
LC record available at https://lccn.loc.gov/2021010003

Portions of chapter 4 first appeared in *American Jewish History* 100, no. 1
(January 2016): 25–50. Copyright © 2016 The American Jewish Historical
Society.

Letter from Erich Fromm to Thomas Merton quoted with permission
of the Thomas Merton Center and the Erich Fromm literary estate.

For Jonathan and Hannah

Contents

PROLOGUE

Faith in Democracy   1

CHAPTER 1

A Catholic Message for America   12

CHAPTER 2

Cold War Disclosures   43

CHAPTER 3

The Fear of False Belief   67

CHAPTER 4

A Kind of Oneness with the Jewish People   92

CHAPTER 5

I Know the Truth   121

CHAPTER 6

Redemption   143

EPILOGUE

Authentic Politics, Passing Faiths   175

Acknowledgments   181

Notes   187

Bibliography   211

Index   243

Figures

Clare Boothe Luce, 1944   15

Bishop Fulton J. Sheen, 1952   23

Clare Boothe Luce in *McCall's*, 1947   33

Elizabeth Bentley, 1951   50

Whittaker Chambers, 1948   53

Marilyn Monroe's certificate of conversion, 1956   97

Elizabeth Taylor and Eddie Fisher,

    with Rabbi Nussbaum, 1959   101

Sammy Davis Jr. and May Britt, 1960   108

Muhammad Ali at the annual Saviour's Day

    celebration in Chicago, 1974   140

Susan Atkins at her trial, 1969   144

Poster for the *Born Again* film, 1978   164

Prologue Faith in Democracy

Picture the scene: The towers of Rockefeller Center cloak the gray stones of St. Patrick's Cathedral in afternoon shadow as a car slows to a stop by the curb. Clare Boothe Luce, an acclaimed playwright, member of Congress, and wife of publisher Henry Luce, alights. Fashionably lean and expensively attired, she ascends several steps to a small plaza and passes through a massive bronze door. On this Saturday in February 1946, a few weeks shy of her forty-third birthday, she stands on the threshold of a new chapter in her storied but privately troubled life. She has experienced too much loss to be idealistic, but she now believes in redemption, for herself and for the world. Pain and hope led her to this cathedral and to the man facing her. In moments he will cast out her demons, consecrate her conversion, and baptize her a Roman Catholic.

Monsignor Fulton J. Sheen is as meticulously clothed and coiffed as Luce is. A silk skullcap covers his immovable black hair; his deep-set eyes seem to blaze with intensity. For occasions such as this Sheen wears his formal vestments: a floor-length black cassock and a long, narrow stole that drapes downward from his shoulders. Famous for converting ex-Communists, several world-renowned musicians, and business titans including Henry Ford II, Sheen is minutes away from his most celebrated conversion of all. Luce and Sheen: even their names glow.[1]

Clare Boothe Luce was one of the most admired women in the mid-twentieth-century United States, even if little remembered after her death in 1987. Her actions that February day at St. Patrick's Cathedral made international news. Conversion to Roman Catholicism from Protestantism was the consequence of her most intimate struggles, but she and Sheen deliberately transformed it into a public confession of political resolve. At a time when a majority of Americans suspected Roman Catho-

1

lics of being unpatriotic, Sheen and Luce insisted that their faith provided the best defense against Communist persuasion. They argued that the truths of Roman Catholic theology upheld democracy.

To her critics, Clare Luce's Catholic conversion was outrageous. It was especially audacious coming from the wife of Henry Luce, the notably Presbyterian son of missionaries and the publisher of *Time*, *Life*, and *Fortune*. Surely, Clare was the victim of nefarious, authoritarian priests who co-opted her free will. The barrage of irate letters she received in response to the announcement of her conversion—an announcement she amplified in an article published across three spring issues of *McCall's* magazine in 1947—indicated how much her public expression of personal faith pushed the acceptable boundaries of religious identity. So hostile were so many of these letters that she even lost a deal with *McCall's* to write a regular advice column. The vitriol directed at Clare Luce presaged the upheaval that greeted other controversial religious converts in the decades after World War II.

The religious conversions of certain well-known writers, entertainers, athletes, and politicians elicited frenzied responses. The importance of these conversions extended beyond questions of why certain faiths appealed to a particular individual or how believers experienced their spiritual journeys. Some notable converts described how they discovered their "real" self when they changed or discovered religion. Others spoke of spiritual transformations. In doing so, they offered ways for other people to imagine the outer limits of self-invention. Yet religious conversions in the decades after World War II equally raised fears as well as hopes. They provoked unsettling questions about the survival of individual autonomy amid a seeming surge of mass conformity. Had a person truly transformed, or were they "passing" or even brainwashed?[2]

Consider the example of Whittaker Chambers, a former Soviet spy. Chambers rose to national notoriety in 1948, when he identified Alger Hiss, a former State Department official with a sterling reputation, as a member of the Communist underground. Over two trials that became emblematic of domestic anti-Communist fervor, Hiss swore that he had no connection to Communist espionage activities, but he was found guilty of perjury and spent eight years in prison. For his part, Chambers credited his newly adopted Christian faith with inspiring not only his rejection of Communism but also, he privately confessed, the end of his sexual interest in men. Liberals who defended Hiss were unconvinced. They circulated rumors that Chambers was a "queer" and sought proof that his conversion was a fraud. If religion could help individuals like Chambers go straight, evidence of religious artifice might illuminate sexual as well as political deceptions. The authenticity of one seemed to bear consequences for the veracity of the others.

Other religious conversions sparked allegations of racial masquerade and ethnic betrayal. When the entertainer Sammy Davis Jr. converted from Protestantism to Judaism in 1960, his white and Black critics accused him of trying to pass as white or curry favor with Jewish audiences. Cassius Clay, who became Cassius X and then Muhammad Ali when he converted to the Nation of Islam in the 1960s, instigated even more outrage. His conversion cost him his title and the best years of his career. Allegations flew that the Nation's leaders brainwashed him. Brainwashing, a term coined to describe supposed Communist mind control, became the default explanation for politically unpalatable religious choices.

Fears of false witness, imposture, and mind control influenced the very ways in which Americans responded to public confessions. Those fears grew from the often unspoken presumptions people held about what an authentic convert looked like or how one behaved. Individuals learned about these conversions with their own expectations already in place about what made a man masculine or a woman feminine, which behaviors signaled that a person was heterosexual or homosexual, and whether racial identities were permeable or fixed. They felt they knew what was normal—and what was not. The religious conversions this book discusses challenged those expectations, with the result that formerly unspoken expectations about sex, race, and authenticity grew more urgent within American politics.

In the early 1970s, evangelical Protestant conservatives transformed fears of brainwashing into a campaign to catapult their faith to the center of American politics. No event better encapsulated the effects of evangelical assertions of religious and political authenticity than the news in 1973 that Chuck Colson, President Richard Nixon's former advisor, had been born again in Christ. Colson was convicted in the Watergate cover-up and went to prison, emerging months later more convinced than ever that Jesus Christ paved the road to salvation. Evangelicals eagerly promoted Colson's story and those of other surprising Protestant converts. They contrasted their authentic Christian faith with the coercive methods of "cults," which attracted American young people in seemingly growing numbers from the late 1960s through the early 1980s.

Such publicly important religious converts as Luce, Chambers, Davis,

Ali, and Colson moved claims of religious authenticity to the center of American political debates. Not all of these individuals attained celebrity status, but their renown among their contemporaries generated wide-ranging interest about their lives. In family magazines, radio and television programs, lecture tours, best-selling books, and films, their stories played upon the stage of public imagination, acting out the drama of self-discovery and transformation. Their conversions spoke directly to questions of whether and how different kinds of faith variously anchored or undermined American freedoms.[3]

Why all the fuss? Religious conversion has not attracted much media attention or shaped American politics significantly since the 1990s. That disinterest is likely in part due to a Protestant-Catholic rapprochement that coalesced in the 1970s, as conservatives forged alliances in defense of "Christian America." This partnership prioritized comity on issues such as abortion and gay rights and minimized formerly divisive theological differences. The public response to Protestant-Catholic conversions in the 1990s and later hardly resembles the animus that Clare Boothe Luce faced in the 1940s. Newt Gingrich, former Speaker of the House and Georgia congressman, converted to Roman Catholicism in 2009 as he married his third wife, Callista, having left the Lutheranism of his childhood for the Southern Baptist Church years earlier. The *New York Times* noted that the very uncontroversial qualities of his conversion attested to the strength of conservative political partnerships among Catholics and evangelical Protestants. As historian Bethany Moreton writes of Gingrich, "only his conversion to Catholicism actually convinced many that Gingrich had sincerely been, in effect, born again." In the case of Marco Rubio, the presidential candidate and senator from Florida, his journey from a Roman Catholic childhood into the Church of Jesus Christ of Latter-day Saints and then back to Catholicism (while attending his wife's Southern Baptist congregation) may illustrate his tendency to calibrate his beliefs according to his audience. It also indicates the extent to which political conservatism has become a big tent for a variety of religious affiliations. A majority white conservative movement prized issues like small government, "family values," and muscular militancy over doctrinal details.[4]

Religious conversions mattered far more to American politics at mid-century because they encapsulated the era's religious enthusiasm and its spiritual panic. Part of that enthusiasm emerged out of a relatively new movement for interfaith partnership. Starting in the 1930s, members of interfaith coalitions argued that Jews, Catholics, and Protestants shared

"Judeo-Christian" values. Those values helped forge American democracy; American democracy likewise depended on a defense of the freedom of conscience. This ecumenical vision inspired President Franklin Roosevelt to include freedom of worship among the "four freedoms" the United States and its allies pursued in World War II. At the same time, a parallel celebration of the phrase "Judeo-Christian" ethos argued that Christianity, having superseded Judaism, was democracy's anchor. Even liberal Protestants worried about full-throated pluralism. In the 1940s, editors of the *Christian Century*, which encompassed primarily nonevangelical Protestant viewpoints, published a multipart series about whether Catholicism could "win America" and what might happen to the nation's "Christian" character if it did. These mainline Protestants presented the nation's moral direction as a choice between Protestant, Catholic, and secular values; they worried that both Catholics and secularists were steadily outstripping Protestants as shapers of the nation's politics and culture.[5]

The horrors of the Nazi genocide of Europe's Jews awakened many Americans to the fragility of religious freedom, but it was the start of the Cold War in 1947 that thrust questions about democracy and religion to the center of U.S. politics. As the Soviet Union shifted from ally to antagonist, American military and political leaders pitted a God-loving America against a faithless Communist threat. President Harry Truman, cabinet secretaries, and foreign policy advisors explained that America's religious values enabled the nation to prevail over the atheistic materialism of Communist authoritarianism. Democracy, the dominant U.S. political narrative went, insured freedom of worship and free markets. As a politics of consensus dominated U.S. politics in the 1940s and 1950s, major partisan differences briefly subsided to forge a centrist opposition to Communism, one that was premised on the connection between piety and freedom.[6]

Religion grew even more publicly political in the 1950s. "In God We Trust" was added to currency and "under God" to the Pledge of Allegiance. These slogans were not merely the products of political hucksters but the consequences of partnerships among businessmen and politicians that took shape in the 1930s. By the early Cold War years, that merging of interests was on display at National Prayer Breakfasts and conferences where corporate leaders prayed with elected officials. The federal government, meanwhile, launched a public relations campaign against Communism at home and abroad. That campaign emphasized the difference between American "religious freedom" and the anti-religious activities of Communist dictatorships. U.S. government-sponsored performances by patriotic musicians, actors, and other celebrities were meant to demonstrate the fruits of democracy and capitalism. Together, these efforts promoted the twin meanings of "Judeo-Christian America": support for religious pluralism and faith in the Christian and capitalist foundations of American democracy.[7]

It was amid these high-stakes political maneuvers that more Americans than ever made time for prayer and gave money to religious organizations. Baptism numbers rose and the membership rolls of church and synagogue lengthened. By 1949, religiously affiliated people in the United States collectively spent $1 billion on new construction of churches and religious schools, indelibly shaping the landscape of new, mostly white suburbs. Whether or not religious affiliation correlated to religious practice, surveys showed high levels of faith, belief in God, and prayer. Religious conservatives later pointed to these decades as a time when the Supreme Court clamped down on religious speech with decisions that limited prayer in school, but religion unquestionably flourished at mid-century.[8]

Protestant leaders of the Black freedom movement of the 1950s and 1960s complicated the conversation about the partnership between faith and democracy. Mainstream civil rights leaders agreed that Judeo-Christian faith aligned with freedom, and they argued that racism defiled the American experiment. Certainly, the United States, despite its religious heritage, had not guaranteed their rights. Civil rights activists demanded remedies to address failures of American democracy at home and support for the struggles of oppressed people around the world. Contrasts they drew between Jim Crow segregation in the United States and the formal racial equality found in socialist nations embarrassed the U.S. political establishment while revealing the blatant racial exclusions that defined American life. Other Black leaders created new faiths, including the Nation of Islam, that rejected American liberal democracy and demanded racial separation. For groups like the Nation, religious and racial identities combined to create new narratives of their origins, heritage, and places of belonging.[9]

An undercurrent of anxiety thrummed beneath this postwar religious enthusiasm. Arguments for religion's role in sustaining democracy flourished alongside an equally potent fear of false beliefs. Evidence of "Manchurian candidates," such as the American POWs who refused repatriation from North Korea in the 1950s, provoked panic about the weakness of American minds. Even Americans might succumb to totalitarian belief systems. Social scientists likewise observed a troubling loss of individuality under the pressures of mass culture. Anthropologists and psychologists unpacked the mysteries of individual and corporate identities with theories about gender roles, sexual desires, and national character. Psychoanalytic psychologist Erik Erikson named the "identity crisis," while exiled academics of the Frankfurt School debated the existence of an "authoritarian personality" that preferred totalitarian rule. Mid-twentieth-century academics and their audiences examined the coercive tendencies of mass culture and the vulnerability of individualism. Perhaps these converts displayed not authentic belief but the consequences of coercive mind control.[10]

Clare Boothe Luce exemplified these overlapping enthusiasms and fears, and her story riveted the public. By making religious conversion public, Luce and others showed that the discovery of one's inner truth could guide the course of American politics. She spoke and wrote prolifically about the "real reason" for her conversion to Roman Catholicism. Luce's model of religious commitment and sacrifice varied widely from the superficial advice that men like the Reverend Norman Vincent Peale circulated. Peale warned as early as the 1930s that the world must choose between Christ and Marx, and he promised that a choice for Christ paved the way for personal success. In his sermons, *Guideposts* magazine, and his best-selling book, *The Power of Positive Thinking* (1952), Peale championed a model of Christian faith as positive self-talk, one that resulted in concrete financial and personal rewards. Plenty of serious religious thinkers worried that not only Peale but also the evangelical superstar Billy Graham made faith captive to capitalism and mass culture, their messages of salvation simplified for wide distribution through books, magazines, televised revivals, and radio spots. (Former president and television personality Donald Trump grew up in Peale's church and adopted Peale's mantra of transactional faith. That preference for positive thinking carried over to his reliance on Paula White-Cain, a preacher within the prosperity gospel tradition, as his spiritual advisor while he was in office.)[11]

Mass-circulated religious stories did not so much co-opt sincere religious identity as create pathways for the believer's expression of an authentic religious self. Unlike many media stars, well-known converts advertised not a superficial or imagined ideal but a promise of authenticity grounded in religious truth. Stories of religious choice, reproduced and circulated through mass culture, helped people puzzle through the problems of modern life.

The Christian model of conversion as the beginning of a new or reborn self originates with Saint Augustine of Hippo. He lived in the fourth century CE, a time of rising and falling empires, when conversion often meant the external movement of people from one faith or ethnic group to another (or from pagan to Christian). Augustine added a second meaning, about an interior journey. He wrote in his *Confessions* of his libertine youth, when his faith in secular and scientific authority blinded him to his sin. When he awoke to his errors and accepted God's grace, his new faith illuminated all that once seemed opaque. He wrote that he had been working hard in the field, "and the field of my labors is my own self."[12]

The Augustinian model of a self transformed is not the only way to narrate conversion's arc. A convert may experience an "awakening" or describe his or her spiritual journey as a homecoming. When the British writer and future Catholic cardinal John Henry Newman described his adoption of Roman Catholicism in the nineteenth century, he used metaphors of familiarity. Becoming Catholic, he wrote, was "like coming into port after a rough sea." About 100 years later, as chapter 4 describes, American entertainer Sammy Davis Jr. said that when he became a Jew, he found the faith that best expressed the self he already possessed; deep down, he explained, he had "always been a Jew." Many faiths require more than a shift in self-perception for an authentic conversion. Their converts must learn a sacred language or memorize a liturgy. Conversion may require the abrogation of ethnic bonds or the loss of family relationships. The individual changes his or her outlook and behavior to conform to "truth"; the soul's discovery of religious principles reveals a true self.[13]

Perhaps a conversion narrative can never provide a factual description of what "actually happened" during a conversion. The writer or speaker is creating a representation of him or herself; each word choice is like a stroke of a paintbrush on canvas, creating a portrait that resembles, but cannot fully replicate, the person who inspired it. The portrait usually conforms to the expectations of its genre. That representation may appear "authentic" to its creator and to others who encounter it, but we are aware that we are viewing a subjective account rather than documentary footage. This interpretation of conversion narratives diverges sharply from the ways many converts describe their experiences as "true," "real," and absolute, and it also challenges the work of scholars who continue to insist on the transparent knowableness of a person's religious identity.[14]

A conversion nevertheless seems to explain something fundamental about the arc of self-discovery. A spate of memoirs by white southerners published since the mid-twentieth century describe a kind of ideological conversion: after upbringings immersed in white supremacist culture, the authors experienced revelations about society's sins and rejected their families' racist values. Feminist anthropologists concluded that many women who participated in the women's liberation movement in the early 1970s had experiences akin to conversion, including the "bridge-burning" actions that often accompany a convert's rejection of a prior belief system. Early twenty-first-century "conversion" narratives often featured stories of apostasy, of rejecting an encompassing faith in favor of secular knowledge. Spokespeople for the "new atheism" explained that scientific evidence repudiated their former theologies; ex-Scientologists described their physical and intellectual escapes from the captivity of the group's strict roles and orthodoxy. The list goes on.[15]

Religious conversions suffuse U.S. history. At the time of the nation's founding, with few preachers and vast square acres of territory, the newly independent nation had much to say about religion in print but very little of organized religious practice on the ground. Untold numbers of babies went unbaptized, and many marriages remained informally acknowledged. Methodist and Baptist revivals in the early nineteenth century transformed American religious life, spreading faiths that embraced dramatic conversion experiences. Young people whose parents lived in common-law arrangements hired preachers for their weddings; congregations sawed lumber to build chapels and fashion pews. Sanctuaries filled each Sunday morning and the weekdays in between with the fervently devoted. Protestant and Catholic missions spread across the states and territories of the United States, Bible societies and Christian newsletters proliferated, and religious societies launched overseas missions throughout the world. Missions expanded the resources and power of American Protestant and Catholic groups. They missionized each other, and they focused their energies on people who seemed ripe for transformation, whether Native Americans or Jews, even when their success rates were consistently low.[16]

By the late nineteenth century, Americans insisted that religion was a choice rather than an inheritance or imposition. Conversion combined the exercise of free will and the intercession of the divine. Americans largely relegated to the historical past the idea that conversion occurred at the tip of a sword—or the barrel of a gun. This understanding of conversion as proof of religious liberty persisted despite evidence to the contrary. American imperialists wielded religious freedom like a cudgel to punish non-Christians and, very often, nonwhite people. In the Philippines in the late 1890s, U.S. military and political leaders justified their violent colonization of the islands as a way to introduce (Christian) religious freedom to a foreign people (most of whom were already Catholics).[17]

An American flair for spiritual innovation created faiths that drew converts in from agnosticism and away from mainline Protestant denominations. Religious movements such as the Church of Jesus Christ of Latter-day Saints, Seventh-day Adventism, Christian Science, and Jehovah's Witnesses grew from the rocky soils of New England and the fertile plains of the Midwest like untended weeds, spreading and reshaping the landscape. Holiness and Pentecostal believers gathered in barns in the South and, by the early twentieth century, on street corners in Los Angeles. The drive for converts survived the industrial transformations that made the United States a global economic power by the late nineteenth century and that drew a majority of the American population to its cities by the 1920s. Religion ascended the elevators of skyscrapers, animated the daily toil of men digging wells for oil in Texas, and moved along the assembly lines of factory floors. Christian businessmen's associations opened branches in Omaha and Chicago; in the 1940s and 1950s, southern evangelicals migrated westward to establish Pepperdine College in Los Angeles and teach the gospel of the free market. Capitalism nurtured rather than undermined Americans' spiritual devotions.[18]

Devout Americans worshipped God in novel ways. They received revelations and transcribed new scriptures; they evangelized and congregated; they published and circulated, preached and mourned. Apostates left their families; other converts convinced their immediate and extended family members to join them in separating from their inherited traditions or communities. Sometimes conversions appeared in waves, the ripple effects of revivals and the charismatic presence of spiritual virtuosos. At other times conversions occurred less dramatically, as two people of different faiths met and wed, with one partner adopting the faith of the other.

Tales of conversion have mattered throughout U.S. history as stories about faiths lost and found and of meanings rediscovered. In the immediate decades after World War II, religious conversions and the responses they elicited bore unique, political significance. Personal motivations certainly shaped why Clare Boothe Luce chose Catholicism, Whittaker Chambers became a Quaker, Sammy Davis Jr. converted to Judaism, Cassius Clay/Muhammad Ali joined the Nation of Islam, and Chuck Colson became a born-again Protestant. Far beyond their importance to particular religious traditions or as life events for the individuals concerned, these conversions galvanized associations between spiritual, sexual, racial, and political authenticity. Close attention to these stories illuminates the prolific intellectual production that occurs outside the walls of the academy or seminary. In living rooms and on television screens, in the pages of magazines and in stadium arenas, public confessions made religious authenticity matter to American politics.[19]

As news of Clare Boothe Luce's conversion spread in 1946, eight secretaries employed in her congressional office could not keep up with the volume of letters that poured in. Converting to Catholicism was a personal decision intended to satisfy an intrinsic need, but its effects were immediately political. Luce marveled, disingenuously, at how her personal story mattered to the public; that was, of course, her point.[20]

Chapter 1 A Catholic Message for America

Clare Boothe Luce entered St. Patrick's Cathedral in February 1946 eager to devote herself to the church that she believed embodied the truest form of Christianity. Roman Catholic doctrines satisfied her supple mind; the church's theology of sacrifice reverberated with her own experiences of pain and loss. The cathedral's soot-darkened windows permitted little daylight to illuminate the arches that bracketed the vast ceiling, but Luce and Monsignor Fulton Sheen gathered with a small group that radiated an energy of its own. A Jesuit priest who served as an early source of spiritual encouragement joined them, along with an aide from Luce's congressional office, a journalist who was also planning to convert, and a childhood friend who was her chosen godmother. Clare Luce's husband, the publisher Henry R. Luce, was not among this small but serious party; he was likely in California with his girlfriend. Clare Boothe Luce declared aloud her faith in Jesus Christ. Sheen made the sign of the cross on her forehead and chest, then laid his hands on her head and spoke a Latin blessing. Lifting his hands heavenward, he prayed for God to send a protecting angel to lead Luce toward the grace of baptism. In Latin he may have addressed the "foul fiend" of demonic powers: "I cast you out, unclean Spirit." Then Sheen led Luce's party deeper into the cathedral.[1]

They must have sensed that they were making history, attuned as they were to how their actions united them with a powerful, eternal truth. The cathedral was quiet but for the occasional tourists staring up at its famed rose windows, believers whispering devotions to one of the saints in the ornate side chapels or praying the rosary in the pews, and perhaps a few priests reciting prayers. If any of these people looked toward the small group walking down the aisle they might have recognized Luce. She was famous, known as the author of the plays *The Women* (1936), a scathing examination of wealthy women's relationships that became the first

Broadway play with an all-female cast, and *Kiss the Boys Goodbye* (1939). Luce was also well known as a journalist, and she was one of only seven women then serving in Congress. She was fair, blond, and slender. Sheen turned heads as well. Perhaps the best-known American Catholic of his age, he preached his message of faith and anti-Communism to millions during NBC radio's *Catholic Hour* on Sunday evenings and received thousands of letters each week from listeners.

Within hours of her conversion Luce became one of the most famous Catholics in the world. Sheen issued a statement later that afternoon. Radio broadcasts carried news of Luce's conversion into hundreds of thousands of U.S. homes before she even sat down to dinner. Luce issued a statement announcing that because she did not want her faith to become a political liability, she would not seek further elective office. The next morning, Catholics who missed the radio announcement heard about it in their priests' homilies. The *New York Times* announced, "Clare Boothe Luce Becomes a Catholic," on its front page. The sexism that dogged Luce's career in Congress, and throughout her life, colored the announcement of her conversion: "Pretty, prim, progressive Clare Boothe Luce, dynamic Congresswoman from Connecticut," the *Cleveland Call and Post* wrote, "surprised her constituents and the nation." The conversion was cheered in the Catholic press, with stories featuring a picture of a smiling Luce adjacent to articles about Cardinal Francis Spellman, one of the most prominent Roman Catholic leaders in the United States, or the pope.[2]

Clare Boothe Luce wanted to share her story of spiritual truth with the world because she believed that nothing less than democracy was at stake. In a life full of disappointment and loss, Luce found solace in her chosen faith and purpose in her political work. Surrounded by the engines of mass culture, she recalibrated them to suit her purposes. Luce employed her skills as a writer and orator to portray spiritual Catholicism and materialist Communism as world-historical antagonists, a key contrast within the vernacular of Cold War political discourse. Authentic and free, she argued, Catholic converts held the future for American power and democracy.[3]

Several powerful Roman Catholic priests helped Luce make her case. Monsignor (later, Bishop) Fulton Sheen tutored her in Catholic dogma and in American Catholic anti-Communism. After she converted and began to debate with her Protestant critics, Father Joseph I. Malloy helped her provide learned responses to the most prejudicial accusations about Roman Catholic belief and papal authority. Both men aided Luce in crafting a public argument about how Roman Catholic faith would halt the spread of Communism abroad; her faith served political as well as spiritual ends. In 1941, her husband, Henry Luce, wrote "The American Century," his case for American international superiority, which he grounded in his own Presbyterian faith. Clare Luce did not want American Protestant values imposed abroad. Instead, she believed that Roman Catholic faith could inoculate each person's soul against the infectious thrall of Communist ideology. Amid the popularity of "Judeo-Christian" ecumenism, she championed Roman Catholicism as the faith best suited to what she believed to be the uniquely free qualities of U.S. democracy. Clare Luce used her public profile and journalistic chops to move erudite debates over religious democracy out of the academy and into family magazines and the popular press. She presented religious conversion to the masses as the surest path both to a "real," authentic self and to democratic freedoms.[4]

Roman Catholicism entered Clare Boothe Luce's life at a time when she was seeking a spiritual home. By the time she reached her early forties, her personal life was shattered. Contrary to media profiles that portrayed her as living a life of ease, Clare had a difficult upbringing, especially after her father deserted the family when she was eight. Encouraged by her aspiring mother to marry rich, Clare wed a dissolute millionaire, George Brokaw, in 1923, when she was twenty. A year later she gave birth to her only child, Ann Clare Brokaw, whom she adored, while George busied himself with golf and alcohol. Clare's friend and biographer Wilfrid Sheed wrote that George, when drunk, "swatted Clare around enough, possibly, to have produced her three miscarriages: the school of hard knocks indeed, long before Clare entered public life." Rejecting her mother's advice to stick it out until George drank himself to death, Clare divorced him in 1929. The alimony was generous, and it sustained her lifestyle as she launched a career as a writer at *Vogue*, an editor of *Vanity Fair* by age thirty-three, and an acclaimed playwright.[5]

Marriage to the publisher Henry Luce in 1935 vaulted Clare into the inner circles of American cultural power. At first blush, Henry (called Harry by friends) seemed to be the ideal spouse for Clare, an intellectual partner who never asked her to compromise her ambitions. The publisher of *Time* and *Fortune* when he married Clare, Harry was a serious man with deep insecurities. Of average height, bald, and with thick dark eyebrows and doughy cheeks, he demanded that the world take him seri-

Clare Boothe Luce controversially criticized President Franklin Roosevelt for his handling of World War II—and coined the term "GI Joe"—during a blistering keynote address at the Republican National Convention in Chicago in 1944. (Courtesy Library of Congress, Prints and Photographs Division, NYWT&S Collection, LC-DIG-ppmsca-24312)

ously. His magazine empire, which grew to include *Life* magazine in 1936 and *Sports Illustrated* in 1954, was a personal testament to his own importance and power. When Harry and Clare first met, at a party, they talked about his magazines before he checked his watch and left abruptly. The third time they met, he proposed. She accepted. Clare enjoyed the company of smart men willing to take her ideas seriously, and Harry gave her that. Nicknamed "Arsenic and Old Luce," Clare and Henry Luce became a power couple at the center of American politics and culture.[6]

The price was sex. Harry experienced periodic impotence with various lovers; with Clare, his problem was persistent. As Wilfrid Sheed quipped, "Harry's famous conscience made it impossible for him to conduct two affairs at once." As a devout Presbyterian, Harry struggled to reconcile his rigid moral philosophy with his divorce from his first wife, Lila, and his ongoing infidelities.[7]

What Clare's marriage to Harry lacked in sexual fidelity it compensated for, to a degree, in political access. In the early 1930s, before she met Harry, Clare supported Franklin Delano Roosevelt's 1932 presidential campaign; Wilfrid Sheed explained that she served as "a scullery maid" in FDR's kitchen cabinet. Harry's obsession with "saving" China from Communism likely persuaded Clare to abandon the political Left. Harry's attachment to nationalist China was visceral: he was born there amid Protestant evangelizing, and he believed fervently in the consonance between Christianity, capitalism, and democracy. Apart from Harry's influence, Clare grew disgusted with FDR's isolationism, blasting him in a highly publicized speech in 1940 for failing to build up the U.S. military as Britain and France struggled against Nazi aggression. She announced her support for the Republican presidential candidate, Wendell Willkie, as a man of military action.[8]

Her concerns about military strategy and foreign policy motivated her to run for the House of Representatives in 1942 as a Republican from Connecticut's Fourth District. When she narrowly won election that November, she joined a group of seven female members of Congress, six of them fellow Republicans. She represented the vanguard of a "New Republicanism" that challenged the isolationism of the Republican establishment. She urged others in the GOP to cooperate with Roosevelt on his social programs while demanding a far more aggressive military strategy to combat fascism. Echoing Wendell Willkie's 1940 presidential campaign, Clare delivered a ferocious critique of Roosevelt's leadership of the war. She offered few specifics of what he might have done differently aside from having a unified military command. The voters in her district re-elected her to Congress in 1944.[9]

Luce pursued bold foreign policy ideas and confronted relentless sexism throughout her two terms in the House. Other members of Congress and journalists homed in on her glib terminology, largely ignoring the substance of her policy critiques. She urged a more global and interventionist approach to combating Communism and promoting democracy. The *New York Daily News* called Luce the "3-B candidate"—"blonde, beautiful, brilliant." She developed a reputation as a Republican firebrand after her first speech from the House floor in February 1943, in which she referred to Vice President Henry Wallace's proposal for postwar freedom of the skies as "globaloney," mocking his idea as an ill-advised alternative to existing policies of the sovereignty of the skies. She hardly uttered a word in committee that did not make the papers, and the "globaloney" comment was widely ridiculed; even *Collier's* titled an otherwise favorable profile of her "The Globaloney Girl." Reporters harped on trivial "cat fights" between her and the other female representatives or on what Luce wore. Rumors occasionally flew that her nose was a little smaller or a tad straighter over time. Clare cared about how she looked, but she also had ideas. The press picked apart her personality. On the occasions when journalists and fellow members of Congress conceded that she both was attractive and made substantive contributions to policy discussions, they impugned her character. A 1943 profile described Luce in Congress as both a delicate female, "serene as a fairy queen in a circle of lucent moonlight," and as someone so unfeeling and brittle that she was insulated from "the thin chill that protects dry ice from careless handling." Luce polished her public image, posing for photos in glamorous attire and with her hair stylishly coiffed. That feminine self-presentation had the unintended consequence of overshadowing her intellect, as reporters breathlessly described her as a ditzy blonde. Given that the press denigrated less fashionable women in politics for being dowdy scolds, the problem was not her attire but her sex, so at odds with expectations for political leadership and strategic thought.[10]

Any faith Clare maintained in human reason evaporated by the end of World War II. The success of her career as both a journalist and a politician meant that she witnessed episodes of genocide firsthand. On assignment for *Life* in 1941 she toured decimated regions of Burma, where the corpses of infants clogged rivers. In 1945, as a member of the Military Affairs Committee, she witnessed the liberation of a European concentration camp and the skeletal bodies of the survivors. She feared that humanity was destined to repeat its worst mistakes. A wary observer of Stalin's aspirations for European hegemony, she predicted a global catastrophe between Christian democracies and Communist tyranny. After the suicides of several of her friends in the late 1930s and early 1940s, including the death of her mother by possible suicide in 1938, she searched for answers to questions of existence and suffering. A 1941 profile in the *New Yorker* portrayed her as a woman who never knew adversity, a fairytale princess with "many good fairy godmothers" who blessed her with "Beauty ... Wealth ... Talent ...Industriousness ... and Success"; that was the public persona she cultivated, but it could not account for her intense need for spiritual answers.[11]

Tragedy closer to home ultimately brought Clare's existential crisis to the brink. On the morning of Tuesday, January 11, 1944, her daughter, Ann, by then a student at Stanford University, caught a ride to Palo Alto with a friend from her sorority. Their convertible was about two blocks away from campus when a car emerging from a side street collided with it from behind. Ann was thrown from the vehicle, and her head struck a tree. She died before reaching the hospital. A prolific writer, Clare struggled for words that could express her grief. Clare later described her reaction to Ann's death as a "nervous breakdown." She twice attempted suicide. As she wrote in a widely discussed article in *McCall's* three years later, "the sudden death of my daughter sharply bolted the door on the last happy answer that seemed to exist to the problem of my life. And hers." A serious student, Ann adored her glamorous mother. Although Clare seldom spoke about Ann's death, she described Ann as "my true love." Her search for a faith emerged from agonized thoughts about whether Ann's soul entered heaven or if her daughter was "rotting" in the ground. She and Harry initially grew closer; he "briefly suspended" his affair with the publicist Jean Dalrymple and attempted to supervise Clare's care as she struggled with severe depression.[12]

Clare Luce's political style became harder edged and aggressively partisan after Ann's death. Less than six months after the accident she delivered a headline-grabbing keynote speech at the Republican National Convention in Philadelphia in which she contrasted the fates of "GI Joe and GI Jim": the former returned home to a hero's parade, while the other lay in an unmarked grave. (Coinage of "GI Joe" is one of her many legacies.) She blamed Roosevelt and his Democratic policy makers for mismanaging the war and causing Jim's death. Roosevelt dismissed her critiques of his wartime policies as the rants of "a sharp-tongued glamour-girl of 40 who sometimes, when running around the country without a mental protector, puts her dainty foot in her pretty mouth." That snide assessment denigrated her remarks as mere blather, infantilized her, and scorned her as a woman past her prime, insulting Luce's skill in the one arena where she felt she had anything left to contribute.[13]

Luce's courtship with Catholicism began in 1942, when she received an unsolicited letter from a Jesuit priest, Father Edward Wiatrak. Passionate and possibly obsessive, he began to write to her on an almost weekly basis. He esteemed her third among all women, he wrote, following the Blessed Virgin Mary and his own mother. He professed his love repeatedly; "I'm a better Priest because of you," he wrote in late June 1944. Clare found Wiatrak to be a source of spiritual comfort. By the summer of 1944 he was planning a visit to the Luces' home in Ridgefield, Connecticut. Luce sent flowers to his mother in Chicago and corresponded with one of his sisters. In one of his letters Wiatrak compared Luce to a mother whom he "adores": "Honestly, really I could not deem you a sister or think of you in that term. As a mother, a thousand times 'yes.'" Wiatrak's letters to Clare often combined declarations of passion with assertions of spiritual purity. He most likely did not intend to quote the character Molly Bloom's orgasmic closing words from James Joyce's previously banned novel *Ulysses*. If she caught the reference, Clare was likely unbothered by it. After Wiatrak startled a female friend of Clare's, whom he also mentored, by suggesting that she join him on a solo religious retreat, Luce herself admitted that he was "a little unbalanced" and "very highly sexed." Instead, Clare appreciated Wiatrak's ardent enthusiasm for her conversion.[14]

Positive images of Catholicism on-screen and in print may also have helped draw Clare to the faith. The novel *The Song of Bernadette* (1942) by Franz Werfel, a German-speaking Jew from Prague, told the story of a poor French girl visited by the Blessed Virgin. The 1945 film adaptation garnered Jennifer Jones an Academy Award for best actress. Luce admitted that her earliest positive image of a Catholic was a character played by Bing Crosby, likely a reference to his portrayal of a priest in *Going My Way* of 1944. Family magazine features and television programs increasingly portrayed Catholicism as quintessentially American, a faith that promoted communal and national solidarity in the face of external threats.[15]

When Wiatrak stated his adoration of Luce he invoked a long-standing Catholic rebuke of Communism's materialism: Catholic love was pure because it was spiritual, he implied, not crassly sensual. Roman Catholics often critiqued the morass of materialism, which they associated with Communism and other varieties of atheism. Since the mid-nineteenth century, the Roman Catholic hierarchy had vehemently opposed Communism in Europe. Now, as U.S. foreign policy leaders became obsessed with the potential dangers of the Soviet Union, members of the Roman Catholic hierarchy in the United States began to trumpet their long-standing opposition to Communism as evidence that they were democrats and patriots. Materialism implied a denial of the spiritual or divine realms and an insistence on physical gratifications. It was the opposite of the religious exaltations Catholics associated with the Eucharist, a transcendent transformation when wine and bread become the blood and body of Christ. The Eucharist made God's presence real and proved his authority over the crude impulses of the human body. The culture of material abundance that flourished after World War II only intensified this conflict between spiritually transcendent beliefs and the material rewards of mass culture.

Nearly all we know of the details of Luce's decision to become a Roman Catholic comes from her published account, which she wrote as a three-part article for *McCall's* magazine. By the time these articles appeared in the spring of 1947, Luce was vigorously arguing that Roman Catholicism was the faith best suited to American democracy. According to the article, late one night in August 1945, she experienced an emotional breakdown. She was dragged under by the "vast sour tide" of failed dogmas, "futile and sterile relationships," and memories of the deaths of loved ones and of innocents who died during the war. Overcome by "a black riptide of grief," she searched for a source of comfort. Tears led to prayers, and Luce began to recite the only prayer she knew by heart, the Lord's Prayer. Fortuitously, an unopened letter from Wiatrak lay on her desk. In it Wiatrak asked her if she had read the *Confessions* of Saint Augustine of Hippo (354–430 CE), which he urged her to "take and read." In that book Augustine described the sins of his youth, his immersion in the secular Manichaeism and Neoplatonism that were popular among the day's thinkers, and how an epiphany of God's grace led him to embrace a life in the church. Clare said in the *McCall's* article that she found a phone book instead, with the number for the Jesuit residence where Wiatrak lived, although she likely already knew how to reach him. She described their conversation as a plea from the spiritual wilderness: "'Father,' I said, 'I am not in trouble. But my mind is in trouble.' He said, 'We know. This is the call we have been praying for.'" He urged her to contact Monsignor Sheen to begin studying Catholic teachings. The published account made it appear that Luce and Wiatrak had never met. Nor did it mention what Luce's personal correspondence makes clear, that later that same night, Wiatrak came to her apartment to offer solace in person. Comfortable with attracting and managing men's desires, Luce directed Wiatrak's ardor toward her urgent spiritual concerns.[16]

Roman Catholicism became Luce's lifeboat. By the fall of 1945, she was meeting regularly with Monsignor Fulton J. Sheen at his residence in Washington, D.C., poring over books of Catholic theology. She later claimed to have read "hundreds" of books. They debated the truth of Roman Catholic doctrine. In his autobiography Sheen described Luce as his star pupil: "Never in my life have I been privileged to instruct anyone who was as brilliant and who was so scintillating in conversation as Mrs. Luce. She had a mind like a rapier." They were certainly well matched as intellectual partners. She found in Sheen a "brilliant teacher," and he boasted about his student's intelligence. "I am more proud of you than any child I ever begot in Christ," he told her. "I thank God daily that He used me as His poor instrument." Sheen built a reputation as the king of Catholic convert makers, and Clare was the jewel in his crown.[17]

At last Sheen convinced Luce that the Roman Catholic Church was the "true" church. She was never much attached to Protestantism. Her conversion meant not that she rejected one spiritual practice or theological system in favor of a different one but that she discovered a faith that spoke to her in intimate, nearly inexpressible ways. Catholicism offered what she believed to be God's truth of redemptive love. As she explained to one critic, Catholicism seemed the "most reasonable" solution to her mind's puzzles about human nature and God's interest in humanity's fate.[18]

Too busy commenting on Luce's latest gibe or fashion statement, the press missed the story right under its nose. In January 1946, a month before her conversion, Luce issued an opaque statement notifying the public that she had decided not to seek another term in elective office "for reasons which will soon be evident." She found a vocation that could replace politics, imbue her life with a sense of purpose, and answer her questions about life's meaning. Within an hour of issuing that statement Luce received phone calls from four newspaper reporters, each asking when her baby was due.[19]

Monsignor Fulton Sheen knew how to make an entrance. Carrying the honorary title of "Monsignor" when he first met Luce, Sheen eventually traded the priest's garb for the ornate robes of a bishop; he preferred to appear in his long, satin cassock with a cape. He groomed himself with precision. His style of combing his hair back from his high forehead drew attention to his heavy black eyebrows and penetrating stare. Both an elite academic and a religious star, he was a professor at the Catholic University of America in Washington, D.C., and a prolific writer in the neo-Thomist school that emphasized the natural law philosophy of Saint Thomas Aquinas. His scholarly books argued for eternal, divinely authored truths, etched in nature and available for all seekers to discover. He was also American Catholicism's biggest star of radio and, soon, television, presenting an affable if peculiar persona to argue for Catholicism's consonance with contemporary values. Nicknamed the "convert specialist" by *Newsweek* magazine, Sheen presided over the widely publicized conversions of famous ex-Communists and notable former Protestants. Many years after his death, the two-volume dossier presented to the Vatican to argue for his canonization included frequent mentions of his convert-making abilities.[20]

Sheen undoubtedly appreciated that Clare Luce had charisma to spare. Contemporaries attributed to her a personal beauty beyond what photos reveal; self-confidence amplified her natural attributes. Poised for photos she raised her chin and smiled with the self-assurance of the privileged. She leaned in when people spoke to her, met and held their gaze, and gave every assurance that she found them fascinating. She captivated the most powerful people in the room. Her archive holds stashes of letters from generals, members of Congress, editors, and artists professing their love for her—and wondering why she could not arrange her schedule to meet with them once more, after so much time had elapsed since her last letter.

The truths that Sheen and Luce asserted were at once spiritual and polemical. They embarked on their program of global Catholicism because they believed the future of democracy was at stake. Protestantism, with its internecine squabbles and tendency toward factionalism and schism, was simply not up to the challenge.

Sheen described Communism as an imminent threat to democracy and Christianity in works of scholarship, radio addresses, and his instructions to converts. American Catholics had organized in opposition to Communism since the early 1920s, but Sheen was single-minded. The scope of Sheen's anti-Communism was such that even a sympathetic biographer concluded that "if Fulton Sheen did not directly participate in the Second Red Scare, he was instrumental in laying the foundations for it." Anti-

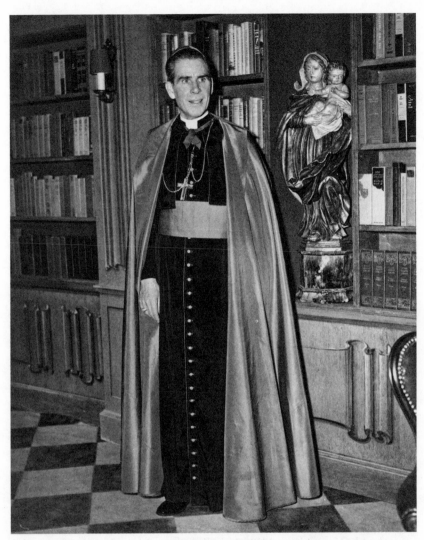

Bishop Fulton J. Sheen, pictured here in 1952, deftly used radio and television, as well as the publicity surrounding the conversions of well-known individuals, to highlight Roman Catholicism's consonance with American democracy. (Courtesy Library of Congress, Prints and Photographs Division; New York World-Telegram *photo by Fred Palumbo, LC-USZ62–123461)*

Communism remained a point of contention among American Catholics, many of whom aligned with the robust Catholic social welfare movement and trade union tradition. Sheen championed anti-Communism without a hint of ambivalence. In the first four months of 1947, he delivered eleven anti-Communist addresses on *The Catholic Hour*, a radio program that reached more than 4 million listeners each week. The argument that Christianity served as a weapon against Communism, the religion of materialism, circulated among Catholic thinkers in the 1920s and 1930s, but it became a kind of Catholic common sense in the 1940s.[21]

Catholics were not the only ones worried about Communism. If Luce and Sheen led the religious anti-Communist charge along the Northeast-mid-Atlantic corridor, evangelical Protestants were at the fore in Southern California. Evangelical preachers in the mold of Billy Graham, as well as fundamentalists such as the Oklahoma-born California preacher Carl McIntire, argued that Christianity was humanity's last buffer against the rising Communist tide. Of course, for these evangelical Cold Warriors, Catholicism was a species of the problem, a false faith whose ecclesiastical power and "collectivism" were as dangerous to Christian democracy as any Communist government.[22]

Luce was convinced that only converts to Catholicism could halt Communism's creep across Europe and Asia. She first delivered this message in a long letter to the *New York Herald Tribune* in November of 1946, and she reiterated it innumerable times thereafter. The stakes were dire: either a world ruled by materialists for whom man "is an animal without a soul"—or a world based on Christian morals. In a speech in 1948 in Salt Lake City, Utah, she called upon Catholics to make converts in order to protect persecuted Catholics abroad and stop the spread of Communism: "If every Roman Catholic made only one convert a year—in seven years the whole world would be Catholic." She was not alone in casting the global situation as an epic confrontation between atheistic Communism and Christian democracies, but she was one of the first to do so. Men said it later and took credit for the idea, and few historians have questioned their version of events.[23]

A vibrant network of Catholic evangelists sought converts. Luce became a supporter of "The Christophers," an anti-Communist Catholic society founded by Father James Keller, who belonged to Maryknoll, a Catholic missionary order. Keller proposed a process of re-Christianization, through which faithful Catholics could create a spiritual bulwark against fascism, Communism, and atheism. In books, pamphlets, and a newsletter, he preached that a deeper commitment to Christ, grounded in a personal relationship with God, could defend American "spiritual values" and help win the war against Communism. In Glendale, California, a laity-focused group called the Convert Makers of America sought to establish Catholic information centers, install racks of pamphlets about Catholicism "in all hotels, bus depots, hospitals, waiting rooms, beauty parlors, and the like," and conduct seminars for interested non-Catholics. Another organization, the Converts' League, hosted speakers, including Clare, and distributed literature. These methods amplified the ongoing efforts of parish priests, many of whom recognized that "never was the time riper for convert-making than today."[24]

Never was the Roman Catholic Church in the United States more self-assured, either. Luce and other famous American converts literally became the poster children of a new form of Catholic outreach that adopted the techniques of modern advertising. The connections between proselytizing for a faith and shucking for customers had precedent; twenty years earlier, a Protestant advertising executive named Bruce Barton innovated many techniques of modern advertising in his best-selling book, *The Man Nobody Knows* (1925), which described Jesus as "the founder of modern business." Catholics apparently took note. In 1943, the Paulist Fathers, an American-born religious order that aimed to bring converts to the church, installed a Catholic Information Center at the prominent corner of Fifty-Ninth Street and Columbus Avenue in New York City. By 1946 one of their attention-grabbing window displays, modeled on "the same business technique" as modern advertising, featured photographs of Henry Ford II, Clare Boothe (misspelled "Booth") Luce, and Senator Robert Wagner: "Why Did These Well-Known Americans Join the Catholic Church? THERE MUST BE A REASON." Ford, Luce, Wagner, and ex-Communist Louis Budenz also appeared in advertisements about inquiry classes that St. Sabina Church in Chicago placed in local newspapers, inviting non-Catholics to discover "Truth, Satisfaction, and Happiness in the Catholic Faith." Luce's fame became an asset for a Catholic Church set on expansion.[25]

Luce's glamor made her an enormously powerful spokesperson for the church. Leaders of the American Catholic Church embraced Luce as their favored messenger to counteract stereotypes of Catholic women: the dull-witted Irish servant parodied as "Bridget" and the celibate nun, portrayed in Protestant print culture as both prudish and as the victim of priests' sexual predation. They recognized that Luce's combination of heterosexual allure, ethnically nonspecific whiteness, literary skill, and charisma could entice a new generation to convert. No priggish nun or dowdy Irish immigrant, she was a white American woman with sex appeal, status, and talent. Wiatrak made no secret of focusing his attentions on attractive female converts. Luce knew that Wiatrak appreciated a physically appealing convert, as well he should, she told a female friend and fellow Catholic convert, "because you can do more for the Church." Luce cultivated her physical appearance her entire life, and she appreciated its value. It helped her navigate a world that discounted her talents, and she could see no good reason to hide it now.[26]

This heroic vision of Catholic Americanism directly challenged Protestant stereotypes about Catholic beliefs and practices. Luce converted to Catholicism at a time when Americans remained deeply divided about the Roman Catholic Church. Since the early nineteenth century anti-Catholicism had roiled American politics and produced a spate of virulently nativist books and plays. Most Protestant Americans suspected that Catholics were more loyal to the pope than to the Constitution. As fascism spread in Europe during the 1920s and 1930s, Pope Pius XI adopted an officially neutral policy toward Italy's Benito Mussolini, and many Italian American Catholics expressed admiration for the fascist leader. During World War II, a new pope, Pius XII, appeared to continue his predecessor's tolerant attitude toward Mussolini and Hitler. The reality was far more complex. Pope Pius XII feigned friendship with Hitler but secretly directed a network of spies who worked for the Vatican to gather damaging information about Nazi campaigns. Critics of Roman Catholicism knew nothing of the church's antifascist espionage and presumed that Pius XI's and Pius XII's public statements in support of Mussolini shaped the church's response to the Axis powers. Protestant anti-Catholicism continued well into the post–World War II years, from scholars who labeled Roman Catholicism antidemocratic, to efforts by Protestant leaders to discredit John F. Kennedy as a credible presidential candidate in 1960.[27]

Anti-Catholic arguments of the 1940s were strikingly similar to those of the 1840s, updated diatribes against the papacy, priestly authority, and Catholicism's incompatibility with democracy for the contemporary political context. Prevalent misunderstandings about the relationship between the Vatican and the Axis powers during World War II revived arguments about the dangers of "Romanism." One woman from Royal Oak,

Michigan, opened her handwritten letter to Luce in 1947 with a sardonic "Congratulations—you have now aligned yourself with the world's greatest force for *war.*" This logic tied Catholicism to criminality; corrupt doctrines produced immoral followers. A man from Amherst, Massachusetts, queried, "Mrs. Luce, tell me this: To what particular creeds or Faiths do the majority of the political crooks, the gangsters, murderers, and lords of the underworld in New York and Chicago belong? Roman Catholic and Jewish, is it not?" The fact that these stereotypes were centuries in the making made them seem true.[28]

Many Protestants saw in Luce's Catholic triumphalism the warning signs of Protestantism's decline. For all the talk about the merits of pluralism during World War II and the Cold War, the idea of any kind of moral parity among faiths did not permeate the broader culture. Some self-identified Protestants wrote to her, probing the reasons for her conversion, proffering their own theories ranging from menopause to the sex appeal of bachelor priests. Others did not question the decision but rather explained to Luce that she erred in overlooking the truth of the Gospels (as understood by evangelical Protestants) and in seeking salvation within a corrupt Catholic faith. Those letters were subtly critical of her choice, as if the writers could not believe that any *rational* person would become a Catholic, least of all a woman they admired as much as Luce. Surely, something terrible in her life must have occasioned so drastic a choice. Others made no effort to disguise their contempt for her or for Catholicism. Men in particular took jabs at Luce's intellect: "No one—and I reiterate no one—of even ordinary intelligence who has been raised a Protestant could ever make a change like this if he or she even half thought about the matter." Her conversion hit a nerve. It was more than a little upsetting to hear that a spiritual seeker did not found the answers she sought within Protestantism. Amid the nasty anti-Catholicism that lambasted "Romanism," the venom directed at Luce revealed how insecure many Protestants felt about their faith's status at the center of American power. People who never met Luce felt that they knew her well enough to take her conversion personally. Her actions seemed to say something about *them.*[29]

Clare Boothe Luce was a woman who refused to silence herself. She enjoyed the privileges of wealth and whiteness, but her achievements as a writer, politician, and ambassador were nevertheless remarkable in an era when men dominated public life. Her audacity, not only in converting to Catholicism but in insisting that the world needed to hear about it, provoked a degree of outrage that seems unlikely to have met a male Catholic convert with a similarly prominent public profile.

Ella W. Page of Steuben, Maine, sent Luce a four-page handwritten note the day she learned of the conversion. She, too, sought an explanation of something she found incomprehensible. In response to those queries, and seeking a way to explain herself and elevate her conversion to a grander plane, Luce sat at her typewriter in the fall of 1946 and got to work.[30]

The intentional use of Luce's renown to win converts to Catholicism stemmed from a long tradition in the United States and Britain of relying on especially well-educated and intellectual converts to explain Catholic ideas to the Protestant masses. Since the nineteenth century, the conversion narratives and works of faith by Anglo-American Catholic converts formed a robust, transnational literary genre. Cardinal John Henry Newman's nineteenth-century conversion narrative, *Apologia pro vita sua*, described how his attempts to return the Anglican Church to its early Christian origins led him, instead, to Roman Catholicism. By the 1940s, the conversions of several Protestants from politically powerful families to Catholicism renewed questions about whether Protestantism or Catholicism was better suited to the defense of American democracy. Avery Dulles came from a family of distinguished statesmen and Presbyterians. His father, John Foster Dulles, was an elder in the Presbyterian Church and became an overtly pious secretary of state under President Eisenhower; his uncle Allen Dulles led the CIA; and his grandfather was a Presbyterian minister. Avery Dulles became a priest and a leading Catholic intellectual. In *A Testimonial to Grace* (1946), he described his conversion during his undergraduate years at Harvard. Dulles's book narrated the story of a soul that experienced the gift of God's grace and of a mind that searched for the theology and doctrine that molded that divine love into a life of faith. Like Clare Luce, Dulles found his way to Catholicism through reading—in his case, books by Augustine, Catholic philosopher (and fellow convert) Jacques Maritain, and Sheen. The ideas of the great Catholic intellectuals supplanted the political liberalism and metaphysics that Dulles discarded. In the fall of 1946, as Luce began to write her conversion narrative, she joined him as a fellow convert intellectual, explaining her faith to the public.[31]

Instead of a densely argued book for the intellectual elite, Clare Luce wrote an accessible article for a popular magazine. Editors from *Woman's Home Companion*, *McCall's*, and *Cosmopolitan* bid on the article. Luce sold it to *McCall's* for $10,000. Editor Otis Wiese understood that her article would cause a stir—and ignite sales—for his middlebrow women's magazine. Women's, family, and hobby magazines were more popular than ever in 1946. *McCall's* was among the most popular women's magazines of the day. By the early 1950s it had 4 million subscribers—about as many as the *Woman's Home Companion*, fewer than *Life*, and more than either the *Saturday Evening Post* or *Good Housekeeping*. Newsstands and bookstores sold hundreds of thousands more copies each month. By one estimate, a monthly issue of *McCall's* circulated among 10 million people, as copies were passed among members of households, families, and friends. The audience for *McCall's* was largely, and intentionally, white: articles and advertisements in *McCall's* never featured people of color; the America they imagined was a white one. (The erasure of African Americans from these "mainstream" magazines helped inspire the creation of new publications like *Ebony* and *Jet*.) Written with the intention of reaching high-school-educated, white, suburban Protestants, Luce's "The 'Real' Reason" struck a unique chord, appearing in print in a form and medium that thrust otherwise erudite conversations about faith, grace, and Catholicism from the lecture halls of seminaries into the living rooms of suburbia.[32]

Clare Luce's desire to make her conversion to Catholicism accessible to a wide public shared more in common with several Black converts than with the erudite apologia of Newman or Dulles. Roman Catholicism's universalism appealed to a growing number of African Americans; by the mid-1940s, converts predominated among the 350,000 "Black Catholics" in the United States. One such convert was the novelist and poet Claude McKay, a Jamaica-born ex-Communist, best known for his 1919 protest poem "If We Must Die" and whose novel *Home to Harlem* (1928) became the first Black-authored best seller. Toward the end of his life McKay began to volunteer with Catholics who cared for the poor, and he was baptized in 1944 in Chicago. Luce may have read McKay's March 1946 article in *Ebony* magazine, "Why I Became a Catholic." Jazz pianist and composer Mary Lou Williams likewise sought to use her gifts to share Catholicism's truths with the masses. After a debilitating depression interrupted her career, Williams became intensely religious. She devoted herself to the poor and studied with a Jesuit priest, becoming a Catholic in the 1950s. She played in clubs and at jazz festivals to pay the bills, but her heart was in religious music. Her most ambitious undertakings were her jazz masses, inspired by the reforms of the Second Vatican Council that encouraged vernacular prayer. She wrote to bishops and cardinals to explain that just as her ancestors invented spirituals, so she created a jazz mass.[33]

Luce understood better than nearly anyone in the United States that the press offered opportunities for famous people to fashion narratives of their "real" selves, that magazine profiles and newspaper coverage could build up or destroy a person's reputation, and that it was crucial to convey sincerity to convince readers of a subject's authenticity. While Clare Luce might never have become a full-fledged celebrity, her proximity to Harry Luce and her professional expertise in publishing and journalism gave her a better chance than most to mold her public image. Her article about her conversion mimicked the formulaic style of a magazine profile. These articles presented celebrities as people who performed in public but who could be their "real selves" at home. The profile promised to bring readers into the inner sanctum of the famous individual's private life, to reveal the "real" person behind the public persona.[34]

Luce played to readers' expectations of sincerity in her *McCall's* articles and adapted the profile for her own ends. Rather than exploring her domestic life, she gave her readers the "real" reason for her conversion. In lieu of demonstrating her authenticity by depicting everyday interiors or leisure pursuits, she described her passionate intellectual pursuit of answers to life's ultimate questions and illustrated those descriptions with ample photographs of her at work and in repose. "The 'Real' Reason" was not simply one woman's story of finding the faith that answered her religious questions; it was a written and visual argument for the centrality of Catholicism to American democracy. She accomplished this in a family magazine that had a largely female readership. Luce directed her argument about Catholicism's value not at (male) foreign policy leaders or theologians but at white, middle-class women. She made the case for Catholicism's place at the American democratic table by writing passionately about how her chosen faith answered her own emotional as well as intellectual needs.

The article was a sensation. A reporter in Washington, D.C., hurried to a newspaper stand to buy the February issue and found that only two copies remained. Editors at *McCall's* recognized that they had hit magazine gold. They split the second installment of the article in half, stretching Luce's more-than-30,000-word narrative, originally commissioned for 5,000 words, into the March and April issues. Part 1 of the article in the February issue alone ran to nearly 14,000 words. For many years the articles were the magazine's most popular reprints.[35]

In the three-part article, Luce described conversion to Roman Catholicism as both an answer to existential questions about the meaning of life and the best response to the global political confrontation between Communism and "the West." She downplayed the personal reasons for her conversion, and she effectively ignored the idea that a sinful past prompted her to examine her conscience. These omissions baffled many Protestants who read the article. To them, the public confession of sin was a ritual through which the convert performed his or her sincerity. Luce instead offered an intellectual history of seeking meaning, an ontological quest to understand each individual's place within an atomic cold war.

The editors at *McCall's* translated this serious fare for their family audience. The February issue introduced Luce to readers who knew little about her and softened her image among readers who disliked her. In a full-page photo that faced the first page, she sat in profile at the base of a large tree, a cocker spaniel in her lap, her wavy blond hair pinned back with a comb. Looking much younger than a woman in her midforties, she smiled as if to a friend just out of the frame. The editors stretched the narrative across more than twenty glossy pages, placing narrow columns of text between as many advertisements as they could fit. Luce's vivid account of her spiritual journey was nestled between ads selling instant coffee, toilet paper, baby diapers, vacuum cleaners, heartburn remedies, Chef Boyardee dinners, laundry detergents, and breakfast cereals.

Readers entered the story amid promises of an intimate confession. The version of events they encountered was, at most, partially true. The most personal piece of writing Luce ever produced for public consumption, the article avoided any mention of her marital difficulties, and it described the devastation of her daughter's death only in passing. She spent more time detailing her frustrations with liberal politics than her inner life. She portrayed her conversion as a journey from liberalism's failures to the logic of anti-Communism, out of the desert of unbelief into the oasis of faith, and from existential crisis to paternal reassurance. Conversion was the result of an intellectual and spiritual quest to understand life's meaning in the midst of overwhelming death—deaths of soldiers and civilians during the war, of friends who committed suicide, and of her mother and daughter. *McCall's* provided a polished, affirmative statement of faith by a captivating and powerful woman. By promising to give her readers the "real reason" for her conversion, Luce rejected any secret motives or hidden family history. She had, she wrote, discovered the "solid objective Truth," the redeeming love of Jesus Christ.[36]

Readers encountered Luce as they always did, adroitly manipulating the narrow gender conventions that demanded that all women, including those of great fame and ability, frame their largest ambitions as iterations of matrimonial submission. Justifying all the publicity she courted after her conversion, she compared it to an engagement announcement: "Even when a woman makes 'the most important personal discovery of her life'—that she loves some man enough to spend all her nights under one roof with him—she generally follows it up with a broadside of publicity." In this metaphor the wedding becomes "the fruit of her conversion to a belief in one man." Luce knew that much of the public's interest in her rested on her combination of beauty, ambition, and wit; she needed her conversion narrative to portray her as simultaneously extraordinarily accomplished and universally understood. She did anything by converting, let alone by talking about it, she explained, that any girl enraptured by her chosen spouse would not also have done. Coming from a woman whose husband missed her baptism to spend the weekend with his mistress, and who carried on a few affairs of her own, this analogy was the biggest lie Luce told in the article.[37]

More earnestly, the articles offered a neo-Thomist's negative appraisal of the secular theories of the day, especially psychoanalysis, Communism, and humanism. Luce wrote in the March issue that she tried psychoanalysis in the 1930s. Her therapy failed because her therapist lacked faith: "My psychoanalyst was a soul-quack." Luce understood that a thorough analysis involved transference, a psychoanalytic concept whereby a patient inevitably projects onto the therapist his or her feelings about someone else. Freud considered transference to be neurotic, but he also explained that transference revealed conflicts buried deep within the patient's subconscious. Realizing that she could never transfer her love for her father or mother to an analyst she found mildly repellant, Luce quit therapy. In her assessment of psychoanalysis Luce drew from her personal experiences to highlight the critiques that Monsignor Sheen made in radio addresses and homilies. This Catholic antipathy to certain forms of psychiatry notably contrasted with the tendency of liberal Protestants and Jews to embrace it.[38]

Luce had different reasons for rejecting Communism. Like many of Communism's critics, she compared it to a religion. It was an all-

The April 1947 issue of McCall's *featured the third part of Clare Boothe Luce's article "The 'Real' Reason," which opened facing this portrait of Luce in her home office. Photographer Toni Frissell was well-known for her portraits and worked as a staff photographer for several major magazines. (Courtesy Meredith Corporation,* McCall's Magazine, *1947)*

encompassing way of seeing the world, a closed community of believers who trusted that their ideology would lead to a new dawn, the end of history, and world peace. She explained that she was interested in Marx and Communism during the 1930s, like most of the liberals she knew, but came to believe that it could not answer life's moral questions. Secular humanism also disappointed her. Luce briefly believed that "man can perfect himself, that he can 'progress.'" The bombing of Hiroshima obliterated that optimism along with so much else. She lost her faith in humanity.[39]

Luce and her editors at *McCall's* presented her as a thoughtful, earnest woman, secure in her femininity even as she engaged the life of the mind. The photograph that accompanied the final installment of the article showed a woman lost in thought. Outdoors and comfortable in February, Clare in April was indoors and contemplative. She sat behind a desk with her hair pinned up by her ears but otherwise falling to her shoulders, pen in hand, her elbows resting on the desk and her head leaning in to touch the pen's tip against her forehead. She wore a dress with a sash at the waist, a pearl necklace and earrings, a bracelet, and a large ring on her left hand. Stacks of correspondence lay in a folder nearby.

The text described a soul on fire. Catholicism was her exit from a burning building. Describing the night she despaired in her hotel apartment, prayed, and called Father Wiatrak for solace, Luce wrote that "on one terrible night the smoke of my doubts burned into the flames of denial. And I fled." In a dig at her husband Harry, she lamented "all the futile and sterile relationships" that left her without emotional support. Instead, she was haunted by the ghosts of individuals who suffered tragic deaths, picturing "the lime pits of Nordhausen [and] a girl's graveyard," and the faces of friends." She pictured her dead mother's face in the "Lethean lagoon" surrounding Hades "and near her, the gay pure face of my daughter, with glowing red brown hair." Rather than about personal sins or failings, she wrote of existential despair.[40]

The multipart article was a publishing phenomenon, a watershed moment for American Catholics, and a harbinger of a cultural fascination with religious conversion. Printed in a magazine for women, the article was widely read; men wrote letters in response to it nearly as often as women did, demonstrating either that *McCall's* often appealed to male readers in the households it entered or that Luce's article was so exceptional that men broke with their usual reading habits. At a time when many, and perhaps most, American Protestants harbored suspicions about Catholics' political loyalties, "The 'Real' Reason" told the story of a woman at the apex of American power for whom the Roman Catholic Church answered her deepest spiritual questions. Above all, it focused readers' attention on the story of religious choice, of conversion as a journey through loss and doubt.

Luce's new faith made all the sense in the world to her; it appalled her critics. She said her rational mind led her to accept the church's teachings after God's freely given grace convinced her of Christ's divinity. Protestants faulted her reasoning and chided her for needing priests to understand the truth that Christ revealed for all to see in the New Testament. Evangelical Protestants in particular rejected her narrative of Catholic self-discovery. They insisted that what was "real" to her was in fact the result of her acquiescence to the dictates of coercive priests. They wrote to her by the hundreds, and she wrote back to nearly all of them with arguments about the truths she found in Roman Catholicism.

Principally, the letters reveal a view of religion as a two-sided, zero-sum game; Catholicism's victory was Protestantism's loss. Many people, not realizing that Luce was newly a private citizen, wrote to her former congressional office. Others sent their letters to *McCall's*. A few sent their letters care of *Time* magazine or simply to "Clare Luce, Greenwich" or "Clare Boothe Luce, New York City" without a street address. She was well enough known that the post office could find her. Most of the letters Luce received directly were congratulatory notes from fellow Catholics, but Protestant complaints reached her at her home and inundated the editorial offices at *McCall's*.

Questions about whether Catholics could be patriotic Americans filled the letters Luce received from critical Protestants. With varying degrees of nuance and civility, they expressed skepticism about Roman Catholic commitments to self-government and to freedom of conscience. Luce heard from Protestant ministers, educated congregants, and individuals who struggled to make their ideas clear. In each case, the people writing to her tended to be knowledgeable about the Bible and ill-informed about the beliefs and practices of Roman Catholics. Very few liberal Protestants commented on Luce's narrative of her discovery of truth. She did not receive a single critical letter from a Jew, Muslim, Hindu, or Baha'i.

Protestants had described Catholicism as a faith inimical to freedom since the sixteenth century, and that critique still flourished in the mid-twentieth century. Boastful of the consonance between Protestant Christianity and freedom of conscience, American Protestants painted Catholicism as a dangerously authoritarian faith that tended toward tyranny. Protestant ministers reinforced popular anti-Catholicism from the pulpit when they delivered sermons promoting a vision of Christian unity that excluded Roman Catholics. These Christians reviled the idea of a celibate priesthood, denying that it had any legitimate basis in early church leadership or in mediating between Jesus and his faithful. One woman from College Station, Texas, wrote, "In searching the Scripture, I cannot find the Catholic Church mentioned, nor can I find authority for many of the practices and beliefs of the Catholic Church." These writers argued that Catholics blindly sustained the papacy and priesthood when Jesus's word in the New Testament was available to all. Catholics practiced infant baptism, but the Bible described baptism as a ceremony for believers old enough to repent. Of course, many Protestant denominations also baptized infants, but the authors of these letters considered Roman Catholicism to be distinctively illegitimate: "Any religious body that cannot justify itself by the New Testament has no authority to exist." It was a point raised again and again in the letters Luce received.[41]

A long-held Protestant complaint objected to Catholics holding public office. When Protestants decried "Romanism," they warned that Catholics answered to the pope first, the Constitution second. The key issue was authority: according to these Protestant prejudices, not only did Catholics give their first loyalties to the pope, but their support for the Catholic hierarchy taught them to prize authoritarianism. "Allegiance to the Vatican ... ahead of that of his country," one man wrote, disqualified Roman Catholics from American public office. If Protestants were not vigilant, Catholics would fulfill their ultimate aim of theocratic dictatorship. In this logic, Catholicism was at once foreign and domestic, an international power broker seeking to steer the American ship of state. One man told Luce that it was not the beliefs of Roman Catholics he objected to but rather the behavior of the church, which was "perfectly ruthless.... She is a Fascist organization from top to bottom." To those who believed that no faithful Catholic could defend the Constitution, it did not seem to matter that Luce was no longer a public servant, especially since many of the people who wrote to her assumed that she still held office.[42]

These allegations bespoke fears of a Catholic conspiracy to "take" the United States from its rightful (Protestant) citizens. The story of wounded hegemony rings familiar: a group that has dominated all aspects of politics and culture reacts to modest assertions of influence with dire warnings about its own imminent extinction. Luce's critics bemoaned the Roman Catholic takeover of the public schools at a time when Catholics were investing deeply in a parallel network of parochial schools; they complained that *McCall's* gave far too much ink to Catholic viewpoints. A Connecticut woman asked how Luce, whom she considered "an intelligent woman, and, until recently, a patriotic one," could join a church "sworn to destroy our right to freedom of religion and of public schools. ... All of us who are descendents [*sic*] of the Mayflower Compact people and the soldiers of the Revolutionary War are heretics to be tortured, to *your* Roman Pope." To those who viewed the Roman Catholic Church as the basest of religious organizations, corrupt to its core and sustained through the abject loyalty of its duped followers, Luce's conversion defied credulity. These exchanges foretold the evangelical anti-Catholicism that grew increasingly prominent in the 1950s. Anti-Catholic tirades appeared in Paul Blanshard's *American Freedom and Catholic Power* (1949) and in Billy Graham's new magazine, *Christianity Today*, which began publication in 1956.[43]

The imperative to "witness" to their faith impelled many Protestants to tell Luce that she was misled in thinking that Catholicism was God's intended path for her. Luce acted similarly in her article, speaking publicly of her conversion out of a conviction that she had discovered the truth and that everyone else should find it, too. Earnest Protestant women wrote page after page to Luce on simple stationery, the ink of their pens showcasing years of penmanship instruction and the length of their missives attesting to their deeply felt convictions. Mrs. J. W. Schwager of Philadelphia, Pennsylvania, was convinced that Luce would soon see Catholicism's flaws the way she did, and she urged Luce not to give up on God when that happened. Dozens of Protestants made similar points, with varying levels of civility. Citing chapter and verse, they wrote that God's grace was available to all who read the Bible. They could not understand why Luce insisted that she needed to be a member of the Roman Catholic Church to experience divine grace. Men were more likely to attribute Luce's choice of Catholicism to ignorance.[44]

Newly a private citizen, Luce employed her devoted secretaries in the work of responding to her supporters and her critics. The resources of the Catholic Church supported her. Father Joseph I. Malloy was a member of the Paulist Society, the order of religious men devoted to converting Americans to Catholicism. The Paulist Society maintained a large presence in New York City, and from those offices Malloy spent hours at his typewriter explaining Catholicism to legions of mistrustful Americans. Luce's secretaries sent him stacks of the critical letters she received and the more theologically inquisitive missives, and he returned them with sample responses attached. Luce also sent draft responses to her secretaries. She was especially interested in anyone who seemed even slightly interested in returning or converting to Catholicism. Her secretaries compiled responses that quoted Malloy at length, omitting some of his longer theological digressions, and edited for tone. The result was something remarkable: a national educational campaign against anti-Catholicism, waged one letter at a time, and phrased with generous civility, at least in letters that bore Luce's signature. Luce and Malloy undertook this work because they believed that their faith was both real and ideally suited to defend American democracy against the authoritarian threat of Communism. Malloy was the right person for the job. The author of *The Catholic Catechism*, a pamphlet-sized guide to Catholic doctrine, he provided theological detail for Luce's defenses of her chosen faith.

Pamphlets and books were the grenades that Luce and her readers lobbed back and forth across the denominational divide. Protestants pointed her to the words of Matthew, Mark, and Luke; she occasionally quoted scripture, but she more often sent pamphlets from the Christophers. She likely understood that claims of biblical authority would not win the day. The Roman Catholic Bible she studied with Sheen and now with Malloy included numerous sacred books that the Protestant version of the New Testament omitted. Luce's critics not only preferred a Bible purged of the Apocryphal and Deuterocanonical books, which Catholics included in their Bible, but also denigrated the great Catholic thinkers whose ideas continued to shape Roman Catholic theology. The true Bible—and the true faith it described—was Protestant. Their exchanges elicit metaphors of the battlefield and also of the poker game: I see your Saint Augustine, the Protestants wrote, and I raise you a Lord Jesus. The Protestant version of the New Testament was the trump card that Luce's critics played in their intellectual battles with her. They refuted Catholic theology—of purgatory, idolatry, and liturgy—point by point, their Bible their ultimate authority. Verse by verse, across the Gospels and into Proverbs, dozens of Protestants enumerated the proof of Luce's error—and urged her to read the Bible. Luce evangelized right back. "You say you have an open mind," she dared one man. "I assure you that I too still have an open mind, and I promise to pray for you."[45]

As Malloy and Luce defended the universality of grace and the legitimacy of the priesthood, they revealed the persistence of anti-Catholicism in American life. The struggle they confronted was not over *whether* faith was necessary to democracy but over specifically *which* faith should guide it. "It is apparent that you have received gross misinformation about the Catholic Church," Luce (and Malloy) wrote to one man. She was not afraid to give back what she received. To the man's accusation that "Roman Catholics are the most bigoted people in the world," Luce chided, "Certainly your statement that 'a Roman Catholic is not fit to hold public office' and your charge that Catholic priests are 'un-Christlike' seem to indicate considerable intolerance and bigotry." In response to a man who sent a letter full of anti-Catholic vitriol while insisting that he meant no harm, Luce wrote, "I am very happy to know you love Catholics. Of course you do, and we agree again."[46]

That mountain of anti-Catholic letters may have inspired an episto-lary interfaith dialogue, but it cost Luce an ongoing role as a columnist for *McCall's*. She had been contracted to start a "monthly question and answer feature" in the issue immediately following the last installment of her conversion article. "In a private meeting with Luce's literary agent, George Bye, *McCall's* editor Otis Wiese confided that he was "quite sure from reading some of the letters that people will say that a department by [Luce] is controlled by the Church." Given the extent to which Mal-loy provided Luce with the text for her responses to her critics, the con-cern had merit. *McCall's* backed away from an earlier promise of $2,500 a month for her advice page. The *Woman's Home Companion* likewise demurred. News of these decisions spread rapidly throughout Ameri-can Catholicism. Many priests seem to have urged their parishioners to write to the editor of *McCall's* to declare their gratitude for Luce's articles and their hope that the magazine would not forfeit future discussions of Catholicism in its pages. Hundreds of Catholics, from Boston and Chi-cago to Petaluma, responded to the call. Most of them stuck close to the recommended text—a few words of congratulations to Wiese, an expres-sion of delight in finding such inspiring and thought-provoking articles in his magazine, and encouragement to the editor to print more of the same. A few Catholics slung the mud right back at their Protestant crit-ics. These lay apologists often made about as much sense as their anti-Catholic counterparts.[47]

Far more than she had in the pages of a middlebrow women's maga-zine, Luce reflected for Catholic audiences on the relationship between grief and conversion, observing that "most convert literature stressed a central theme: that of pain." For these readers, she explained that her dis-covery of the truth of Catholicism emerged in a less dramatic fashion than a midnight crisis in her hotel apartment, the tearing open of a letter, or a desperate call to a priest, but in many ways this version was more emo-tionally profound. She described conversion as the "end of a process that had [the convert's] whole life for its beginning." Without referencing her daughter, whose death was mentioned in the brief biographical statement that introduced her essay, she wrote that "a great grief is a tremendous bonfire in which all the trash of life is consumed. It may turn a man from God, or it may turn him to God. But it never leaves him unchanged." Too often, she wrote in 1950, narratives of new faith dwelled on the effects of an individual's choice rather than the source of their new assurance. For Luce, as for Sheen and Malloy, the only true source of the gift of belief was

God. Without an understanding of or explanation for grace, the hearers of these stories continued to "plead with the convert for the 'real' reason."[48]

Catholicism offered her more than healing words; it gave her a tangible reality of God's presence. In a 1950 article for Catholic readers, she emphasized the transforming power of the Blessed Sacrament—the presence of the "host," the consecrated bread of the Eucharist. She recalled occasions, before her conversion, when she witnessed Catholics at Mass and felt moved by something she could not, at that time, explain. With the benefit of hindsight and the opportunity to ascribe new meaning to her past, she realized that in those moments she was moved by the "real presence" of the Blessed Sacrament, the body of Christ remade through the sacramental rituals of the Eucharist. She traveled in Italy during the closing months of World War II as a member of the House Military Affairs Committee. Riding in a jeep up the mountains on Christmas Day, she saw a group of American troops gathered on a snowy mountainside. The motions of a priest at the front of the gathering showed that they were observing the Mass. Reflecting in 1950, Luce interpreted her presence at that place, in that moment, as part of the working of God's grace on her soul: "And so Providence decreed that on the central day of the liturgical year, I, an unbeliever, should witness the central moment and join in the central act of Catholic worship in a very central context, a battlefield." Like many Catholics in the modern era, Luce believed in the reality of God's presence in human history and in God's literal presence in the consecrated host of the Eucharist.[49]

It was all of a piece for her: the answer to her suffering, the reality of God's divinity, and the global stakes of humanity's search for religious meaning. She soon found another convert to join her in this mission. He was as unlikely a mass cultural superstar as one might find: a monk with a broken typewriter who took a vow of silence.

Clare Boothe Luce's love of literature, Catholicism, and smart men found a new, if chaste, outlet in 1948: the Cistercian ("Trappist") monk Brother Louis, who published under his given name, Thomas Merton. Luce seems to have first learned about him from one of his books, *Thirty Poems* (1944), which garnered attention from readers of serious poetry and a small circle of Catholic intellectuals. Merton converted from Protestantism to Catholicism in the 1930s. He became a monk in 1941 and lived the rest of his life at the Abbey of Gethsemani near Louisville, Kentucky. During the summer of 1948, Clare Luce read the page proofs for Merton's forthcoming memoir of Catholic conversion, and they began an epistolary friendship. As with the other men in her life, Luce lavished this one with gifts. Her personal secretary shipped him a record player, albums of Gregorian chant, and a typewriter, care of the Trappists. A monk read "The 'Real' Reason" aloud in the Gethsemani refectory. Merton's memoir, *The Seven Storey Mountain* (1948), became an international best seller. In it he argued for the truth and necessity of Roman Catholic devotion to God by human beings impaired by their innate sin. When the hardcover appeared in bookstores in October 1948, Luce's blurb joined those of fellow Catholic converts Graham Greene and Evelyn Waugh. That Christmas season, Luce abandoned her usual practice of sending personalized gifts to her friends and instead had her secretary send everyone on her "Xmas" list a copy of *The Seven Storey Mountain*.[50]

Energetic to the point of restlessness, Clare Luce took on new projects that combined her passions for Roman Catholicism, mass cultural entertainment, and politics. Darryl Zanuck of Twentieth Century Fox flew her to Los Angeles in the fall of 1947 to write a screen adaptation of C. S. Lewis's novel *The Screwtape Letters*, a recently published polemical defense of Christianity in the form of letters the devil wrote to his nephew. Lewis was a devout Protestant, but his argument for God's existence resonated with Luce. Despite paying Clare $75,000, the studio rejected her script. She assured Lewis that the screenplay's failure was a "happy abortion," an odd word choice for a Catholic describing the destruction of a creative work but a reflection, perhaps, of Luce's anger at the way the commercial film industry bowdlerized works with religious messages. She wrote screenplays with Catholic themes, including one about two nuns who opened an abbey in Bethlehem, Connecticut. Heavily rewritten, the story became *Come to the Stable* (1949), which won multiple Academy Awards. (Two other Catholic-themed dramas she wrote were flops.) She edited *Saints for Now* (1952), an essay collection in which famous writers discussed their favorite saint. Rev. James Keller awarded the book one of the 1953 Christopher Awards. Reluctantly breaking her vow to stay out of politics, Luce ran for Senate in 1952 but lost in the Republican primary. By early 1953 she was on her way to Italy to serve as the U.S. ambassador, the first woman to head an American embassy. Several years later, when an ambassadorship to Brazil fell through, she took up scuba diving and wrote about it for *Sports Illustrated*. In the 1960s she "retired" to Hawaii and took up painting. She became an avid experimenter with LSD, encouraged by her friend the new age philosopher Gerald Heard, whose vague philosophy mattered less to her than his ready procurement of psychedelics. Perhaps she experienced in those hallucinogenic states a connection to the divine, to the simultaneously sacred and *real*, that she also found in her faith.[51]

She and Harry lived together off and on, a celibate partnership of intellectual equals, until his death in 1967. Her deepest friendships appear to have been with her confessors and spiritual mentors, to whom she confided about her bouts of severe depression. Clare's politics became increasingly conservative as she aged. She served on the President's Foreign Intelligence Advisory Board under Presidents Richard Nixon and Ronald Reagan and died in 1987 at the age of eighty-four.[52]

In the early years of the Cold War, Clare Boothe Luce and others taught the American public that certain kinds of Christian faith fortified their democratic values from the terrifying possibilities of authoritarian government. To a generation that witnessed astonishing degrees of human depravity, from concentration camps to battlefields, and that lived with the looming threat of nuclear annihilation, this message was reassuring, even if Luce's specific advocacy of Roman Catholic faith irked countless Protestants. In writing about the "real reason" for her conversion, she performed her authentic faith and attempted to answer skeptics' questions about whether priestly coercion directed her beliefs. These promises of authentic selfhood came to typify the genre of spiritual autobiography that Thomas Merton and other Catholics popularized. He and other authors became gurus of self-discovery for a transnational audience of seekers.

Another wave of books told stories of faith's discovery with narrators whose credulity was far more difficult to ascertain. These authors asked their readers to trust their stories of journeying from doubt to truth. They presented an unstable self, one that morphed and moved among ideologies and affiliations. The conversions of ex-Communists—especially former spies for the Soviet Union—seemed to showcase the best and the worst of how faith affected the nation.

Chapter 2 Cold War Disclosures

⋯⋯⋯⋯⋯⋯⋯⋯⋯⋯⋯⋯⋯⋯⋯⋯⋯⋯⋯⋯⋯⋯⋯⋯⋯⋯⋯⋯⋯⋯

Whittaker Chambers warned that democracy was dying. He blamed Communism, a false religion that violated God's natural order. He did not blame himself, although he had until lately advanced Communism's aims. Chambers joined the Communist Party in the 1920s, and for several years in the 1930s he engaged in active espionage on behalf of the Soviet Union. Religious conversion saved him, he explained. Faith in God empowered him to escape the "underground" and build a new life as a writer and family man. His new Christian values compelled him to testify about his former espionage activities and supply the names of other known or suspected members of the Soviet underground in appearances before the House Un-American Activities Committee (HUAC) and in numerous FBI interviews. Chambers viewed himself not as an agent of democracy's demise but as its tragically heroic defender. His past gave his present testimony credence; he knew the evils of Communism because he witnessed them. But there was one piece of his story he kept hidden.

On February 15, 1949, Chambers reached the end of a long day's interview at the Federal Bureau of Investigation's New York City headquarters. For hours, he had answered questions about the Communist spy networks that operated along the Eastern Seaboard. Perpetually disheveled, he now stood up in his stained, wrinkled suit and handed an envelope to an agent. It contained a signed confession. Chambers wanted the details of this confession to remain secret. It attested to his clandestine sexual activities with unnamed men during the years in which he ferried copies of confidential government documents to his Soviet and American handlers. This secret sexual life lasted from about 1933 until 1938, at which point, he wrote, he experienced a tripartite conversion. The discovery that year of a new faith in God precipitated his break from Communism and his renunciation of same-sex sexual encounters. By the next day a copy of the contents of that envelope made its way to the desk of J. Edgar Hoover, head of the FBI, in Washington, D.C. It remained hidden from public view until a Freedom of Information Act (FOIA) request revealed it among the FBI's files on Chambers.[1]

Chambers tried to hide his sexual past even as he became one of the most well-known public figures in the early years of the Cold War. Chambers played a central role in the perjury trials of Alger Hiss, a former high-level State Department employee. Hiss epitomized the liberal elites who led the New Deal and the welfare state it created; his conviction in 1950 on perjury charges marked a symbolic triumph of conservative anti-Communism against the perceived excesses of liberal government. Chambers wrote a blockbuster memoir, *Witness* (1952), which made him an intellectual hero for the conservative movement. His story of exiting the darkness of Communism for the light of Christian truth amplified the importance of religious faith to Cold War politics. But in 1949 he feared that his enemies might reveal his nonconformist sexual past to undermine his credibility.

Chambers was one of a cohort of ex-Communist converts who presented their stories as closing arguments in the anti-Communist case against the Left. Like Chambers, these converts narrated an escape from the false faith of Communism to both redemptive Christianity and heterosexual monogamy. Former Communist editor Louis Budenz and ex-spy Elizabeth Bentley each wrote memoirs that described their discoveries of religious truths. As Budenz and Bentley became valued government informants, they grounded their political authenticity in their conventional sexuality, which they in turn attributed to their faith. Former Communists and spies who suddenly declared themselves the defenders of democratic freedom needed to prove that they now spoke the truth. Their varied fortunes in the public eye illuminate some of the ways in which both faith and sex became measures of political authenticity.[2]

When ex-Communist authors described journeys into and out of Communism, they traced a pattern of conversion and apostasy. They "converted" to Communism because Communism itself constituted a totalizing, religion-like worldview, the writings of Marx substituting for the Bible as a sacred text. Richard Crossman, a British MP, cemented that metaphor with his edited volume, *The God That Failed* (1950), a collection of six narratives, each of which attempted to describe "the state of mind of the

Communist convert" between 1917 and 1939. Crossman described the authors' initial fascination with Communism as a religious epiphany: "They saw it at first from a long way off ... as a vision of the Kingdom of God on earth." Subsequent historians have adopted this metaphor, writing of the "conversions" of American intellectuals and activists to Communism or sympathy with Communist goals in the 1920s and 1930s. Many notable ex-Communists became witnesses and informants, whose knowledge of Communist networks and affiliations, or the pretense of such knowledge, made them political celebrities in the feverish early days of the Cold War.[3]

Ex-Communists themselves described Communism as a false religion and compared their decision to become Communists to a conversion. They employed this metaphor even when their political odysseys did not end in an expression of religious faith. The former Communists and fellow travelers within the non-Communist Left who became anti-Stalinists in the late 1920s and 1930s were an ideologically diverse and argumentative bunch. Many of them remained atheists (or secular Jews) as they moved toward either liberal or conservative politics. For these ex-Communists, devotion to liberal democracy, rather than conversion to Christian beliefs, was sufficient to mobilize their exit from Communism or socialism.[4]

Some ex-Communists described both joining and leaving Communism as religious awakenings. Public declarations of religious faith became politically expedient, while past associations with atheism served as political liabilities from which ex-Communists needed expiation. In a sense, then, these ex-Communist narratives described faith as instrumental to the decision to abandon Communism; the authors derived strength from God to resist the party's hold. Linking a rejection of Communism to an embrace of Christianity was an astute move at a time when the United States persecuted anyone suspected of Communist leanings. Catholicism in particular provided an ideological antiseptic for many postwar ex-Communists. They found in Catholicism a holistic system of belief and practice, firmly rooted in a transnational network of social institutions. Roman Catholicism's teachings on sexual morality and monogamous, lifelong marriage additionally salvaged the reputations of men and women who wanted to distance themselves from the sexual permissiveness and easy divorce that were associated with Soviet-style Communism.[5]

One of the ex-Communists that Fulton Sheen converted was Louis Budenz, a former editor at the *Daily Worker* who was born a Roman Catholic but had not practiced his faith in many years. Budenz joined the

Communist Party in 1935 and remained a member for ten years, but he was disillusioned with the party much of that time. The Popular Front, a coalition of leftist and liberal political groups that broadly supported the New Deal, offered Budenz opportunities to get to know socialists and the many Catholics who advocated for workers' rights. Budenz reached out to Fulton Sheen after learning that the Comintern, the Soviet agency responsible for fostering Communist revolutions outside of the USSR, encouraged cooperation between French Communists and proworker Catholics. In 1937 they met for the first time, following a few written exchanges about whether Roman Catholics should align themselves with workers. When the Nazi-Soviet pact of 1939 put an end to the Popular Front, Budenz recognized the extent to which American Communism followed the dictates of its Soviet leadership.[6]

Budenz's common-law wife, Margaret, and his children played prominent supporting roles in his performance of contrition and self-transformation, replacing his past associations with Communist sexual nonconformity with the marital heterosexual traditionalism that Americans valued. Budenz told Sheen about his plans to leave Communism in the fall of 1945. Sheen tutored Margaret, and on October 10, 1945, in front of witnesses in St. Patrick's Cathedral, he presided over the couple's wedding and the Catholic baptisms of Margaret and the Budenzes' three daughters.[7]

The sacramental rites of marriage and baptism complete, Budenz launched a new career as an FBI informant, author, and professional ex-Communist. He gave the names of his former colleagues to government agencies investigating domestic Communism. Sheen found Budenz a teaching post at the University of Notre Dame, his only credential his Catholic ex-Communism. Already by December 1945, agents from the FBI had initiated the first of many debriefings with Budenz at a hotel in South Bend. His memoir followed quickly. *This Is My Story* (1946) traded on the sensationalism of his return to Catholicism and showcased his willingness to tell all and name names about his Communist past. The editors at Whittlesey House (the forerunner of McGraw Hill) were confident enough in the book's prospects that they printed a huge initial run of 45,000 copies.[8]

This enthusiasm for espionage made Budenz a friendly government witness before House Un-American Activities Committee (HUAC). He told HUAC that the American Communist Party was not an independent political organization but rather "a direct arm of the Soviet Foreign Department." Such assertions, along with his declarations that the Soviet Union sought to destroy the United States, gave credence to the efforts of many anti-Communists to define membership in the Communist Party as equivalent to treason and thus grounds for deportation. That fall, Budenz took to the lecture circuit and radio programs, often under the auspices of the Catholic Church, warning about the dangers of Communism. He testified approximately twenty-five times before six different congressional committees, seven times in court trials, and four times in administrative proceedings. His devotion to the Catholic Church, and to its fervent anti-Communism, bolstered his credibility. Budenz remained a valued government witness even when many of his assertions under oath were revealed to be false. Most of the people Budenz accused of Communist loyalties turned out not to be affiliated with the Communist Party. Rather, Budenz seems to have assumed that anyone he encountered during his heady days in the Popular Front had Communist leanings—and was thus, in his estimation, a concealed Communist. He became a key figure in the informant system's assault on the American Left.[9]

When Budenz and others linked Christian faith and democracy, they highlighted as well their heterosexual respectability. Media coverage about Budenz's rehabilitation as an anti-Communist crusader highlighted not only his rededication to Roman Catholicism but also the new legal status of his marriage and his wife's decision to align her faith with his. By saving himself, he saved his family.

The appearance of sexual rectitude mattered even more to the fortunes of the former Soviet spy Elizabeth Bentley, nicknamed the "Red Spy Queen." Bentley transformed herself from a former Communist into a valued U.S. government informant in several infamous cases that struck at the heart of the New Deal's legacy. Bentley joined the Communist Party during the mid-1930s, while she was living in New York City and eking out a living as a secretary and copy editor. In her 1951 memoir, *Out of Bondage*, when Bentley described her time in the party, she portrayed her younger self as a naïf, indoctrinated by expert recruiters and overcome by her emotional attachments to the party's ideals. She fell in love with the party's struggle on behalf of the oppressed, and she fell for Jacob Golos, a former member of the Soviet secret police. Despite the thrills of espionage and nonmarital sex, she feared being double-crossed and becoming a target of Soviet retaliation against suspected dissenters. In 1945, she wrote, she left the party and headed straight to an FBI field office, lest one of her former colleagues in the underground name her first. Who or what drew her away from Communist atheism, Soviet espionage, and socialist free love to the baptismal font of the Roman Catholic Church is not entirely clear. Subsequent revelations about Bentley's loose relationship to the truth make *Out of Bondage* an unreliable source.[10]

Bentley attempted to rehabilitate her sexual as well as her political reputation at a time when American conversations about sex and religion were heating up. Alfred Kinsey and his research associates at Indiana University published *Sexual Behavior in the Human Male* in 1948. The book compiled data that Kinsey and his team of researchers at Indiana University gathered over years of interviews with men from across the United States about the minutiae of their erotic lives and the "sex history" of each person's experiences with heterosexual sexual intercourse, same-sex sexual acts, masturbation, premarital sex, and "petting." Covered widely in the press and excerpted in family magazines, the book was a major cultural event. Kinsey and his team did not judge whether their interview subjects were "normal" or "moral" people but calculated statistical averages about how often American men engaged in specific sexual acts. To the surprise of most Americans, the book showed that more than 30 percent of American men experienced orgasm through a sexual act that involved another man. The book documented rates of premarital and extramarital sexual intercourse that similarly confounded any presumptions of premarital chastity or marital monogamy.

Five years later, Kinsey's second volume, *Sexual Behavior in the Human Female* (1953), elicited far greater condemnation when it documented similarly diverse nonmarital sexual behaviors among American women. Premarital and extramarital sex, which many people associated in the 1920s with "Bolshevism" and in the 1940s and 1950s with atheistic Communism, appeared in the Kinsey report to be fairly widespread practices. Maybe the Communists were winning. Evidence of American women's nonmarital sexual behaviors created a rash of accusations against the Kinsey researchers for circulating filth and undermining the nation's morals. If the monogamous marital household was the bedrock of American democracy, as the popular thinking presumed, perhaps women's "promiscuity" augured a slide into socialism. Kinsey's books raised the stakes for ex-Communists seeking to demonstrate their complete transformation from socialist hedonism to democratic morality. For women in particular, sexual behavior appeared to reveal political loyalties.[11]

By the late 1940s, Bentley was famous less for what she did while she was a member of the Communist Party than for the staggering numbers of alleged Communists she named to federal authorities after she left it. She was a key informant and a witness at trials that epitomized the government's domestic surveillance of leftist politics during the Cold War. She explained that she gave the names of her Communist friends to federal authorities in order to free them from the clutches of Communist tyranny; she thought her former comrades would be grateful. In 1948 Bentley was an expert witness in the government's case against William Remington, a Commerce Department employee whom Bentley identified as a Communist. His lawyers sued Bentley for libel after she repeated these charges during an NBC radio interview on *Meet the Press*. Unlike many of Bentley's other targets, Remington did not invoke his Fifth Amendment rights and refuted her accusations under oath. Remington's lawyers wanted to depose Bentley in the libel case in the fall of 1948. The problem was they could not find her; the "ex–Red Spy" vanished from the scene. After five weeks of searching, journalists tracked the "plump blonde" to a Catholic retreat center in the Bronx, where she had been for a week, studying with Fulton Sheen, following several weeks at another Catholic retreat. By the time U.S. marshals and reporters located her, she was already a Catholic: she was baptized on November 5, 1948, at a Catholic church in Washington, D.C.; Louis and Margaret Budenz were her godparents. On the basis of Bentley's inconsistent testimony, Remington was found guilty of perjury and sentenced to federal prison in 1950. In 1954 he was murdered by fellow inmates.[12]

Bentley lacked the accouterments of heterosexual respectability that Budenz and Clare Boothe Luce possessed, which were essential to the performance of politically conservative religious sincerity. Far from embodying an ideal of feminine domesticity, Bentley was single, sexually experienced, childless, and rumored to be bisexual. The solution her publisher and ghostwriter devised was to play up her (hetero)sexual allure. Whatever prompted her religious transformation, her memoir portrayed it as a romantic, even erotic, awakening to truth, however theologically incoherent. In a scene set in 1945, the book places her away from the noise and danger of New York City and instead amid the serenity of Old Lyme, Connecticut, its Congregational church's spire symbolizing the town's ties to "old values." Walking along the shore of the Long Island Sound, she found herself on the cusp of conversion: "My faith in my old Communist ideals was gone now; even the embers were growing cold. And yet, I thought wistfully, I shall never feel like that again—never again will I be able to think and feel and live with such intensity and passion." In answer

Former government informant Elizabeth Bentley wrote in her 1951 memoir that conversion to Roman Catholicism gave her the strength to break with Communism and become more conventionally feminine. (Courtesy Library of Congress, Prints and Photographs Division; New York World-Telegram photo by C. M. Stieglitz, LC-USZ62–109686)

to that lament about the death of romance, the Congregational church beckoned her like a beacon drawing her toward its shores: "Almost without knowing what I was doing, I opened the door and walked in." Despite the fact that she ultimately became a Roman Catholic, the book characterized her conversion as a return to the Protestant morals of her New England forefathers. Like other converts before her, Bentley described a moment of epiphany in the form of prayer, of the divine speaking through her and directing her speech: "Then, suddenly, without any volition on my part, I found myself trying to pray—calling out for help to Someone whom all these years I had denied. Oh, God, I cried out desperately; help me to find the strength! As if in answer, the old familiar words of the Twenty-third Psalm came throbbing into my mind." The scene reads blue; she is attracted, overcome, cries out during the throbbing intensity of sensation, and is then awash in a sense of calm.[13]

Out of Bondage did not mention that shortly before Bentley's ecstatic visit to the Congregational church in 1945, she read in the newspapers that Louis Budenz had left the party, returned to his Catholic roots, and shared what he knew about Soviet espionage on American soil with the FBI. Fearing that Budenz might name her as a Soviet agent, she broke with the Soviet underground and looked for ways to make herself into a valued informant rather than a target of FBI interest. Her memoir offered little explanation for why she then turned to Fulton Sheen and the Catholic Church. Within a year of her baptism, she held a teaching post at Mundelein College, a Catholic women's school that is today part of Loyola University, where she gave talks to the Philosophy Club about Communism's failure to address "social injustice." Bentley infuriated the Left but gained few admirers on the Right; her legacy was in the names she gave to the federal government.[14]

Contained within the hours of testimony that Bentley provided in the Remington case was her assertion that former State Department employee Alger Hiss was a Communist. Time magazine writer Whittaker Chambers, himself a former Communist spy newly converted to Christianity, emerged as the key witness in the case against Hiss. Called before Congress in August 1948 to verify Bentley's statements, Chambers named Alger Hiss as a Communist. A few weeks later, in an interview that aired on NBC radio's Meet the Press, he went a step further, identifying Hiss as a member of a D.C.-based Communist "apparatus" intent on infiltrating the highest levels of the U.S. government in order to shape policy according to Soviet priorities. The eventual results of those statements were the two perjury trials of Alger Hiss, between 1949 and 1950, after he denied under oath that he was a Communist or knew Whittaker Chambers as a member of a pro-Soviet spy network. The case set the stage for the rise of Senator Joseph McCarthy, whose speech in Wheeling, West Virginia, on February 9, 1950, came within weeks of Hiss's conviction. The trials also launched Richard Nixon's national political career. Still a young representative from Southern California, Nixon began to make national headlines as one of HUAC's most avid anti-Communists.[15]

The Hiss-Chambers case drew international attention to one of the most startling, and unsettling, religious conversion narratives in American political history. By the time Chambers came into the national spotlight in the late summer of 1948, by accusing Hiss of being a member of a Soviet spy apparatus, he lived with his family on a substantial farm, attended Quaker meeting, and earned a living as a journalist for *Time*. Ten years earlier, he fled the Soviet underground and searched for a spiritual home.

Chambers joined the Communist Party in the 1920s, but he testified that it was a Soviet spy network based in Washington, D.C., that introduced him to Alger Hiss in the 1930s. Hiss served in the federal bureaucracy under the Franklin D. Roosevelt administrations, starting in 1933 at the Department of Agriculture and then at State, where he was the assistant secretary of state, eventually heading the UN desk and participating in the 1945 Yalta Conference. In 1946 he became head of the Carnegie Endowment. According to Chambers, in the mid-1930s Hiss also belonged to an underground network of Communist sympathizers within unions, government offices, and other organizations. These informants funneled information to "handlers," who in turn reported this information to Moscow. By 1937, Chambers asserted, Hiss was involved in a Soviet cell in Washington, D.C., that transitioned from a "sleeper apparatus" to "active espionage." Chambers, as a kind of middleman between embedded spies within the government and the Soviet agents, gathered and hid documents and photographs. Over the course of the hearings and trials, Chambers revealed a stash of stolen State Department documents, all dated 1937 and 1938, which he said were copied on the Hisses' typewriter or in Hiss's longhand. Hiss's lawyers insisted that the documents were forgeries and disputed the authenticity of the typewriter, by then in the possession of the Hiss family's former maid. Because Hiss testified

The sworn testimony of Whittaker Chambers before Congress in 1948 ensnared former State Department employee Alger Hiss in the anti-Communist investigations of the early Cold War. (Courtesy Library of Congress, Prints and Photographs Division; New York World-Telegram photo by Fred Palumbo, LC-USZ62–114739)

before a New York grand jury that he neither saw Chambers after 1935 or 1936 nor ever belonged to the Communist underground, he was indicted on two counts of perjury. The first perjury trial began in late May 1949 and ended in a deadlocked jury. A second trial commenced that fall. Hiss's guilt or innocence hinged on forensic analyses of typewriter fonts, the provenance of microfilmed documents that Chambers hid in a pumpkin on his Maryland farm, and other details over which the men's partisans, critics, and historians pored with inexhaustible curiosity.

Then and since, one's view of Hiss's guilt or innocence served as a political litmus test. The accusations created a proxy for widening divisions in American politics over the legacy of the New Deal. Hiss embodied the influence of East Coast elites in creating and staffing the growing federal bureaucracy and in promoting international cooperation. Progressives saw a sterling résumé in domestic and foreign affairs; conservatives viewed the same career and found appeasement of Communists and an unfounded willingness to see Communists as diplomatic rather than military concerns. Liberals of many stripes flocked to Hiss's defense as Chambers became a hero of the conservative movement.[16]

Accusations of religious and sexual deviancy surrounded the Hiss trials. Gossip about Chambers's homosexuality dated to the 1920s. At one point, Chambers and a younger man lived together with a woman, who was possibly a sexual partner to both men. Investigators working for the Hiss defense team needed to discredit Chambers, and they seized upon his sexual history to illustrate his intrinsic untrustworthiness. Their principal strategy was to paint the Harvard Law–educated Hiss as a paragon of masculine etiquette, refinement, and rectitude and to cast Chambers as a sexual deviant. This plan reflected the widespread idea, enshrined in popular culture, medical texts, and policy guidelines, that "homosexuals" were emotionally and mentally unstable. Stigma surrounding same-sex desire resulted in a far-reaching ban on federal employment of suspected homosexuals because they were presumed to be security risks. Similar employment policies went into effect in many states. More Americans lost their jobs as a result of this "Lavender Scare" than as a result of the Cold War "Red Scare." Not surprisingly, then, investigators for the Hiss defense team questioned Chambers's friends and acquaintances about both his past same-sex relationships and possible hospitalizations or outpatient mental health treatments. Proving Chambers's homosexuality, which was considered a symptom of mental instability, would demonstrate his untrustworthiness. Without overtly describing Chambers as a homosexual,

Hiss's lawyers deployed innuendo to cast Chambers as a rejected suitor, whimpering and wounded.[17]

Insinuations of homosexual desires included Alger Hiss, too. Rumors circulated in the fall of 1948, as the HUAC hearings were under way, that the case was a "battle between two queers." In one of his sessions before HUAC, Chambers described Hiss as being of middling height and slender: "In his walk, if you watch him from behind, there is a slight mince sometime[s]." Investigators for the FBI also collected information about Hiss's stepson, Timothy Hobson, who was dishonorably discharged from the U.S. Navy in 1945 because he engaged in homosexual activity. Hiss, meanwhile, described Chambers as "somewhat queer" four times in a memo he sent to HUAC in September 1948. The word "queer" principally connoted oddness, but among gay men it already suggested same-sex desire or gender nonconformity. Hiss likely used the word intentionally.[18]

In a further effort to cast Chambers as a fraud, Hiss's supporters scrutinized Chambers's conversion. The conversion unfolded in two stages, beginning with baptism in the Episcopal Church. Episcopalian colleagues at *Time*, including editor Samuel Gardner Welles, the son of an Episcopal minister and brother of a bishop, inspired Chambers to join their faith. At the Cathedral of St. John the Divine, the seat of the Episcopal bishop of New York, Chambers was "instructed and baptized" in September 1940. With hindsight, Chambers later explained that even as he prepared to enter the Episcopal Church, he longed to attend a Quaker meeting: "Some instinctive sense of my need, abetted by a memory of a conversation with my grandmother Chambers, ... drew me powerfully to the Religious Society of Friends, the Quakers." After initially hesitating to affiliate with a Quaker meeting because of the group's opposition to war, he went to a meeting in New York City. In 1941 he and his family joined the Pipe Creek Monthly Meeting in Maryland. Like Clare Luce, Chambers insisted that only Christian faith could supplant Communism's infiltration of U.S. politics.[19]

This religious journey became a liability in the prosecution's case against Alger Hiss. During the second Hiss trial, one of the expert witnesses for the defense, Dr. Henry A. Murray, a psychologist at Harvard Medical School, characterized Chambers's shift from the Episcopal Church to the Quaker meeting as evidence of the mental instability that contemporary psychiatry associated with homosexuality. The judge in the second trial even allowed a psychiatrist, Carl Binger, to offer his expert opinion, based on observations of Chambers from reading his work and observing the man in the courtroom, that Chambers was a "psychopathic personality." That diagnosis encompassed a range of symptoms of mental instability, including, Binger noted, "abnormal sexuality." This was the first time that a judge permitted a psychiatrist to provide expert testimony about a witness's mental state. Just a few years after the Hiss trials, the Immigration and Nationality (McCarran-Walter) Act of 1952 barred individuals diagnosed with a "psychopathic personality" from entering the country, a restriction that effectively barred openly gay or lesbian people from legal immigration. That same year, the American Psychiatric Association published its first *Diagnostic and Statistical Manual*, which described homosexuality as a paraphilia, a clinical term for disorders that involve intense and often harmful sexual fantasies directed toward children, nonconsenting adults, animals, or inanimate objects.[20]

The defense team's gay-baiting strategy failed to convince the jury that Chambers was a sex deviant, despite the homophobia of most Americans during these years. Nor did the attempt to portray Chambers as a religious imposter diminish the government's case against Alger Hiss. Hiss was convicted and served eight years in a federal prison. Such was the intensity of American anti-Communism in the early 1950s that the man rumored to be a sexual deviant had more credibility in court than the Ivy League–educated career civil servant he accused of spying for the Soviet Union.

In writing *Witness*, his account of those trials—and of the life that preceded them—Chambers made the case both for his own historical importance and for the righteousness of his Christian battle against Communism. Despite its length (800 pages) and overweening prose, *Witness* was an immediate best seller and a Book-of-the-Month Club selection. The book became a perennial favorite among American political conservatives, earning Chambers a place at the heart of the intellectual Right. *Witness* became required reading for the political conservatives who gathered around William F. Buckley at the *National Review* and inspired generations of conservative activists. President Ronald Reagan awarded Chambers a posthumous Medal of Freedom in 1984. The book helped educated white men, including Buckley and Reagan, see themselves as the victims of history, appreciated by few and redeemed only by their patriotism and faith.[21]

Chambers employed a literary style that brought passionate conviction to the precipice of histrionics. *Witness* comprised both memoir and polemic, detailing his family history, involvement in Communism and espionage, and the religious awakening that drew him away from Soviet influence. "The finger of God was first laid upon my forehead" one morning in the summer of 1935, he wrote in the book's prologue, when the beauty of his young daughter's ear awakened him to the mysteries of God's creation. Chambers juxtaposed that now-famous description of the discovery of God against stories of atheistic amorality that accompanied his Dantean descent into the inner circles of Communist hell: "The thought passed through my mind: 'No, those ears were not created by any chance coming together of atoms in nature (the Communist view). They could have been created only by immense design.'" By 1935 he had been working in the Soviet underground for several years but was increasingly fearful of reprisals and betrayal. *Witness* explained how his faith in Communism declined as his awareness of God increased.[22]

Faith in God, combined with love for his children, enabled Chambers to break with Communism despite his fears of being hunted down by Soviet agents. *Witness* recounts the details of his escape from the underground in 1938, a story replete with all-night vigils, as he waited with a loaded pistol for Soviet goons who never arrived. The task of the book—and its great accomplishment—was to transform a physically repellent social outcast and political traitor into a heroic defender of American democracy. Described even by his friends as having black teeth, body odor, filthy clothes, and uncouth manners, Chambers relied on his literary gifts to claim his place at the center of American intellectual life. Perhaps more than any writer of his generation, Chambers solidified a Cold War consensus politics that opposed "materialism," the atheistic principle that human activity derives from tangible rather than supernatural forces. Chambers loved "the West," and warned that without an authentic (Christian) faith to stop them, Communists destroyed bodies and souls alike.[23]

Many of Chambers's main ideas overlapped with those of Will Herberg, another former leftist who combined a newfound religious devotion and right-leaning politics by the late 1930s and early 1940s. Most famous for his book *Protestant, Catholic, Jew* (1955), Herberg found his own religious faith only in adulthood. Herberg was the child of Russian Jewish parents and immigrated to the United States when he was very young; he grew up in a secular household. In the 1920s and 1930s he became enamored of Marxist ideology, but like many American socialists, he recoiled at the Soviet purges. The Nazi-Soviet pact of 1939 was the final straw, proof for Herberg and others that Soviet-style Communism, and possibly all forms of socialism, inevitably devolved into totalitarianism. Searching for explanations of why socialism failed, Herberg studied the moral teachings of Protestant theologian Reinhold Niebuhr, who described the world as mired in human sinfulness that only God could redeem. Herberg even considered converting to Catholicism. Niebuhr guided him toward Orthodox Judaism instead. Herberg studied at the Jewish Theological Seminary, but his subsequent conclusions about the religious foundations of American democracy remained indebted to Niebuhr's Christian realism.[24]

Herberg argued that Marxism was a kind of religion that challenged the free world. Like Chambers, he explained how Marxism once provided him with a set of beliefs that constituted the entirety of his worldview. It was "a religion, an ethic, and a theology: a vast, all embracing doctrine of man and the universe, a passionate faith endowing life with meaning, vindicating the aims of the movement, idealizing its activities, and guaranteeing its ultimate triumph." Herberg now insisted that democracy rested on "religio-philosophical" truths of human fallibility, with theology (of the right sort) providing the only defense against totalitarianism. Freedom, on its own, could not guarantee democracy's survival. And much as Chambers warned that the fate of the world depended on whether totalitarianism or free faith in God prevailed, Herberg cast the conflict between democratic nations and Soviet-style Communism as a "religious conflict"; as he told an interfaith gathering of clergy in 1952, "quite literally, it is a struggle for the soul of modern man." Anti-Communist and antisecular, Herberg championed religiously based national values as the best defense against Communism. In the pages of Buckley's *National Review*, Herberg reiterated his theory that authentic conservatism required religion and explained his opposition to "the pseudo-religion of secularism." Religion was the sphere within which authentic individualism flowered, the alternative to a "naturalistic" secularism that reduced the richness of human experiences to materialism.[25]

Not all ex-Communist conservatives, of course, found God along the road that led them out of Marxist ideology. The formerly leftist writer John Dos Passos was increasingly conservative by the early 1950s; in 1952, he supported Robert A. Taft in the Republican primary election, finding Dwight Eisenhower too moderate a Cold Warrior. In a review of *Witness* in the *Saturday Review*, Dos Passos praised Chambers for illuminating the nobility of suffering. Liberals trying to tarnish Chambers's reputation, he warned, were more dangerous than Communists. Their "moral lynching of Whittaker Chambers" posed a grave threat to America. That was a view that James Burnham and Max Eastman, both prominent former Communists who joined the ranks of the *National Review*, rejected. Burnham urged fellow conservatives to base their ideology on logic and evidence, not the religious narrative of pain and self-transformation that Chambers, Budenz, and others displayed. Many ex-Communists across the political spectrum rejected the conflation of certain kinds of religious faith with democratic values. Eastman shared with Dos Passos a past alignment with Communism and a post–World War II conservatism, but he differed sharply over the question of religion's relationship to power. An atheist, Eastman criticized Chambers and conservatives like Arizona senator Barry Goldwater for attributing the historical foundations of freedom to God's will. Chambers, he wrote in 1955, was "very profoundly wrong" for casting the struggle between Communism and the free world as a contest between atheism and religion. Eastman proffered a free-market rationale for opposing New Deal liberalism.[26]

William F. Buckley gave the book a more enthusiastic appraisal. Even though Buckley's own faith and politics did not undergo any profound shifts or transformations, he was drawn to other men's religious and political conversions. Born into a devout Roman Catholic family, he remained a Catholic throughout his life, and his conservatism was likewise consistent. He appeared eager to amplify the agonizing disillusionment and self-abnegation that infused the life histories of men such as Chambers, Herberg, and Dos Passos in the pages of the *National Review*. They illustrated for him the importance for conservative politics of religious faith born out of a man's public suffering.[27]

Writing his life story as a political parable allowed Chambers to assign himself a starring role in the drama of democracy's life-or-death struggle against totalitarianism. His was a scandalous story of an American family mired in madness and sexual depravity. If Chambers's childhood was even a fraction as bad as he portrayed it in *Witness*, then it was repellent. Then again, Chambers had a keen ear for metaphor; fact and fantasy often blurred. Chambers described his life—from the moment of its beginning in 1901—as a brutal struggle against death, with the grotesqueness of his own existence causing the suffering of everyone around him. "Mine was a dry birth," Chambers wrote. He weighed twelve pounds: "After this frightful delivery, Dr. Dunning sat for several hours beside my mother, holding together the edges of a torn artery." That medically incoherent passage conveys a sense of his mother, Laha, as a stoic, suffering figure destined to bring him into the world, whatever the cost. *Witness* relayed crass anecdotes of childhood bullying, including an episode where a few boys peed on a lollipop and then offered it to another, unsuspecting child: "I think it was at that point [in the first grade] that I developed a deep distrust of the human race." As he described it, the family home on the South Shore of Long Island descended into disarray, its peeling wallpaper a metaphor for the nation's moral decline. His father, Jay, was an artist who worked in the city and met lovers there; for a time in Chambers's childhood, his father rented a room in Brooklyn. Biographer Sam Tanenhaus believes that some of these lovers were men. Laha was dramatic and talented, her ambitions thwarted by the constraints of middle-class domesticity and a husband who was both unfaithful and stingy. Paranoia was a family hobby. After Jay moved out, Laha began to keep an axe in her bedroom; young Whittaker slept with a knife under his pillow.[28]

Chambers linked his irreligious upbringing to his family's faults: "My parents were nominal Episcopalians," and he attended Sunday School at an Episcopal church until another child afflicted with whooping cough blamed the Chambers children for spreading it. His paternal grandmother came from a family of Quakers. Chambers described himself as religiously adept, sensitive from an early age to the aesthetic intimations of divine presence. His appreciation of the natural world offered him early awareness of God: he shared a childhood memory of seeing "a field covered from end to end, as high as my head, with thistles in full bloom," alight with goldfinches. "The sight was so unexpected, the beauty was so absolute, that I thought I could not stand it and held to the hedge for support. Out loud I said: 'God.'" This "intuition," he wrote, lay buried within his subconscious for the next forty years.[29]

As a young adult, Chambers bore witness to his own sanctified persecution. He ran away the day of his high school graduation and worked under an assumed name as a laborer in a Washington, D.C., rail yard. He went to New Orleans, where he nearly starved, and then asked his parents for train fare home. Gaunt and righteous, he moved back in with his parents. In the fall of 1920, when he was nineteen, he entered Williams College but stayed only a few days before deciding it was not for him. He attended Columbia instead, where he remained through his junior year. He studied with English professor Mark van Doren, who also influenced Thomas Merton; took a part-time job in the New York Public Library newspaper room; and committed himself to becoming a writer.[30]

With a literary flair that inspired generations of American conservatives to appreciate their martyrdom, Chambers urged his readers to recognize that it was he who suffered most of all from his family's tragedies. After his mentally ill maternal grandmother moved in with them, she took to wandering about the house at night while holding a knife, which was a terrible inconvenience to Whittaker. His younger brother, Richard, experienced some kind of psychological break during his freshman year of college and began to rant about the meaningless of life. He dropped out and moved back to the family home, too, helping his mother repair the dilapidated house in between drinking and bringing sex workers back to a small garage in the yard. Twice Chambers interrupted his brother's attempted suicides in their parents' home. After Richard married and moved to an apartment, his drinking and depression worsened. Whittaker was not present to intervene at Richard's third, and successful, suicide attempt. Inured to empathy, Chambers questioned not why his brother killed himself but why he (Whittaker) had not. He determined that the reason was his moral superiority; "deep within me there was a saving fierceness that my brother lacked." When his father died, Whittaker ruminated on the awesome responsibility of being his family's last remaining procreator: "The promise of new growth lay wholly within me—in my having children.... But by then I agreed with my [deceased] brother that to repeat the misery of such lives as ours would be a crime against life." A heterosexual ethos that celebrated male-female sex was implicit in Budenz's and Bentley's books; it suffused the narrative of *Witness*.[31]

Chambers discovered Communism while a student at Columbia. He claimed in *Witness* that he dropped out of college in 1925 to become a full-time Communist organizer, but in truth he was disappointed after university faculty found some of his poetry blasphemous. He had no clear idea of what to do with his life. In *Witness*, he described the decision to drop out as prophetic; the world needed him. Existential dread about the "dying world" compelled his choice. Communism provided "faith and a vision, something for which to live and something for which to die." Communist Party involvement also enabled a kind of sexual adulthood for Chambers, although he regretted his initial immorality. He moved out of his parents' house and into a "party marriage" with another Communist, similar to the nonmarital union between Louis and Margaret Budenz during Louis's years in the party. These arrangements, which lacked legal formalities, reflected Communist antipathy to state regulation of sexual relations. A few years later, in 1931, Chambers married

Esther Shemitz, a pacifist fellow traveler and artist who had been born in Russia. (Laha Chambers, Whittaker's mother, referred to Shemitz as "my Jewish daughter-in-law," but Shemitz was not a practicing Jew.) Esther gave birth to a daughter, Ellen, in 1933 and a son, John, in 1936. Early in their marriage Esther and Whittaker lived in an apartment that adjoined the rooms of another Communist couple, and rumors circulated of illicit, varied sexual pairings among the four friends.[32]

Throughout those years, Chambers worked as a spy, passing government documents to his Soviet handlers. He lived in fear of notoriously violent agents and noticed when several spies disappeared under mysterious circumstances. Disillusioned both with Communism and with the perils of life as a spy, he broke from the underground sometime between 1937 and 1938. Scraping by with work as a translator, he hid with his family in Florida and then moved to Baltimore. He soon found a job writing for *Time* and began commuting to New York from his family's home in rural Maryland. The job at *Time* put Chambers on a path to religious, political, and sexual legitimacy.

Reactions to *Witness*, much like the response to the Hiss trials, split along political lines. For anti-Communists, the book proved that they were correct all along to search out and punish Communists working in the federal government. The *New York Herald Tribune*, a longtime Republican newspaper, declared that *Witness* was an "amazing autobiography." It was a great piece of literature, arguably "the book of the year, and possibly of the decade." The centrality of religious faith to Chambers's journey out of Communism impressed many reviewers. Richard Nixon, a fellow Quaker, wrote an appreciation of *Witness* for the *Saturday Review*, a weekly publication that featured reviews of literature, describing it as "an amazingly accurate account of what happened during the ... investigation of the Hiss Case." Nixon hailed Chambers for treating Communism as a religion and for insisting on "a counter-faith to combat the Communist idea—a faith based not on materialism but on a recognition of God." As the leading member of HUAC to have pressed for Hiss's prosecution, Nixon certainly had a stake in whether Chambers's version of events was truthful.[33]

Leftist and liberal critics struck back at the idea that religious belief or conversion had anything to do with political truth, and they did so with unbridled nastiness. These critics advocated for secular solutions to political problems. They objected to the idea that the defeat of Communism depended on belief in God. One of these critics, the historian

Arthur Schlesinger Jr., lambasted *Witness* in the *Saturday Review*. He found much of the book objectionable. Schlesinger took offense at Chambers's graphic descriptions of his suicide attempts, his brother's death, and his family's violent behavior. He disagreed with Chambers's conclusions about the significance of whatever espionage may have occurred. Schlesinger was especially outraged by Chambers's argument that the antithesis of Communism was Christian belief. A centrist supporter of the New Deal, Schlesinger called for a rationalist government of expert managers, something that religion alone could not accomplish: "To divide the world between those who reject God and those who worship God would put some curious people in Mr. Chambers's camp." Other reviewers were unable to mask their contempt for Chambers. One reporter who covered the Hiss-Chambers case characterized the author of *Witness* as "the bland, dumpy, and devious Chambers," who composed "a fat volume of 799 pages, unevenly compounded of fact, of faith, and of metaphysical mush." Writer Irving Howe, a socialist and secular Jew, despised the sanctimoniousness of both the book and its author: "From 'Witness' an unsympathetic reader might, in fact, conclude that God spent the past several years as a special aid to the House Committee on Un-American Activities." (Howe was similarly dismissive of Herberg's defense of religious anti-Communism.)[34]

The shame of sexual deviance slipped into these reviews, alluded to but never mentioned explicitly. When reviewers noted the book's baseless claims and exaggerations as evidence of Chambers's insecurities, they occasionally referenced unnamed personal failings that clouded his character. "Some of the more unpalatable personal facts have been omitted," one wrote. Charles Alan Wright, who called *Witness* "the longest work of fiction of the year," alluded to the sexual innuendos that surrounded Chambers during the Hiss trials: "It is a too-well-scrubbed Chambers who is depicted here. Many of the lies, eccentricities, and immoralities in his past are forgotten." For readers familiar with the trial, these euphemistic immoralities connoted sex with other men. The FOIA documents released in the 1970s proved what many students of the Hiss-Chambers case long suspected about Chambers's sexuality. The revelations about his same-sex sexual encounters during the 1930s reveal, moreover, that he needed his religious conversion to accomplish even more than *Witness* suggested it would. Faith not just led him out of Communism, but it reoriented his sexuality away from men and toward monogamous fidelity to his wife.[35]

Witness asked a lot of its readers, but even readers who recoiled at the book's length or grim details could find other ways to glean the main points. The *Saturday Evening Post* published a condensed, serialized version during the spring of 1952, before the book's publication, a mere 40,000 words spread across two months of weekly issues, compared to the finished book's 200,000 words. *Reader's Digest* published a similarly condensed version in the early fall, cut from 800 to about 150 pages. These expurgated editions in no way diminished the book's overpowering tendentiousness. Some readers, at least, found in them a noble story. After the *Chicago Daily Tribune* published a favorable review of *Witness*, one reader thanked the newspaper for giving the book its due. "Having read his story in a magazine," Mrs. Dora K. Bent hoped that more people would recognize its merits.[36]

The popularity of *Witness* among American conservatives presaged their emerging embrace of right-leaning religious anti-Communism—whether Roman Catholic, Quaker, or fundamentalist Protestant—by the 1970s. In the 1950s, Chambers became a superstar for a conservative movement that argued for Christianity's importance to democracy, the defense of free markets, and aggressive military actions to defeat Communism. Ideological conservatives honored him as a voice for "freedom." What they had in mind was not religious liberty writ large but a much more specific vision of religious faith tied to a critique of New Deal liberalism and to support for sexual traditionalism.

Striking, in hindsight, is how effectively these religious narratives shored up a conservative political ideal of the Christian defender of American freedoms. Protagonists in stories about religious absolutes captivated the Right, even as they wove narratives of drastic dips and swerves on their road to Christian Americanism. Because these writers insisted on the consonance between their religious beliefs and their political activities, they invited questions about how the sincerity of one affected the veracity of the other.

The emerging consensus that Hiss was guilty of espionage undermined the Left's earlier dichotomy between a duplicitous Chambers and a virtuous Hiss. When historian Allen Weinstein set out in the 1970s to write the definitive history of the Hiss-Chambers case, he presumed that he would document a story of false conviction. Amid revelations about the FBI's domestic spying program, COINTELPRO, and the crimes of the Nixon administration, left-leaning scholars like Weinstein (who has expressed more conservative political views in the years since) were inclined to believe that the New Dealer Alger Hiss was the scapegoat of politically conservative efforts to discredit liberalism. Instead, supported by FBI files and previously unreleased evidence, Weinstein concluded that Hiss indeed passed classified U.S. government information to his Soviet handlers.[37]

Further confirmation of Hiss's guilt arrived in the mid-1990s, when the National Security Agency released documents from the Venona project, a covert effort from the early 1940s until 1980 to intercept and translate Soviet diplomatic cables. Historians pored over the documents, identifying code names for Americans who spied for the Soviet Union. The Soviets referred to Julius Rosenberg, who passed along top secret information about the American atom bomb project, as "Liberal." One document mentioned "Ales," which many scholars believe was Alger Hiss's code name. The principal historians of the Hiss-Chambers case assert that the documents conclusively prove that Hiss was a spy; a few insist that "Ales" might refer to someone else.[38]

The gay-baiting sexual innuendos and outright allegations against Chambers persisted long after the trial's conclusion. In 1967, the psychiatrist Meyer Zeligs argued in his psychohistory of the trial, *Friendship and Fratricide*, that Chambers became an Episcopalian and then a Quaker as a manifestation of his fantasy of "suffering and salvation," the Episcopal baptism a ritual of "rebirth." Zeligs argued that Chambers accused Hiss in a misguided attempt both to woo him and to punish him for rejecting his sexual come-ons. Chambers converted to the Quaker faith, Zeligs postulated, because he incorrectly believed that Priscilla Hiss, Alger's wife, was a "birthright Quaker," and he wanted to identify as closely as possible with the Hiss family. Zeligs and other Hiss partisans thought they spied a suspicious lack of emotion in the way Chambers described his conversion to the Episcopal Church, and for years after the trials concluded, they attempted to document the inauthenticity of his faith. In his research, Zeligs sought to discredit the religious transformation that Chambers described in *Witness* by discovering inconsistencies between Chambers's accounts of the witnesses at his baptism, church records, and the recollections of the priest and friends who supported his conversion. If ex-Communist converts declared their newly discovered faith as a badge of truth, Hiss's lawyers wanted to rip that badge from Chambers's grubby lapel.[39]

Zeligs substantiated his argument that Chambers lusted in vain after Hiss by drawing conclusions from ambiguous evidence of same-sex encounters involving Chambers. One informant, Leon Herald, sent Zeligs a letter in which he described an experience of sexual assault (although he did not name it as such) in the 1930s by a man who might have been Chambers. At the time, Herald lived in Chicago, the site of a meeting of the John Reed Society, a leftist cultural organization popular among Communists. Like many local activists, he offered to provide housing for out-of-town attendees who could not afford a hotel room. The man who stayed with him appeared to be homeless, wearing filthy, rumpled clothing, his teeth blackened and rotting. Herald described how he awoke in the middle of the night in the midst of an orgasm, his penis in the visitor's mouth. From subsequent media coverage of the Hiss trial, he identified his assailant as Whittaker Chambers.[40]

The political stakes in the case have abated, but a few voices from the political Left, including that of Alger's son, Tony, cast Alger Hiss as the innocent target of Whittaker Chambers, the duplicitous schemer. Tony, who is openly gay, wrote in the mid-1970s about Chambers's sexual motivations for damaging his father's reputation, reviving the theories of thwarted same-sex desire that the Hiss defense employed at the second trial. As late as 2001, Tony Hiss maintained a website on the New York University server that gathered evidence to disparage Chambers and assert his father's innocence.[41]

The lingering ambiguity surrounding the Hiss-Chambers case only amplifies the intertwined salience of religious confession and sexual normality in the narratives of ex-Communists. For Chambers and the others, religious conversion promised the pronouncement of a coherent identity as a person whose words could—and in these high-stakes cases, must—be believed. These authors asked their readers to trust their stories of journeying from doubt to truth, while admitting that they were serial liars. Their books claimed that the journey concluded, and that their identity crisis resolved, within a faith—and a politics—of defined boundaries and definite values.

The domestic Cold War linked unionism to socialism, and it associated same-sex desires with traitorous blackmail. In that atmosphere of sexual suspicion, narratives about the Christian foundations of American democracy did more than defend the merits of capitalism. They made assertions about sexual "truth" central to the operations of American power.

Chapter 3 The Fear of False Belief

....

A vision of democracy that required public confessions of spiritual truth faced an unavoidable dilemma: sometimes those confessions turned out to be false. Corrupt belief systems could subvert an individual's mind; people who professed to hold sincere beliefs might be discovered as liars. Surveying the damage from European and Asian fascism, and intensely anxious about Communism's global creep, many Americans worried that authoritarian governments could rob an individual of his or her ability to make autonomous choices. Closer to home, critics feared that Americans were too willing to let other people—and new media such as television—do their thinking for them, creating captive minds that might succumb to false prophets. These concerns permeated both social science and popular culture throughout the 1950s and 1960s. Two episodes from the mid-1950s—of an ex-Communist government informant who admitted that he lied profusely under oath and of American POWs in North Korea who refused repatriation—offered uncomfortable evidence of how much was at stake.

Harvey Matusow was an inconsequential American Communist who became a staggeringly prolific government informant. Between 1950 and 1953, he provided the federal government with the names of more than 200 suspected Communists, including prominent union leaders who faced jail time as a consequence of his testimony. Just as suddenly, in 1954, he said that a new religious faith inspired him to confess that he fabricated much of what he told the government. If Clare Luce, Louis Budenz, and Whittaker Chambers tied their religious commitments to their American patriotism, Matusow's narrative of religious searching loosened those bonds. He promised to reveal truths, but instead of proving the dangers of Communism, he offered a revelation about the moral bankruptcy of American politics. Even the title of his memoir, *False*

Witness (1955), undercut the political aims of Whittaker Chambers's treatise on faith-based anti-Communist conservatism. Like a pin in the inflated balloon of postwar religious anti-Communism, Matusow drained the air out of the informant system. In his guile and self-regard, Matusow personified the tenuousness of the links between American democracy and authentic faith.[1]

The consequences of the American military engagement on the Korean peninsula in the early 1950s ratcheted up these fears about how antidemocratic or anti-Christian leaders controlled their followers. After the Communist government in North Korea invaded the anti-Communist military dictatorship based in Seoul in June 1950, the first major military conflict of the Cold War began. President Harry Truman committed tens of thousands of American servicemen to the United Nations' "police action" in Korea. Three years and nearly 40,000 American casualties later, the U.S. government declared strategic victory despite gaining no new territory for South Korea. When twenty-four American POWs in North Korea refused repatriation in 1954, claiming that they came to agree with the Communist philosophy they learned from their captors, they instigated widespread fear about "mind control" and influenced the neologism "brainwashing." The term seemed to explain the behavior of Cardinal Jósef Mindszenty of Hungary, a former anti-Communist who emerged from months of Communist interrogations in 1948 to confess to absurd crimes that discredited the Roman Catholic Church in Eastern Europe and ensured the Communist Party's sweep of regional power. (In the late 1960s and 1970s, as chapter 6 explores, evangelicals and others deployed the term "brainwashing" to explain "cults" and religious experiments.)[2]

The U.S. government defined its strategic interest as halting the spread of Communism and committed troops to conflict zones for that purpose; captive servicemen's acquiescence to Communist ideology exposed vulnerabilities in the freedom of conscience necessary for American democracy to thrive. Declarations by the American POWs that "there is no freedom of speech in the United States" and that they found "real democracy" under Communism became proof positive that their captors controlled their thinking. There could be no other explanation for why young American men refused to return home to "college on the GI Bill if they want it, or a job in a free country if they do not." It was all well and good for Communists to become Christian crusaders, but the idea that American Christians might become Communists undermined the premises of Cold War anti-Communist faith.[3]

Psychologists and other social scientists validated these fears. They produced theories about mass culture's deadening effect on individuality and about the power of authoritarian regimes to silence dissent. Even science fiction books and films cast the American family as easy prey for body snatchers. Sociologists, novelists, and social observers produced a trove of books about the risks that mass society posed to authenticity. They adapted principles from psychoanalysis to the study of entire societies. In 1950 a group of exiled German Jewish scholars produced *The Authoritarian Personality*. In an attempt to explain the fascist leaders who arose in the prior decades and the millions of people who obeyed them, the authors proposed a typology of traits, cultivated in childhood, that informed an adult's predilection for authoritarian governance. Perhaps the rise and strength of Nazism revealed something inherent in German national character, or perhaps it exposed the susceptibility of all individuals to authoritarianism.[4]

A new psychology of "identity" studied these questions. "Identity" usefully combined a psychological concept of the personality with a sociological idea of social location or associational life. It became the dominant way in which Americans named both their individual and collective personhood. The age knew no finer thinker on the subject of authentic identity than German Jewish émigré scholar Erich Fromm. One of his books, *Escape from Freedom* (1941), examined the conditions that produced authoritarian regimes in order to prevent more of them from arising. *Escape from Freedom* described the "loss of identity" that led to mass conformity. Authoritarian regimes waged wars, centralized capital, destabilized social institutions, and otherwise convinced individuals of their isolation and powerlessness. Fromm explained that freedom could be terrifying for the unmoored individual confronting massive concentrations of power. Dependent on external affirmations of intrinsic worth, the individual living in these conditions fused his or her identity to an external source of power "in order to acquire the strength which the individual self is lacking." Reduced to a "pseudo self," this insecure individual "has in a measure lost his identity." Fromm characterized the pursuit of authentic selfhood not as navel-gazing self-indulgence but as a necessary precondition for the expansion of human freedom. Fromm and other mid-twentieth-century social theorists warned about internalized self-deceptions rather than intentional masquerade.[5]

This twentieth-century concern about individuals whose internal identity had been corrupted differed from much older fears of con men and imposters. Knowing whether to trust that people are who or what they say they are has long been a conundrum for people who encounter strangers and travel long distances. In the 1850s, the fragile American economy suffered from the long cons of counterfeiters who printed money with the names of phony banks and evaded the nascent central government's reach. "Confidence men" and tricksters populated nineteenth-century fiction and inhabited its towns and cities; no one was sure whom to trust if they did not grow up amid these people and did not know their pedigree. Nineteenth-century Americans grappled with the deceptions of professional grifters and impersonators. Circus impresario P. T. Barnum's genius was in fashioning an entertainment empire premised on the appeal of artifice and the profusion of doubt. He dared his customers to disprove that the woman on the stage was the 160-year-old former nursemaid to George Washington, as she and Barnum claimed. He and others created a popular culture that mass-produced "humbug" and teased audiences about their susceptibility to "bunk." Fears about one kind of masquerade merged with others; tales of enslaved people who charted a path to freedom often involved both racial passing and cross-dressing; impersonations of racial identity also challenged assumptions about gender and sexuality.[6]

Explanations for religious choices that fell outside the mainstream likewise emphasized imposture or mind control. In the nineteenth-century United States, Protestants who viewed the growing population of American Catholics as a threat to their political and cultural power described nuns as deviants who "seduced" innocent Protestant women into joining their ranks. Anti-Mormon literature of that time portrayed the women who joined the Church of Jesus Christ of Latter-day Saints (LDS) as deluded; as one historian explains, "female participation in the 'degradation' of plural marriage was comprehensible only as a consequence of fanaticism or mental magnetism." Centuries after the Reformation, people in Britain continued to fear the presence of converts to Catholicism who passed undetected among their Protestant neighbors. In the United States as well, religious and erotic deviance overlapped in descriptions of the darkly mysterious confessional booth, conversely suggesting that Catholics were adept at disguising their spiritual and sexual nonconformity. The con man who intentionally deceived others declined in cultural importance by the mid-twentieth century. Far more threatening was the corrupted mind, one that thought it was sincere but was in fact controlled by a nefarious external force.[7]

Fromm and other experts with guidance about authentic identity and self-knowledge entered into a rich tradition of American advice literature. Advice books for middle-class women flourished in the nineteenth century with words of wisdom about how a wife's attention to domestic details might improve the lives of her husband and children. In the 1920s, advertising executive Bruce Barton offered parables about Jesus as a self-made businessman to give other men hope for their own career advancement. Throughout the twentieth century, readers of local newspapers and family magazines encountered columns with tips for self-improvement penned by psychologists, physicians, clergy, and self-styled experts. Radio and television brought this advice to new media. But whereas earlier advice givers tended to focus on external changes, whether by creating a cozy living room or by cooking a wholesome meal, a new genre, self-help, emerged in the 1950s and 1960s that paid more attention to internal self-discovery.[8]

Surpassing Fromm as a popular authority on authentic identity was psychiatrist Erik Erikson, a Denmark-born Jew who trained in Vienna to be a child analyst. His work propelled academic conversations about identity into the public culture. Erikson moved to the United States in 1933 to escape rising anti-Semitism in Europe. Breaking from the Freudian orthodoxy of his colleagues in the close-knit field of psychoanalysis, he introduced the concept of "identity" to theories of the ego. Psychoanalysis described the ego as one of the three components of the subconscious, mediating between the impulses of the primitive id and the rule-abiding strictures of the superego, to offer the self a rational way to interact with the world. Erikson argued that the ego experienced a process of "synthesis" over time that created "self-sameness and continuity." He argued that the ego's chief purpose was to provide individuals with a "sense of identity." In *Childhood and Society* (1950) Erikson described eight stages of a person's development. He formulated a theory of the "identity crisis," which occurred when individuals lost their sense of uniqueness and began to feel that their lives possessed no unifying purpose. Likewise, in *Young Man Luther* (1958), a psychohistory of Martin Luther and his motives for criticizing the papal hierarchy, Erikson analyzed the "conversion" that drew Luther into an Augustinian monastery in Saxony in the early sixteenth century. Erikson argued that an adolescent identity crisis prompted the young German monk to renounce both his father and his obedience to the pope and eventually to author critiques of Roman Catholicism that helped inaugurate the Protestant Reformation. The book did not sell especially well, and Protestant and Catholic theologians scoffed at Erikson's musings about Martin Luther's identity crisis. Despite *Young Man Luther*'s commercial and critical shortcomings, Erikson succeeded in popularizing the idea that adolescence represented a confusing but pivotal life stage. The adolescent individual's identity was malleable and thus easily enticed by the allure of external belief systems.[9]

Anthropologists contributed to these conversations eagerly. They presented themselves as public intellectuals able to explain the cultural dynamics that shaped individual personalities and concepts of the self. Franz Boas, a professor of anthropology at Columbia University, trained a generation of students, including Ruth Benedict and Margaret Mead, who promulgated the "culture and personality" theory of identity and values. Their far-ranging and widely read studies argued that a society's or nation's "culture" shaped how people within that society understood themselves. Even more important, these social scientists argued that many of the constitutive parts of identity, from race to gender and sexuality, were the products of cultural processes, not merely biological inheritances. By the 1930s, cultural anthropologists were publishing major scholarly works (sometimes also published as mass-market paperbacks) to show that racial origins bore no more imprint on biology than the consequences of ancestral geographic proximity. The result was what one historian has described as an "epistemic shift in social thought that reverberated throughout the rest of the twentieth century." Social scientists questioned the biological basis of race and of gender roles, reconceptualizing them as products of culture and reflections of circumstance. These theorists linked the emergence of race with their theories of sexuality, describing each as socially constructed. Their work resonated with an established body of African American intellectual production that challenged the science of racial differences and argued that racial determinism was anathema to democracy. By the 1950s, so much of what determined a person's personness seemed bound to culture.[10]

Sociologists of the 1950s made a point of blaming mass culture for squashing individualism and "open-mindedness." Conformity squelched rational debate and autonomous thinking, without which a free and democratic society could not survive. Liberal intellectuals praised autonomous selfhood as essential for social and economic progress. David

Riesman studied with Erich Fromm, and he shared his teacher's concern with the pursuit of authentic individuality. In *The Lonely Crowd* (1950), Riesman distinguished between older "tradition-directed" societies, transitional "inner-directed" types, and the modern problem of the "other-directed" social character. "Inner-directed" people had "acquire[d] early in life an internalized set of goals." Americans found themselves by 1950 living in a society dominated by "outer-directed" types. Lacking an internalized set of norms or character ideals, employees of tertiary management and service jobs instead sought guidance from external sources, whether those be their friends or the mass media.[11]

For some of these social scientific thinkers, religious faith promised a way out of mass culture's malaise. In *The Quest for Community* (1953) sociologist Robert Nisbet bemoaned the loss of nineteenth-century individualism and self-sufficiency. Contemporary Americans were beset by "insecurity and disintegration" and obsessed with external markers of status. The results were "moral estrangement and spiritual isolation." Nisbet explained that contemporary social forces were damaging men's and women's spiritual selves. He echoed theologians who argued that secularism produced social alienation.[12]

Religious writers were eager to popularize their advice about how to remain true to one's self in a world of terrifying absolutes. Sales of inspirational and devotional religious books broke all previous records. In the 1920s, Harry Emerson Fosdick grew famous for leading the Protestant defense of modernity against Protestant fundamentalism, a movement that argued for biblical inerrancy and a complex theory of the end times. Fosdick soon found an appreciative audience for his blend of liberal Protestantism and psychology. In his book *On Being a Real Person* (1943), Fosdick shared insights from more than twenty years of pastoral counseling at Riverside Church in New York City. He presented liberal Protestantism as utterly consonant with modern psychiatry. The central problem of human existence, he explained, was the desire to be a "real person." Fosdick told his readers that they could live fuller, more authentic lives if they combined faith in God with psychological introspection.[13]

Fosdick was not alone in arguing that the combination of a theologically liberal faith and the principles of psychiatry offered the best way to discover one's authentic personhood. *Peace of Mind* (1946), by Rabbi Joshua Loth Liebman, sold over a million copies within two years of its publication. With psychology's help, Liebman cheered, "*we find out who we are*! Psychotherapy is a method by which we stop being someone we thought we were (or have been told we ought to be) and become *our-selves*." Liebman invited his readers to see themselves as active agents in the shaping of their identities. Published just a few years later than Liebman's best seller, Fulton Sheen's *Peace of Soul* (1949) relocated the "confession of sins" to the confessional. He spoke for many Catholics who considered psychiatry incompatible with their faith. Sheen's book, too, reached a mass audience of readers eager for wisdom.[14]

Americans' search for meaning drew them to serious books about the search for God and faith as well. Among these texts, the most influential was Thomas Merton's Catholic conversion memoir, *The Seven Storey Mountain* (1948). The book won Clare Luce's admiration and made Merton a spiritual role model for millions of readers, but it was an unusual text. Unlike most other religious best sellers of the day, Merton's book was theologically dense. Where other authors promised peace of mind or soul, Merton called for personal sacrifice. The title itself invited readers to enter a 500-page book named for the term Dante used for purgatory in *The Inferno*. Merton argued that religious conversion—and inward transformation of the self in relation to the divine—produced the "real" person otherwise obscured by materialistic and temporal concerns.[15]

Merton's book alternated among charming descriptions of childhood and family life, scenes from his youthful jesting with bohemian friends, and sustained discussions of Catholic doctrine and philosophy. His interest in Catholicism began while he pursued his PhD in English at Columbia University. In the midst of his studies, he read works by Catholic theologians, and these books changed him. He was baptized into the Roman Catholic Church at Corpus Christi, a parish church near Columbia's campus, on November 16, 1938, when he was twenty-three years old. Merton wanted his conversion to Catholicism to be totalizing, and he grew increasingly dissatisfied with being "in the world." In December 1941 he entered the Cistercian order of "Trappist" monks at the Abbey of Gethsemani, near Louisville, Kentucky. He took vows of silence, poverty, and chastity. In the book, Merton admonished readers who sought a deeper love of Christ to abandon their pursuit of personal gratification and instead "sacrifice your pleasures and comforts for the love of God and give the money you no longer spend on those things, to the poor." Merton offered an austere vision of worldly renunciation for the sake of spiritual truth and enlightenment.[16]

A surprise literary sensation, *The Seven Storey Mountain* helped make Catholic conversion narratives commercially successful in a thriving religious publication market. Merton's memoir stayed atop the best-seller lists for a year. Within a month of the book's publication, the Catholic magazine *America* predicted that *The Seven Storey Mountain* would become "a spiritual classic." In 1950, the Catholic Writers Guild of America bestowed its Golden Book Award for nonfiction on Merton's narrative. Signet published a twenty-five-cent paperback edition in 1951. By January 1955, the combined hardcover and paperback sales topped 900,000 copies.[17]

Merton sought solitude at Gethsemani even as he found fame as a writer. The abbey exercised strict control over the public identity of the book's cloistered author. His face obscured from readers' view on the book jacket, Merton became, through his words, the most widely read and intimately known mid-twentieth-century American convert. *The Seven Storey Mountain* offered a counterpoint to another top-selling book that year, Paul Blanshard's anti-Catholic diatribe, *American Freedom and Catholic Power*, and to Liebman's *Peace of Mind*. Other authors capitalized on this cultural interest in religious conversion with group biographies and collected essays by and about converts from Saint Augustine to Clare Boothe Luce.[18]

The Catholic poet Horace Gregory grasped that *The Seven Storey Mountain* addressed the spiritual thirst of a reading public. Interest in Communism in the 1930s, Gregory wrote, was but a prelude to a deepening quest for spiritual meaning. Searching for "theological" insights, Americans in the 1940s now looked not to "the scientific materialists" but to spiritual adepts like Merton. Thomas Merton's autobiography, Gregory wrote, "has arrived at precisely the right moment."[19]

Not all of the advice focused on contemplative self-realization. Another blockbuster book that year, Rev. Norman Vincent Peale's *Guide to Confident Living* (1948), previewed the ideas Peale offered in his spectacularly successful 1952 book, *The Power of Positive Thinking*, about the instrumental use of prayer to attain success in family life and career. In these books and in advice columns in family magazines, popular religious authors tapped into the reading public's desire for guidance about finding answers to questions about their careers, sex lives, and relationships. Peale, Liebman, and their ilk promised quick results from relatively simple acts of faith, prompting many critics to warn that they allowed mass culture to co-opt religion. Peale in particular described faith as transactional: pray to God, and God will provide.[20]

Peale's advice and the evangelist Billy Graham's televised crusades troubled Thomas Merton and Erich Fromm. Graham crisscrossed the United States, Europe, and Australia from the late 1940s through the early twenty-first century leading massive revivals, many of them televised, that invited individuals to accept Jesus into their hearts and be "born again." Seated at his desk in the Abbey of Gethsemani, Merton may have rolled his eyes. He struck up an epistolary conversation with Fromm after reading Fromm's *Psychoanalysis and Religion* (1950). Fromm shared Merton's disapproval of easy faith. In 1954, Fromm told Merton that he recognized the chasm between Merton's moral seriousness and the pablum of Graham, Peale, and Sheen: "I am shocked by the blending of alleged religious teaching with the profoundly irreligious spirit of the modern business world. I am afraid that to 'sell' religion, and the idea of God[,] is a worse sacrilege than any denial of God can be." Though not a believer himself, Fromm was wary of the creation of idols. Merton's narrative about the sacrifices required for religious authenticity offered a far different message from other popular religious texts, one that impressed trained academics and a mass audience.[21]

Fromm and Merton did not exchange letters about Billy Graham's 1957 televised revival in New York City, when Graham and his team secured sixteen weeks of live, prime-time television coverage. Had Fromm and Merton discussed the "Billy Graham Crusade," they almost certainly would have observed the advent of the "electric church" in those broadcasts and in programs like Graham's *Hour of Decision* and Fulton Sheen's weekly program *Life Is Worth Living*. While serious theologians viewed the televised crusades as signs of the further erosion of religious sincerity, television evangelists knew that they had a novel means of channeling religious connections. Graham in particular understood that he validated his authenticity with the people he most hoped to reach when he used mass media. Radio, television, and film brought the timbre of his voice and scenes of large-scale conversion into intimate spaces of home.[22]

Scholars scoffed at Graham's stadium-sized revivals and their message of easy faith. The theologian Reinhold Niebuhr deplored what one scholar has called the "cult of reassurance" offered by Peale and Graham. The mainstream of American culture embraced it. President Dwight Eisenhower, whom Graham supported and advised on his decision to be baptized upon taking office in 1953, likewise viewed religiosity as a good in and of itself, with little interest in theological debate or doctrinal differences. The religious revivals of the 1950s exploited the power of mass media. They further enmeshed free-market economics with American politics. As growing middle-class prosperity brought television sets into nine out of ten American households by 1960, entrepreneurial religious leaders seized their opportunity.[23]

Few figures in the 1950s embodied these questions about how religion mattered to democracy, mass culture, and authentic identity more than Harvey Matusow, one of the most influential, if largely forgotten, liars of the mid-twentieth century. Between 1946 and 1955, Matusow became a Communist, a paid government informant, an outspoken ex-Communist, and finally a converted truth-teller who exposed the excesses of McCarthyism. With equal parts manic energy and inflated ego, he willed himself into the center of American politics at breakneck speed. When his lies and counter-lies caught up with him, Matusow confessed his duplicity in a conversion memoir that strained credulity. The story of how one young man moved from Communist to valued informant—only to recant much of his testimony within a few years—offers a striking window onto the power of public confessions in the 1950s.

Matusow changed his mind drastically, numerous times. He leaned on popular psychology to explain his inconsistencies. A nagging inferiority complex, he wrote, drove his quest for fame. His memoir, *False Witness* (1955), gave a brief account of a middle-class childhood in the Bronx. His recollections were notable for their crushing self-loathing: "The Bronx didn't cheer on the week I was born," he begins. The narrative omitted details about his family and offered few illustrative examples other than those that emphasized his mediocrity. In sports and in school, "there was always somebody who made me feel inferior." Matusow was seventeen when he enlisted in the U.S. Army to fight in World War II, following in his older brother's footsteps. The war was a tragedy for the Matusow family; in 1944 his brother's plane went down over Nuremburg, Germany. When Matusow came home from the war he found himself, he explained years later, "with no identity. And I wanted an identity."[24]

Matusow joined the Communist Party after he returned home from his military service. In 1946, at a friend's invitation, he attended meetings of American Youth for Democracy, a progressive group, and found himself drawn to the Communists he met there. Soon thereafter, he joined the party. During his years as a Communist, Matusow sold subscriptions to the *Sunday Worker*, but he otherwise made few positive contributions to the socialist revolution. He was an ancillary and unpopular member of the party's local organization. His reasons for admiring and then despairing of Communism seemed to revolve around matters of bureaucratic protocol: after experiencing the thrill of gathering signatures for petitions, he discovered the party's offices were closed when they should have been open; appointments were not kept. Comrades who dealt with Matusow found little to admire in the young man. Matusow recalled a "feeling of hurt and envy toward those who were criticizing me." Just like the kids in grade school, the Communists did not like him.[25]

Federal indictments against leaders of the United Auto Workers (UAW) in 1949 gave Matusow an idea: he could parlay his brief, tangential Communist years into access to national political power. At the time, agents of the federal government were bringing chargers against labor leaders and progressives for violating the Alien Registration Act of 1940, which outlawed affiliation with the Communist Party. Popularly known as the Smith Act, the law reflected the desire of its sponsor, Virginia senator Howard Smith, to curtail the rights of workers and unions by targeting Communists. The Smith Act empowered the federal government to arrest, detain, and deport any U.S. resident found to have believed in Communist principles or even to have spoken about them. Left-leaning civil rights and labor leaders faced federal indictment, as leaders in both the Democratic and Republican Parties saw little daylight between progressivism and Communism. Louis Budenz provided crucial testimony against the UAW leadership in Smith Act cases. Budenz's testimony inspired Matusow to become a government informant. In February 1950, while still a member of the Communist Party, Matusow contacted the FBI and offered to tell them what he knew. Within the year, he was a full-time government informant.[26]

At last Matusow discovered an identity as a gallant savior, one worthy of his estimation of his importance. Communists were deeply unpopular in the Cold War United States, but Matusow believed that "the informer was a hero." He gave the FBI the names, addresses, and phone numbers of people he met at Communist Party and Labor Youth League meetings. He took photographs of his friends as they marched in a May Day parade. The FBI paid him between seventy and seventy-five dollars a month. Word of his activities soon reached Communist Party leaders in New York, and in January 1951, they expelled him from the party. As Matusow gave the names of his former associates to FBI investigators, he "found it hard to accept as a fact that I done them any harm." He was boorish, boastful, and almost universally disliked. These qualities troubled Matusow's FBI handlers, who reported to the Department of Justice that army physicians diagnosed him with "psychoneurosis of a mild but acute form." Supervising FBI agents overlooked this and other concerns, including indications that Matusow stole from his employers, because he seemed so useful to their campaign against domestic Communism. Working as an informant offered Matusow the chance to demonstrate to the world what all the naysayers overlooked: rather than a megalomaniacal man-child, he was a courageous soldier for truth.[27]

Matusow's national profile rose after an encounter with lawyer Roy Cohn, whose most notorious client was Wisconsin senator Joseph McCarthy. Cohn was employed in the early 1950s as an investigator for the New York City Board of Education, which fired teachers and other employees suspected of having Communist sympathies. With Cohn's recommendation, Matusow worked for McCarthy's reelection campaign in 1952 and became one of McCarthy's prime surrogates in contested congressional races throughout the country. Matusow later confessed that many of the claims he made under oath—such as that he knew that 100 employees of the *New York Times* and about seventy at *Time* were Communists—were based on rumors he heard from the senator.[28]

Matusow listed the names of suspected Communists in testimony before the House Un-American Activities Committee, the Senate Internal Security Subcommittee (SISS), and the Senate Permanent Subcommittee on Investigations, which was known as the McCarthy Committee. In testimony before SISS he said that he knew "by sight probably 1,000 (Communist) Party members in New York," a patently ridiculous assertion that none of the senators challenged. He also gave interviews to the FBI to aid its investigations into suspected Communist affiliations and networks. In the end, over the three years that he worked as a paid government informant, he provided a staggering 216 names of suspected Communists to the federal government. He was one of at least eighty-three ex-Communists who worked as paid informants for the Department of Justice between 1952 and 1954.[29]

The government's case against Clinton Jencks illuminated the impact of Matusow's falsehoods. Jencks was a leader of the International Union of Mine, Mill, and Smelter Workers and a hero of the Left; he played a character based on himself in the film *Salt of the Earth* (1954) about a strike in New Mexico. In 1953, the Justice Department charged Jencks with lying on the statement that the 1947 Taft-Hartley Act required of all labor union leaders: an affidavit attesting that they did not "believe in" or "support" Communism. Passed by Congress over President Truman's veto, the Taft-Hartley Act became a principal vehicle of domestic anti-Communism, a means of bringing the anti-Communist witch hunt deeper into the labor movement and diminishing the power of unions.

Matusow's testimony insinuated that Jencks covertly obeyed the Communist party line. The two men met in 1950 at a dude ranch in New Mexico that was popular among leftists. Matusow explained to the FBI that he never attended a Communist Party meeting in New Mexico and never heard Jencks identify as a Communist. Those details aside, he asserted that "there is no question in my mind but that Jencks is a member of the Communist Party." Matusow additionally affirmed that Jencks discussed plans to call a strike to disrupt copper production and thus stymie the U.S. military's efforts. After a hearing before SISS, at which both Matusow and Jencks testified, a federal grand jury indicted Jencks for perjury for having allegedly misrepresented his allegiances when he signed his Taft-Hartley affidavit. Convicted and sentenced to five years in prison, Jencks appealed.[30]

The outcome was more than Matusow's conscience could bear. He briefly disappeared from public life. When he resurfaced a few months later, he confessed his lies, announced a newfound faith, and embarked on a new career. At last, it seemed, he found the identity he sought.

The road that led Matusow to moral clarity passed through the offices of Methodist bishop Bromley Oxnam. Why Matusow twice confessed his lies to Oxnam remains a mystery. Oxnam was a well-known progressive and was himself a casualty of Matusow's red-baiting. Years earlier Oxnam served as the president of the Federal Council of Churches, a consortium of "mainline" Protestant denominations. In that role he embraced the post–World War II call for "a revival of religion," a global mission to convert souls to Christ and thus stop the spread of Communism. Even a defender of Christian nationalism like Oxnam was vulnerable to the excesses of American anti-Communism. He soon found his name on a list of suspected Communists because he supported labor rights and other progressive causes. In 1952, Matusow gave Oxnam's name to the House Un-American Activities Committee. How surprised Oxnam must have been, then, when in April and again in May of 1954, Matusow appeared at his offices and confided that he had lied under oath. Matusow told Oxnam that he "had had a religious experience that made him a new man" and wanted forgiveness from those he harmed. Perhaps Matusow viewed his admission as a means of apologizing to Oxnam. Perhaps he reveled in the drama of disclosing his sins to a man of faith, mistakenly assuming that

Methodist bishops were like Catholic priests, bound by the confidentiality of the confessional booth.[31]

His secret confession entrusted to Oxnam, Matusow mocked the political culture that nurtured his lies. In June he booked a five-night gig at a Washington, D.C., restaurant, performing a spoof of the army-McCarthy hearings. His act included puppet-like figures fashioned out of pipe cleaners. The former star of the federal government's anti-Communist obsessions now played the lead role in a weird one-man show about its absurdities. Ironic distance proved insufficient, and by summer Matusow put hundreds of miles between himself and Washington. Living in Dallas, he became a stand-up comic, a theater usher, and a puppeteer who performed skits about Hebrew Bible characters for children. From Dallas he hitchhiked and cycled to Utah.[32]

The inchoate theistic awakening that drew Matusow to Oxnam's study led, in Utah, to a religious conversion. Matusow was raised in a Jewish family, and Jewish teaching shaped his lived experience. He told a story about walking past the elaborate stone facade of Temple Emanu-El on the Upper East Side of New York City during his time as an informant. As he read the inscription, "Do justly, love mercy and walk humbly with thy God," he was overcome with shame. In Utah he learned about the LDS Church from the renowned columnist and investigative journalist Jack Anderson and from Senator Arthur Watkins (R-Utah), who was both an LDS Church elder and one of McCarthy's harshest critics. Matusow started attending church with Anderson and Watkins several times each week. Even in describing his adoption of this faith, Matusow struggled to tell the truth. He was baptized in October 1954 in the LDS Church, but he told friends that he did not convert. (LDS baptism implies a prior conversion.) Perhaps Matusow simply misunderstood the religious implications of becoming a Mormon. Members of the LDS Church have consistently affirmed that they are Christians who accept Jesus Christ as Lord, but other Christians argue that the Mormon faith lies outside Christian confessions. Matusow insisted that in joining the church he simply expanded on his Jewish identity, a son of Israel finding common cause with members of the lost tribe of "Anglo-Israelites," as LDS Church members understood themselves. In the 1950s, the LDS Church's marginal relationship to Protestant and Catholic forms of Christianity may have helped Matusow understand his new faith as an extension rather than a rejection of his family's Judaism.[33]

Matusow explained that part of the LDS Church's appeal was the faith's lack of anti-Semitism, as compared to most Christian groups. At least some survey data from the 1960s supported this impression, finding that the church's theological understanding of its Semite origins made its members less inclined to adopt contemporary anti-Semitism. In LDS theology, Israelite heritage served less as a source of empathy with actual Jews than a way of marking chosenness. Matusow did not explain why Judaism no longer appealed to him. Perhaps he identified Judaism with an ethnic identity—a peoplehood—and thus saw no incompatibility between becoming a Mormon and sustaining his self-identification as a Jew.[34]

Matusow's western solitude ended abruptly when Bishop Oxnam testified before the Subversive Activities Control Board, a committee of Justice Department employees and other lawyers empowered to investigate suspected Communist influence within the American government. The case before the Subversive Activities Control Board concerned the Abraham Lincoln Brigade, a group of Americans who fought on the side of the Spanish Republic in the Spanish Civil War in the 1930s. During his time as an informant, Matusow told the committee that several veterans of the brigade were Communists. The defense counsel called Oxnam as a witness who could counter those allegations. In testimony that made Matusow's private confessions a matter of public record, Oxnam asked the board to justify its reliance on Matusow's account, given that Matusow admitted to fabricating so much of his prior testimony. Tracked down by reporters to his new home in Taos, New Mexico, Matusow claimed that Oxnam exaggerated and misunderstood his comments. Matusow protested that he merely confided to the bishop about his tendency toward embellishment, not falsehoods: "I took things out of context, but I never lied before a committee." Called back to testify before Congress in various ongoing investigations in the fall of 1954, Matusow tried to dodge a perjury charge by refusing to say whether Oxnam's statements were accurate.[35]

Left-leaning editors Angus Cameron and Albert E. Kahn (of Cameron and Kahn publishers) saw in Matusow's tortured responses the seeds of vindication against anti-Communist excess. Both men had direct experience with the anti-Communist machine; Cameron left a job at Little, Brown, after refusing to respond to questions from a congressional committee about whether he was or ever had been a member of the Communist Party. The editors paid Matusow's airfare from New Mexico to New York and began to gather documents that could verify his version of events. Neither Cameron nor Kahn much liked their author. In his preface to Matusow's memoir, Kahn noted that he was struck by Matusow's "deep-rooted sense of inferiority and an intense unease," which his "obvious acting talent" did not obscure. Matusow maligned Cameron and Kahn for their leftist ties at congressional hearings and in comments to reporters, but more than anger at his past aspersions made them wary. Kahn described Matusow as unable to translate his life into an intelligible narrative. To get the story straight, they gave him prepared lists of questions and transcribed his answers. Matusow refused to write the book himself or have it ghostwritten, preferring to speak it aloud to a stenographer. The editors knew that they needed to convince readers that such an effective liar now spoke the truth. Their task was complicated by obvious doubts about Matusow's honesty. As the *New York Times* asked, "What is believable from the lips of an admitted false witness[?]"[36]

Federal law enforcement took the resolution of that question out of the hands of the media and made it a matter of law. Officials at the Department of Justice received phone calls from liberal columnist Stewart Alsop, who heard about Matusow's lies from Oxnam. The Justice Department started an investigation. In an affidavit presented in federal court on January 31, 1955, and in testimony before SISS on February 21, 1955, Matusow finally admitted that he perjured himself repeatedly. His new faith led him to renounce his earlier testimony, telling one senator, "Sir, I believe in God, very strongly. . . . I believe in God and Christian charity, and I understand the meaning of it, sir." He recanted his testimony against Jencks and two other people convicted under the Smith Act. Matusow claimed that Roy Cohn pressured him to provide false testimony. Still just thirty years old, Matusow stood before reporters in New York wearing a bow tie and tweed jacket. He described his perfidy as a manifestation of his identity crisis: "I'm a kid from the Bronx, and I'm looking for an identity." This convinced few of his critics. *Time* called him "the biggest phony of them all." The lies piled up, and Matusow's confession rang hollow.[37]

The legal implications were immediate. Defense attorneys filed motions for new trials for defendants convicted under the Smith Act, several of whom were already serving prison terms. Jencks had his conviction voided in 1957. A jury found Matusow guilty of lying about his lies, and he served three and a half years in a federal prison in Lewisburg, Pennsylvania. Alfred E. Kahn served six months for contempt of court after he refused to comply with a federal court request for the documents that supported the claims in Matusow's book. The Cold War informant system also took a hit. As a consequence of Matusow's confession, the Justice Department stopped using paid informants against suspected Communists. False declarations of sincere beliefs threatened the conservative argument for Cold War American religious patriotism.[38]

Entertainment for children, rather than politics, held Matusow's attention over the next forty years. Matusow moved (and married) often. He renamed himself Job after seeing similarities between the biblical character's suffering and his own, seemingly missing the point that Job's traumas were not self-inflicted. He organized a theater troupe in the 1970s that performed for children in the Southwest, with shows on radio and television. By the early 1990s, he lived in Utah and produced a children's television show, *Magic Mouse Magazine*, which aired on public-access television stations in California, Iowa, Michigan, Texas, Massachusetts, Arizona, and Utah. Unverifiable stories in a 1999 profile in Utah's *Deseret News* claimed that Billie Holiday hosted a going-off-to-prison party for him, that he introduced Yoko Ono to John Lennon, and that he got a small role in *Touched by an Angel* after praying to make enough money to help a Hopi reservation buy the corn it needed to survive a prolonged drought. He founded a "peace center" in the 1980s and completed a "peace walk" across the United States with Mahatma Gandhi's great-nephew. Job Matusow died in 2002, survived by his eleventh wife.[39]

Harvey Matusow's cross-country trek and pursuit of enlightenment captured a romanticized ideal of (white) men's self-discovery in the post–World War II era. American literature long featured tales of men "lighting out for the territory." As the literary historian Timothy Melley notes, an established literary tradition showcased men seeking escape from the confinements of domestic spaces. After World War II, American literature portrayed conflicts that played out in men's very consciousness. "Society," usually represented as female, threatened men's agency and individuality. That journey reverberated in the late 1950s in novels by the Beat author Jack Kerouac, whose *On the Road* (1957) and *Dharma Bums* (1958) semi-autobiographically described his abandonment of domesticated life on the East Coast for the pursuit of spiritual enlightenment out west.[40]

Matusow's bizarre life thus left one more legacy. Remembered for his role in bringing down the informant system (through his own brazen manipulation of it), he also embodied the modern American search for a religious "identity" as an object of adult self-knowledge. Unlike Clare Luce, Louis Budenz, Whittaker Chambers, and others who forged associations between religion, patriotism, and American democracy, Matusow placed less emphasis on the consequences of his actions for world-historical events than on his own peace of mind and soul. The privileges of whiteness smoothed his uncertain path, as they would for other seekers to follow him. No Jim Crow restrictions hindered his physical mobility, no prohibitions on African Americans in the priesthood affected his conversion to Mormonism, and no presumptions of intellectual inferiority clouded the public's reception of his statements. He was a kook and a confessed liar; he got a book deal and a second chance.

Matusow's lies came to light amid international fears of mind control during the first major military action of the Cold War. Fighting erupted on the Korean peninsula in 1950, a region where the United States established a military bulwark again Communist expansion. In 1943, President Franklin D. Roosevelt and China's nationalist leader Chiang Kai-shek agreed to pursue Korea's independence after years of Japanese occupation. Roosevelt and the Soviet Union's Joseph Stalin in 1945 formed a trusteeship in Korea, and both leaders agreed to keep their troops off Korean soil. After Japan's surrender in August 1945, American and Soviet diplomats divided their spheres of influence at the thirty-eighth parallel and almost immediately violated their earlier pledge to constrain their militaries. The Soviets and Americans, unable to agree on which government represented the entire Korean nation, each propped up their respective Communist and anti-Communist leaders. Korea was already strategically important because of its proximity to Japan, which was under U.S. occupation. Its geopolitical significance escalated in 1949, when Communist leader Mao Tse-tung in neighboring China defeated Chiang Kai-shek's nationalist army. Both China and the Soviets now supported North Korea's Communist government. News in the summer of 1950 that the North Korean military had crossed the thirty-eighth parallel and launched an invasion of the South caught officials at the U.S. State Department completely by surprise. Within days, the United Nations Security Council authorized an international force, led by Gen. Douglas MacArthur, to support the South Korean government.[41]

The U.S. war in Korea—and the U.S. government's justification of it—changed how Americans understood the stakes of the Cold War. When President Harry Truman announced his policy of "containment" in 1947, he described an intention to assert U.S. military power abroad in order to limit Communist governments to the countries in territories in which it already existed. The Korean War transformed "containment" into a global effort to deter Communism from spreading further across the Korean peninsula. By the fall of 1950, after an initial rout nearly put Seoul under Communist control, UN forces drove the North Korean military out of South Korea. The UN had a mandate to reestablish the status quo, but General MacArthur defied the mandate and President Truman's wishes. He ordered his troops northward to unify the peninsula under a single, anti-Communist government. That decision not only ensured significant Chinese military support of the North Korean government at its border but also led to two years of stalemate, costing tens of thousands of lives. The situation remained fraught when a July 1953 armistice reinstated the thirty-eighth parallel as the international border. The conflict left the border between South Korea and North Korea unchanged, but it cemented perceptions of the U.S. military as an essential resource in the war against global Communism. The military budget, which shrank in the immediate aftermath of World War II, entered an era of perpetual growth.[42]

The "police action" in Korea personalized the dangers of Communism for many in the United States and amplified Cold War fears. It revved the engine of anti-Communism. Tens of thousands of American soldiers died or returned home gravely wounded. The Soviet Union or China, Korea or East Germany: Communism seemed to lurk everywhere. Ideological and geopolitical nuances faded as schoolchildren practiced "duck and cover" drills and foreign policy leaders called for "massive retaliation" against a Soviet nuclear attack. Air-raid sirens pierced the soundscape of urban and rural areas alike. Domestic panic about Communism galvanized a new Red Scare. On suspicions of left-leaning political allegiances, thousands of people were fired, thousands more were threatened with deportation, and the entertainment industry blacklisted dozens of writers, directors, singers, and actors.

A critique of Cold War panic emerged just as quickly. The ironies and even absurdities of American anti-Communism inspired novelist Joseph Heller to write *Catch-22* (1951), a book that satirized the predicament of fighter pilots in World War II but which he based on the U.S. government's rationale for its military aggression in Korea. Heller's brilliant send-up of a military policy that required pilots to fly their planes unless they were mentally ill—when, in the main character John Yossarian's view, the fear of death was profoundly rational—excoriated the military-industrial complex with its pompous, convoluted rationales for expending men's lives. The commercial success of *Catch-22* suggests the popularity of Heller's critique of Cold War ideology (or, perhaps, it indicates the failure of many readers to recognize that critique). Militaristic machismo cost men's lives, he showed in his book. The gender politics of the era were unsparing. Anti-Communist conservatives described liberals as "effete" and "limp"; foreign policy experts cast the Cold War itself as a sexual contest between a Soviet seductress and a virile, heterosexual, and democratic United States. Anti-Communism was pervasive and punitive in U.S. politics during the 1950s and 1960s. Even left-leaning public figures asserted their aggressive, "manly" commitment to rooting out Communist influence.[43]

Such associations between American manliness and anti-Communism could not explain why twenty-three American POWs in North Korea refused repatriation to the United States and chose to live in China instead. The peaceful exchange of POWs between the former antagonists figured prominently in the armistice negotiations that began in July 1951 and dragged on until 1953. More than 4,400 American soldiers lived in North Korean POW camps at the time of the July 1953 armistice; 2,730 American prisoners died in captivity. The UN Command held 150,000 North Korean and 21,000 Chinese soldiers in its prison camps. American POWs endured horrific conditions, near-starvation diets, and forced marches without adequate shoes or clothing. Neither the American-led UN forces nor the Chinese-backed North Koreans initially knew how to handle prisoners who refused repatriation, which was never considered a choice for the prisoner to make. Two of the twenty-three Americans eventually agreed to go back to the United States, but despite letter-writing campaigns by American schoolchildren and stern words from Defense Department spokesmen, the remaining twenty-one preferred to relocate to China.[44]

Reports about the POWs in U.S. newspapers emphasized that the men must have been coerced or had their thoughts co-opted by their captors. Given the option, surely everyone chose American-style democracy. No rational explanation, these reports emphasized, accounted for men who did not at least try to escape their Communist captors. The men themselves reiterated their conviction that Communism was superior to capitalism, but few Americans believed those statements were sincere. The term "brainwashing," coined by American journalist Edward Hunter in 1950 to describe Chinese "reeducation" methods, offered an explanation for an otherwise politically incomprehensible choice.[45]

News reports about the American GIs explained that the men acted in response to stimuli and cues that their captors inculcated in their subconscious minds. Popular knowledge about psychological experiments proved useful in explaining what transpired. *Life* magazine described the soldiers as "prisoners of Pavlov," conditioned (and tortured) like the subjects of behaviorist Ivan P. Pavlov's early twentieth-century studies to respond automatically to conditioned stimuli. If Pavlov famously made a dog salivate by ringing a bell associated with the arrival of food, Communists programmed the minds of their U.S. captives until they subordinated themselves to the totalitarian state. Armchair social scientists fed theories about which men might be especially vulnerable to brainwashing's power. As reporters, politicians, and others puzzled over the twenty-three unrepatriated American prisoners of war in North Korea, they noticed that African Americans resisted Communist brainwashing: only three of the unrepatriated soldiers were Black, and the rest were white. Many came from rural and lower-income backgrounds. Some commentators admitted that they could understand why Black Americans might find the Communist critique of the United States compelling, but the behavior of the other captives baffled them.[46]

Sexual deviance held the key to explaining the inexplicable. A weak-willed, feminine individual fell under the thrall of a seductive man. Media reports about the American POWs in Korea portrayed them as long-haired homosexuals and cross-dressers, whose overbearing mothers practiced a psychologically damaging variant of mother love that psychiatrists dubbed "momism." A timely book described brainwashing as "the rape of the mind." Journalists and critics questioned why so many American prisoners had seemingly "given up" rather than resist their captors. Some postulated that the prisoners' lack of faith or close family bonds left them without the resources they needed to resist indoctrination. Images of emasculated prisoners circulated amid a broader Cold War American panic over endangered masculinity, homosexual infiltration of the government, and weakness in the face of Communism's seductive secret agents.[47]

Evidence of how often Americans relinquished their free will offered little reassurance. Too many people seemed happily fooled by the propaganda machines of mass culture and advertising, dupes of public relations and dependent on an expansive bureaucratic state. Urban boosters trumpeted mass consumption as the key to economic prosperity, but social critics worried about the mind-dulling effects of consumerist complacency. These authors bemoaned how the postwar consumer economy not only constrained the economic horizons of white men but also subjected these men to soul-numbing conformity. Writers including C. Wright Mills (*Middle Class*, 1951), Sloane Wilson (*The Man in the Gray Flannel Suit*, 1955), and William H. Whyte (*The Organization Man*, 1956) expressed what historian Lizabeth Cohen describes as the "concern among cultural critics of the fifties that the standardization inherent in mass consumption was breeding social conformity and homogeneity." As Mills wrote, "the twentieth-century white-collar man ... is always somebody's man, the corporation's, the government's, the army's." More ominously, William Whyte warned of the collectivist creep within middle-class manhood. For all the talk of individuality and personal initiative, he argued, freedom became nothing more than a corporate slogan, an advertising gimmick to prod the masses into desiring new consumer purchases that mirrored the desires of their comparably consumerist suburban neighbors, all in the name of the American Dream.[48]

History provided additional examples of individuals who were complicit in their own enslavement. In perhaps the most literal iteration of this idea, the historian Stanley Elkins argued in *Slavery: A Problem in American Institutional and Intellectual Life* (1959) that the plantation mentality kept enslaved people from revolting against their owners. Psychiatrist Bruno Bettelheim, himself a refugee from Nazism, similarly wrote about cowardice and submission among the inmates of Nazi concentration camps. These authors described people who willingly put themselves under authoritarian control, a phenomenon one scholar describes as "a relinquishment of the burdensome self." Critics in the 1950s described passive Americans as "Cold War captives," unable to exercise their freedom because they sacrificed themselves to the promises of affluence and security. Maybe modern people longed not for freedom and choices but for authority and the semblance of options. These themes enlivened popular culture as well, with best-selling books and films that featured characters subjected to mind control and coercion. The message was dismal: Americans were not that "free" after all.[49]

These fears coalesced in Richard Condon's novel *The Manchurian Candidate* (1959), which was adapted into a 1962 film. *The Manchurian Candidate* coined another term to describe brainwashing's victims. It told story of American Korean War veterans who were subjected to brutal Communist mind-control experiments while in captivity in Manchuria. The film, starring Frank Sinatra as Maj. Ben Marco and directed by John Frankenheimer, depicts Marco's flashbacks about his indoctrination in China. He tries to warn a fellow veteran, Raymond Shaw. Neither man realizes that Shaw has been programmed by his Communist captors to assassinate the U.S. president. Shaw has an overbearing mother in the extreme; she is a Soviet agent (played by Angela Lansbury) who seeks to prop up the political ambitions of her husband (Shaw's stepfather), Senator John Iselin, whom Condon modeled on Senator Joseph McCarthy. Frankenheimer explained that the film, like the book on which it was based, critiqued both Communism and right-wing anti-Communism. The film was released amid the October 1962 Cuban Missile Crisis and garnered nominations for various Academy Awards.[50]

Brainwashing tapped into fears of an unseen enemy, about weaknesses within the American psyche that exposed the mind to subjugation. Cultural critic Vance Packard warned of the "hidden persuaders" in the mass media and advertisement industries who manipulated the consuming public's desires. Popular culture and literary productions of the post–World War II era rehearsed these anxious images of mass conformity. If Raymond Shaw could be triggered to assassinate someone simply by seeing the queen of hearts playing card, ordinary Americans might find themselves drawn to purchase certain brands or products when they heard a jingle or recalled a pleasing slogan.[51]

The psychologist Robert Jay Lifton, considered the country's foremost expert on brainwashing, enumerated the strategies that groups used to achieve "ideological totalism" in his influential book *Thought Reform and the Psychology of Totalism* (1961). Lifton spoke to the fears that animated the social psychology of Fromm and the Frankfurt School's study of authoritarianism. His book was not merely an investigation of the mind's processes but, more grandly and ominously, "a psychological study of extremism or totalism." Lifton explained how authoritarian groups controlled their followers: milieu control, "mystical manipulation" to convince followers of the group's higher purpose, a demand for moral purity, a "cult of confession," a profusion of jargon-laden but "definitive-sounding" phrases, and a prioritization of doctrine over personal well-being. This definition of brainwashing was nothing if not capacious. What religion did *not* do some of these things?[52]

Fears that coercive mind control might lurk within each person added to these warnings about coercive captors and cult leaders. Madeleine L'Engle's popular young adult novel *A Wrinkle in Time* (1963) featured a perilous journey to the planet Camazotz (itself a play on the Kennedy administration's "Camelot"). There a disembodied brain dictated the thoughts and actions of the inhabitants. Their identical suburban homes and anonymous office towers represented the terrifying apotheosis of postwar pressures to conform. As the 1960s progressed, American politics and culture had less to say about Communist captors and anti-capitalist indoctrination. Popular fears focused instead on the leaders of controversial religions derisively called cults, who directed their followers' every thought and action like a massive, tyrannical brain.[53]

Insinuations of inauthentic faith likewise dogged the conversions of African Americans like Sammy Davis Jr. and Muhammad Ali in the 1960s. As the next two chapters describe, each man insisted that he acted of his own free will and chose the faith that expressed his authentic self. The complex politics of racial identity surrounded their public confessions.

Chapter 4 A Kind of Oneness with the Jewish People

In November 1954, the entertainer Sammy Davis Jr. awoke in a Los Angeles hospital bed, uncertain of the events that landed him there. Nurses explained that he had been in a car accident on his way back from a performance in Las Vegas. During the collision a raised emblem on the steering wheel punctured his left eye. Still groggy from anesthesia, Davis noticed that one of his hands was bandaged and asked a nurse why that was, when the surgery was for his eye. She opened his side table drawer and took out "a gold medal the size of a silver dollar. It had St. Christopher on one side and the Star of David on the other." Days later, after surgeons removed the damaged eye and treated his other injuries, Davis recalled friends Tony Curtis and Janet Leigh walking alongside his gurney as orderlies wheeled him through hospital corridors "and of Janet pressing something into my hand and telling me, 'Hold tight and pray and everything will be all right.'" Gripped so tightly that the Star of David left a scar on the palm of his hand, this religious object proved to Davis that he was destined to become a Jew. As he recuperated, Davis began to study Judaism, mapping his journey of spiritual self-discovery across the geography of the American West. From the night-darkened highway between Las Vegas and Los Angeles to the synagogue study of a Hollywood rabbi and nightclubs in Vegas where white audiences roared with laughter at his new Yiddish-laden shtick, he charted a path of Jewish identification with American freedoms and of an African American historical consonance with Judaism.[1]

Jewishness offered a way for Davis to perform his authentic self and assert his political voice. He insisted on the alignment between his racial and religious identities: becoming a Jew expressed his most deeply felt desires as an African American for full civil rights and freedom. Blacks and Jews had similar histories of oppression and marginalization, he explained. He admired Jewish people's tenacity. Davis defended his choice of Judaism by arguing that it amplified his commitment to African American civil rights. Judaism gave him an authentic faith and affirmed his political convictions. When he became a Jew he found the faith that best expressed the self he already had and that validated his lived experiences. Rather than experiencing a dramatic conversion or transformation, he came home: "I have always been a Jew in my thinking and my own undefined philosophies." In a way that white converts to Judaism never had to, he developed an explanation of the inherent harmony among his racial, ethnic, and religious identities.[2]

It was an argument that left Davis politically isolated, particularly as both he and a segment of American Jews shifted to the political right after the 1967 Arab-Israeli war. Conversion to Judaism initially subjected him to mockery from Jewish and non-Jewish friends in the entertainment industry and to derision from some African Americans who interpreted his conversion as an abandonment of his racial heritage. By the late 1960s, when he cheered the State of Israel's military victory over its Arab neighbors, his Jewish pride in the small nation's survival was at odds with many Black nationalist and civil rights critiques of the Israeli occupation of Palestinian territory. His subsequent, unfounded confidence in Richard Nixon as a champion of civil rights cost him friends. Fellow entertainers Harry Belafonte and Sidney Poitier saw Davis's rightward turn as a betrayal of racial solidarity. Values at the heart of midcentury American Jewish culture—of ethnic distinctiveness, empathy with the stranger, and pride in Jewish histories of generational survival—coalesced in primarily positive Jewish responses to his conversion. The nuances of Jewish particularity meant less to Davis's African American critics, who identified Judaism with white, middle-class access to material comforts and power. Statements about the naturalness of Black-Jewish partnership grew stale as American Jewish Zionism, Black Power, and Nixonian politics blew apart former political alliances. For Davis, Judaism and Zionism promised a form of belonging outside of the fraught racial politics of the United States, a homecoming to a faith self-consciously concerned with its history of dispossession. As Americans scrutinized the sincerity of religious conversions, people like Davis, who did not "look" like the identity they claimed to know themselves to possess, bore the burden of proof. Responses to the Jewish conversions of Davis and other famous entertainers in the 1950s and 1960s exposed how profoundly Judeo-Christian pluralism presumed the white, Christian character of American citizenship.

Jews hit the big time in American popular culture decades before Davis became a Jewish celebrity. Most Jewish celebrities in the century's early decades, like the early twentieth-century magician Harry Houdini, the son of a rabbi, obscured their religious identities as they became national and international stars. Jewish influence in popular culture was simultaneously pervasive and discreet. Never more than a tiny fraction of the U.S. population (2 or 3 percent at most), American Jews exercised an outsized influence on the vaudeville, music, and film industries. American Jews shaped the vision of "America" that coursed through Christmas carols and flickered across the country's earliest movie and television screens, even as many of them performed under Anglicized versions of Eastern European names. Their experiences underlined a common thread in American culture: the longing for home, coupled with a nagging awareness of being on the outside.

Once denigrated as members of the nonwhite "Hebrew" race, Jews over time became representatives of white American success. While restrictive covenants in many suburbs continued to exclude Jews in addition to African Americans, American Jews themselves began to feel increasingly "at home in America." Even when some novelists portrayed Jewish characters as shape-shifting racial chameleons who "passed" as white, these characters did so successfully. Jews' relatively rapid move from poverty to affluence and their disproportionate visibility on stage, radio, and screen suggested the possibilities of white ethnic success. By the 1950s, Jews, like Catholics, appeared more often than before in American popular culture and played greater roles in shaping it.

The entertaining Jew was a novel American icon in the 1950s and 1960s. A new cohort of performers drew attention to their Jewishness. Listeners who heard Benny Goodman on the radio in the 1940s might not have known that he was Jewish, but everyone who encountered the brilliantly profane comedy of Lenny Bruce in the 1950s and 1960s knew that he was. Even Bob Dylan (Robert Zimmerman) wrote a few lines about the "Hava Nagila." These midcentury celebrities made Jewishness part of their public identities as their careers ascended.[3]

The Jewish conversions of actors Marilyn Monroe and Elizabeth Taylor amplified the American public's fascination with Jewishness in the 1950s. Monroe converted in 1956 before her marriage to Arthur Miller, and Taylor became a Jew in 1959 as she prepared to marry singer Eddie Fisher, having previously married another Jewish man, Mike Todd. Monroe's and Taylor's new roles as glamorous Jewish wives, rather than their ethnic identities, drove the public response to their conversions. Their conversions demonstrated how racially uncomplicated it was for a white Christian woman to become a Jew. They might even teach other Jewish women a few things about femininity, some writers jabbed. Newspaper and magazine reports depicted the conversions of these international celebrities as understandable, even necessary, accommodations to their husbands' faith. Conversion domesticated them. Their spiritual journeys took them from a rabbi's study to the marriage altar and the benefit hall, where they fundraised for Jewish causes. A columnist for the American Jewish press mused over whether the recent spate of Jewish wedding ceremonies—involving Monroe, Taylor, and the film actress Carroll Baker, "three of the most ravishing actresses"—meant the dawn of "a fad for the American glamor girl to be married by a rabbi." (In 1955, Baker converted before marrying a man who survived Auschwitz.) As converts, Monroe and Taylor in particular embodied an ideal of white, feminine sex appeal that defied negative stereotypes of Jewish women and set them apart from historical associations of Jews with suspect ethnic and racial inferiority.[4]

Interfaith marriages between Christian women and Jewish men intrigued American audiences. *Abie's Irish Rose* (a 1922 play, followed by the 1928 film version) and its imitators portrayed Irish Catholic American women who loved and married Jewish American men. Such story lines emphasized strategies of ethnic accommodation while sidestepping the thorny question of religious conversion. These plays and films also made digs at Jewish women, inaccurately representing them as sexually inadequate and unfeminine. Jewish women appeared in these popular culture productions as unappealing nags, unable to compete with Christian women for Jewish men's attentions. In reality, Jewish interfaith marriage, still fairly uncommon in the mid-1950s, was extremely rare in the 1920s. Jewish audiences likely enjoyed these plays and films as parables about romantic solutions to ethnic difference without worrying too much about the potential for large-scale interfaith couplings.[5]

The 1950s story line of Hollywood icons choosing to become Jewish reassured Jews who feared that they were subject to coercive conversions or cultural decline. Since at least the third century CE, when Emperor Constantine made Christianity the official religion of the Roman Empire and launched a vast missionary effort, Jews encountered violent and often deadly attempts to convert them to Christianity. Christians valued the conversion of the pagan, traditionally understood as a person without a monotheistic faith, but they especially prized the conversion of Jews. Conversion in the United States proceeded absent the violence that marked it in Europe. By the early twentieth century, as one historian explains, Christian missions worked to convert American Jews "in virtually every city in America that had a community of a few thousand or more Jews." These missionary efforts yielded a mere 12,000 American Jewish converts to Protestantism by 1930. Conversion was a contentious topic for Jews, a minority religion whose conversion and thus elimination has been a goal of various Christian majorities throughout Western Christian history. What a relief, then, for American Jews to witness Hollywood stars who chose to become Jews.[6]

No celebrity convert endured more public exposure or scrutiny in the mid-1950s than the actor and former pinup model Marilyn Monroe. Her erotic charisma captured the sexual ambivalence of the decade, combining demure innocence and female desire. In 1956, the thirty-year-old film star was engaged to marry the playwright Arthur Miller, having divorced Joe DiMaggio the year before. She met with a Reform rabbi, who gave her a book about Jewish history, and she explained her reasons for converting. She learned how to recite a few Hebrew prayers. In the presence of Marilyn's husband Arthur Miller, his brother Kermit, and one other witness, on July 1, 1956, Marilyn Monroe renounced all other faiths, declared that she freely chose Judaism, and she recited the *Sh'ma*, the Jewish prayer declaring the oneness of God. About an hour later, at the upstate New York home of Miller's agent, a location chosen to avoid the paparazzi camped outside Miller's home in Connecticut, the same rabbi who presided over her conversion officiated at the couple's wedding.[7]

Monroe's sex-goddess public image contrasted with contemporaneous stereotypes about Jewish women. One of the most publicly sexualized celebrities of the twentieth century, Monroe began her career as a model, later finding fame with film roles that drew attention to her physical appearance. Monroe recognized the costs of a career built around her sex appeal. In a 1960 interview she described what it was like to be a sex object for an international audience, how men "pawed" her in front of her various husbands and treated her like a machine: "My body turned all these people on like turning on an electric light." In the 1950s and 1960s,

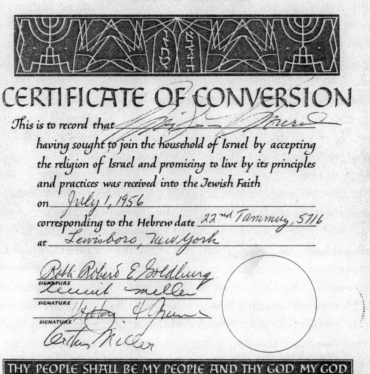

שמע ישראל יהוה אלהינו
HEAR O ISRAEL THE LORD OUR GOD
יהוה אחד
THE LORD IS ONE

CERTIFICATE OF CONVERSION

This is to record that *[signature]*

having sought to join the household of Israel by accepting
the religion of Israel and promising to live by its principles
and practices was received into the Jewish Faith

on _July 1, 1956_

corresponding to the Hebrew date _22nd Tammuz, 5716_

at _Lewisboro, New York_

Rabbi *Robert E. Goldburg*
SIGNATURE

SIGNATURE

SIGNATURE

Arthur Miller

THY PEOPLE SHALL BE MY PEOPLE AND THY GOD MY GOD

BOOK OF RUTH

COPYRIGHT, 1955 BY UNION OF AMERICAN HEBREW CONGREGATIONS

*Marilyn Monroe converted to Judaism the morning of her wedding
to playwright Arthur Miller in 1956. (Courtesy Jacob Rader Marcus
Center of the American Jewish Archives, Cincinnati, Ohio)*

many male Jewish comics built routines around jokes about how their mothers, by contrast, impeded their romantic lives and thwarted their attempts at independence. Jewish wives who ran their husbands ragged with materialistic demands were punchlines. Erotic appeal dropped from the equation in these representations of conflict-driven Jewish marriages. The adult Jewish woman in these jokes misdirected her passion away from her husband and toward her sons. With the publication in 1969 of Philip Roth's best-selling novel *Portnoy's Complaint*, the humor of the Jewish mother's overinvolvement in her children's lives and preoccupation with feeding them hardened into the grating, perverse figure of Sophie Portnoy. Monroe's hypersexualized self-presentation and blond hair added to a fascination among other Jews about whether she could maintain her shiksa (stereotypically non-Jewish female) sexuality while becoming a Jewish homemaker. As reporter Elsa Maxwell wrote in the *Washington Post and Times Herald*, "Marilyn is trying—as she did in her two previous marriages—to be the woman she believes her husband's wife should be."[8]

Preparation of gefilte fish, arguably the least sexy food in Jewish cuisine, came to signify how thoroughly Monroe embraced her new vocation as a Jewish wife. A standard Eastern European–derived dish of heavily seasoned baked white fish, gefilte fish tested the abilities of Jewish home cooks to take an oily fish, often carp, and transform it into a savory treat, often served at the Passover seder. Gossip columnists and reporters noted that Monroe was learning how to cook Jewish food from her mother-in-law. In perhaps the most Jewish description of the recent convert ever uttered, the Austrian actor Walter Slezak reported overhearing "the two girls ... [exchange] recipes for gefilte fish. Marilyn described how she used whitefish instead of carp." Speculation that Monroe was pregnant amplified rumors that Miller tamed her sexuality, as one reporter noted in the *Jewish Advocate*: "At this writing, Marilyn is a happy, pregnant Jewish wife, who delights in cooking gefilte fish and other such favorite dishes for Arthur." (Monroe suffered from endometriosis and miscarried multiple times.) As men who wrote in to Jewish newspapers reminisced about how much better their mothers' homemade gefilte fish was than the supermarket brands their wives prepared, they considered whether a blond bombshell could become not only a good Jewish wife but a good Jewish mother—according to Jewish men's expectations. Their musings turned into a critique of Jewish women's talents in the kitchen: "Maybe [Monroe's] example in cooking gefilte fish will start Jewish girls toward doing the same again." Monroe's culinary skill became evidence of marital domestication, of a sexual radiance no less brilliant but rechanneled toward the domestic arts.[9]

Organizers of fundraisers for Jewish and Zionist organizations realized the value of Monroe's fame. The United Jewish Appeal, which dispersed funds to social service organizations, scheduled Monroe to talk about her decision to convert to Judaism, an event certain to draw a crowd. Organizers canceled the event when Miller refused to comply with a House Un-American Activities Committee request to testify about any Communist ties in his past or present. Once the courts cleared him of wrongdoing, the fundraising invites resumed. Monroe and Miller made at least one joint appearance at a Jewish fundraiser, when they helped raise funds for the American Friends of the Hebrew Union College in Jerusalem in September 1959.[10]

Jewish newspapers and philanthropic organizations praised Monroe-as-Jew because the very details of her physical appearance and the vastness of her fame affirmed Jewish desirability—particularly, the desirability of Jewish men. Just as Monroe drew fans to her movies and to gossip about her love affairs, she seemed by the very whiteness of her alabaster skin, dressed in clothes that drew attention to her physical gifts, to affirm the gaze of the people who gawked (and "pawed") at her. After she died in 1962, at age thirty-six, she was buried in the Westwood Village Memorial Park Cemetery in Los Angeles following a ceremony arranged by Joe DiMaggio. Arthur Miller, whose new wife was nine months pregnant, was unable to attend. Newspaper reports described the ceremony as nondenominational, although a Lutheran minister officiated.[11]

The possibilities of a glamorous celebrity convert appealed to Rabbi Max Nussbaum, who presided over Elizabeth Taylor's conversion at Temple Israel of Hollywood. Nussbaum appreciated the appeal of the celebrity convert as a spokesperson for "the Jews." Physically attractive and articulate converts proved to the American public and the world the merits of his faith. These converts represented a people who in the very recent past faced mass extermination and the failure of anti-Semitic democratic governments to save them. Nussbaum wanted Taylor to become a model convert, much as Fulton Sheen and Edward Wiatrak urged Clare Boothe Luce to make her religious conversion the basis for a global mission. In March 1959, flanked by Nussbaum, a cantor, her parents, and her fiancé, Eddie Fisher, Taylor made her statement of commitment to Judaism. She recited the *Sh'ma* using a mix of Hebrew and English. Nussbaum offered remarks that exemplified his view of the Jewish people as an embattled but resilient minority, eager to welcome her as a full member of the community. A native of Germany who fled in 1938, Nussbaum spoke in heavily accented English about the challenges facing Taylor as she joined "not only a new religion ... [but] a people. And a people which has suffered much, as you know." Having himself survived an anti-Semitic attack, Nussbaum welcomed Taylor, "because I know that you will be a great asset to us." Her celebrity and art were good for the Jews: "You have so much to give to the community ... in the light of your talents, and so much to give to the world. I am proud that from now on, your name will be associated with us." In interviews and in later memoirs, Taylor insisted that her conversion was unrelated to her marriages to Mike Todd and Eddie Fisher. Some Jewish women of her generation scoffed at this insistence, but aside from being the butt of perhaps Lenny Bruce's most famous joke ("I hear Elizabeth Taylor's become bar mitzvah!"), Taylor's conversion provoked little public scorn. Two months later, Nussbaum presided at her wedding to Fisher at Temple Beth Sholom in Las Vegas.[12]

Uncontroversial among American Jews, Taylor's conversion nevertheless embroiled her in the racial politics of Jewish identity and of the State of Israel. An international dispute over Israeli citizenship took aim at the ease of Taylor's acceptance by the Jewish people. Under its founding principles and constitution, the State of Israel granted the right of any Jew to become a citizen. Sometimes referred to as the "right of return," this expansive immigration and naturalization policy was a direct response to the Nazi extermination of 6 million Jews during the Holocaust, the horror of which was compounded by the refusal of nearly every democratic nation (including the United States) to provide a safe haven for Jewish refugees. The internal religious politics in Israel meant that ultra-orthodox rabbis exercised wide discretion to implement policies governing marriage, divorce, and immigration. Their decisions often reflected the class and racial biases of the majority of Israelis, who descended from European, or "Ashkenazi," Jews and who considered themselves racially white. In 1961, the Israeli Chief Rabbinate banned marriages in Israel between members of the Indian Bene Israel congregation and other Jews because members of the Bene Israel community did not meet the chief rabbi's criteria for Jewishness. While the ruling reflected the belief among Orthodox Jews that other varieties of Judaism lacked legitimacy, it also smacked of racial prejudice. Amid meetings in Bombay and elsewhere

Elizabeth Taylor and Eddie Fisher were married in 1959 in Las Vegas, at a Jewish ceremony officiated by Rabbi Max Nussbaum, who also presided over Taylor's conversion. (Courtesy AP Images, ID 5905120209)

in India, a nonsectarian Indian newspaper covered the issue on its front page: "Recently a gentile—Elizabeth Taylor—was admitted to the Jewish community and married a Jew. Is she a purer Jew than those Indian Jews who have been practising [sic] Judaism for two thousand years?" In Israel as in the United States, white converts enjoyed presumptions of religious authenticity that converts of color—and even, in this case, long-standing members of the tribe—did not.[13]

Taylor's financial support for the State of Israel politicized her films in the Arab world. A few weeks before her conversion, when Taylor pledged to purchase $100,000 in Israel bonds (Fisher pledged $10,000), the United Arab Emirates announced a ban on her films. In 1959, Egypt banned Monroe, Taylor, and Baker. These bans hardly affected Taylor's fame or career. Her whiteness and her Zionism nevertheless underscored Jewish fascination with ancestral descent, which typically prioritized Ashkenazi Jews over those who traced their ancestry to the Middle East or global South. Jewish and Israeli organizations remained among Taylor's philanthropic priorities. In 1959, she gave nearly $70,000 for the completion of a new auditorium at the Chamber Theater in Tel Aviv named in Mike Todd's memory. This largesse may have inclined at least one rabbi to break with usual practice and officiate at an interfaith wedding; when Taylor married the English gentile Richard Burton in 1963, the ceremony was officiated by a rabbi under a chuppah.[14]

American Jews largely appreciated the contributions that Monroe and Taylor made to Jewish households, charities, and Zionist causes. The actors embodied an idealized white femininity that many Jews hoped would inspire other Jewish women's behaviors. Sammy Davis Jr. benefited from no such assumptions about his fitness for Jewish observance or contributions to the community. Instead, the racial politics of both Jewish ethnicity and African American identity meant that Davis needed to explain and justify his Black Judaism again and again. He considered himself to be a Jew for several years before he converted in the fall of 1960. About a week after his conversion, he married the Swedish actress and fellow convert May Britt. Their union was one of the most high-profile interracial marriages in the United States at the time. It became a liability for Davis, who found himself disinvited to the Kennedy inauguration. The president's advisors sought to avoid provoking the rancor of Kennedy's segregationist southern Democratic supporters. For Davis, battling Jim Crow and being Jewish were two fronts in the same war for social acceptance and self-respect. In his performances and in interviews, he at once acknowledged and undermined the ways in which being a person "of color" complicated his ability to claim a Jewish identity.

Sammy Davis Jr. earned his reputation as one of the greatest American entertainers of the twentieth century. He was a virtuoso tap dancer (a "hoofer"), a capable singer (especially talented at doing impressions), an actor, a musician, and a comedian. Born in 1925 in Harlem to impoverished vaudeville performers, he entered "the business" as a young child. His mother, who was Catholic, relinquished custody of him when he was an infant. For the rest of his childhood he was either at home in Harlem with his maternal grandmother, who taught him to be a Baptist, or on the road with his father and "uncle" Will Mastin, his father's vaudeville partner. When Davis was three years old he did an Al Jolson impersonation that so impressed his elders that they put him in the act. He debuted in his first film role, in *Rufus Jones for President*, when he was six or seven. Davis wrote in his autobiography that his father and Mastin sheltered him from racism, explaining the Jim Crow discrimination they encountered at hotels and restaurants as prejudice against entertainers. Remarkably, Davis insisted, he had little understanding of Jim Crow or other varieties of white supremacy while under his father and Mastin's protective care. The army draft in 1943 ended his racial innocence. Assigned to one of the army's first integrated units, Davis sustained several broken noses in fights with racist soldiers who taunted him. He also began to break away from the management of his father and Mastin by defying their objections to performing impressions of white men, which was then taboo for African American entertainers. In the army, performing impressions of white superiors, singers, and actors, Davis seized upon the genius of his childhood impression of Jolson—who, of course, performed in blackface—and experimented with a love of racial and ethnic mimicry. Davis wowed audiences with his seeming ability to do everything; during a single performance he sang, danced, impersonated Frank Sinatra, Louis Armstrong, and Humphrey Bogart, and played drums, bass guitar, and trumpet.[15]

Davis struggled financially until his big break at Ciro's, a nightclub in Los Angeles, in 1951. His star rose higher when the Jewish comedian Eddie Cantor invited Davis onto his popular television show in February 1952, giving Davis his first national television audience. The publicity he received after the car accident in 1954 further propelled his career. Film and theatrical roles followed—*Mr. Wonderful* on Broadway (1956), the role of Sportin' Life in a film adaption of *Porgy and Bess* (1959), and *Ocean's Eleven* (1960) with the "Rat Pack's" Frank Sinatra, Dean Martin, Peter Lawford, and Joey Bishop. By 1960 he had severed his partnership with his father and Mastin and become a solo act, selling out clubs throughout the United States. As Davis's career accelerated, he wandered into spiritual doubt. He later described his interest in religion as part of a quest "to cure a spiritual emptiness."[16]

Magical talismans, the loyalty of Jewish friends, and the gratitude of someone who survived a near-fatal accident shaped Davis's explanations of his decision to become a Jew. He changed key details as he retold the story over the years. Davis credited Jewish entertainers, including the television and film star Eddie Cantor (who got his start performing in blackface), with encouraging his interest in Judaism. In 1960, with his conversion still relatively recent, Davis told *Ebony* that when Cantor learned that Davis was curious about Judaism, he gave Davis a mezuzah, a small rectangular box that houses a scroll with the words of a Jewish prayer. Five years later, Davis credited Cantor with giving him the mezuzah earlier in the 1950s, before the car accident. This latter version, which appears in Davis's first memoir, *Yes I Can* (1965), attributes his initial interest in Judaism to Cantor, a form of homage to a senior comedian who shaped Davis's career and gave him one of his big breaks. In both accounts, Davis thereafter wore the mezuzah on a chain around his neck.[17]

The mezuzah held magical, protective powers for Davis. In *Yes I Can* he wrote that during that fateful drive to Los Angeles he realized that he had left the mezuzah behind in his Las Vegas hotel room. Just as with the Star of David that Tony Curtis and Janet Leigh gave him before surgery, Davis transformed the mezuzah into a talisman. The origins of the Star of David shifted in later accounts. By 1971, Davis recalled that Tony Curtis and Jeff Chandler gave him the Star of David at the hospital. (This version of events removes from the story the complicating detail that Janet Leigh, a Christian, gave him an object that had equal parts Christian and Jewish iconography.) Details aside, what is clear is that Davis interpreted his survival of the crash as a sign of God's protection and of the inevitability of his conversion to Judaism. Talking to reporters at the hospital, Davis said, "Baby, all I can say is that God must have had his arms around me. He really did[,] or I would have been killed." He used similar language to describe a suicide attempt (when he tried to drive his car off a cliff) in the year after he lost his eye, telling Alex Haley in a 1966 interview that he survived because "God had his arms around me." Newly confident about his relationship with God, Davis explained his conversion as a discovery of his authentic self and of God's plans for him.[18]

Whether or not Davis found himself protected in the arms of God, his friends, many of them Jewish, saw to it that he received competent medical care after the car accident in 1954. Jeff Chandler was among those who rushed to the hospital in San Bernardino, concerned that the staff might not admit an African American patient or, if they did, might not treat him equitably. When Chandler learned that Davis lost the use of one of his eyes, he reportedly offered to donate one of his corneas to him. Eddie Cantor also visited Davis in the hospital. As Davis recalled these events, he noted that someone retrieved the mezuzah from the Las Vegas hotel room; he once again wore it around his neck. Having already given Davis the mezuzah that served as a kind of shield against harm, Cantor again offered Davis protective guidance. "Never forget what an enormous gift God gave you when He gave you your talent," Cantor told him. By the time Davis left the hospital, he believed that God bequeathed him the talents that made him a star and looked out for him on the road to Los Angeles.[19]

Short and lean, Davis found a masculine style he could emulate as he observed American Jewish men. They prized wit and knowledge, and he dug it. The Reform rabbis he met after the accident impressed him with their sartorial and intellectual sophistication. The first of these rabbis to visit Davis in the hospital was, Davis later explained, "a rugged, athletic looking man in a khaki suit and a button-down collar." So unlike the bearded rabbis Davis encountered during his childhood in Harlem, this rabbi impressed him. More Paul Newman than yeshiva *bucher*, the rabbi exuded urbane confidence. Echoing Cantor's comment about his talent as God's gift, Davis asked the rabbi why God gave him such talent only to punish him with a debilitating car accident. God issued warnings, but he did not punish, the rabbi explained. Davis was soon convinced that Judaism was manly, quintessentially American, and designed to meet his spiritual needs.[20]

Davis identified with the Reform rabbis he met. They were entertainers, just as he was. They were cool. Rabbis possessed qualities that Davis coveted. Lacking a formal education, Davis reveled in the aura of intellectual gravitas that rabbis exuded. The rabbi was the consummate intellectual and a skilled entertainer; he embodied the quality Davis wished for but lacked and the attribute Davis most esteemed in himself. At a benefit in San Francisco in 1955 Davis was seated next to Rabbi Alvin Fine of Temple Emanu-El, who gave one of the speeches that evening.

Here was a charismatic entertainer for Davis to emulate: "With just logic, sincerity, and dignity, he completely wrapped up the audience.... An Old World wisdom poured out of him in combination with the most modern terminology, almost hip." Davis struck up a conversation with Fine, who taught him parables about Rabbi Hillel, an admired teacher from ancient times, suggested books about Judaism, and invited him to visit his temple. For Davis, Rabbi Fine was the real deal: "Everything he said had meaning." When Davis visited Temple Emanu-El in San Francisco he was struck by the "simplicity" of the building's architecture and décor, recalling images of the Mount Sinai tablets embroidered on the altar cloth (curtains covering the ark for the Torah), four satin-covered scrolls (Torah scrolls), and silver ornaments (the mantle, breastplate, and crown for the Torah scrolls). Davis reveled in the thought that men such as Fine, who devoted their lives to studying Torah, represented the sophistication he sought for himself.[21]

The rabbi who most profoundly affected Davis was Max Nussbaum, the same man who presided over Taylor's conversion and officiated at her wedding to Fisher. Davis and Nussbaum began meeting sometime in the mid-1950s. Nussbaum encouraged Davis to consider the faiths of his parents and warned that a decision to convert should not derive from knowledge gleaned from books alone. Practicing a traditional Jewish reluctance to welcome the convert, Nussbaum reassured Davis that his hesitancy was not a reflection of racial prejudice: "Race has absolutely nothing to do with our reluctance to rush you into conversion.... We *cherish* converts, but we neither seek nor rush them." Nussbaum urged Davis to attend religious services and join Jewish organizations in order to gain experiences of a Jewish life.[22]

Nussbaum may have encouraged these practical steps because Davis told him that, in his own mind, he was *already* Jewish. Davis recalled in his autobiography that he told Rabbi Fine in 1955 that he appreciated Jewish law not least because it affirmed what he already believed: "It's more like basic rules for everyday living and it's odd, I'm not a Jew but so much of it is what I believe in—ideas I'd love to be able to live up to ... confirming so much that I'd learned the hard way." Indeed, as Davis often noted, becoming a Jew was for him not as much of a transformation as an affirmation of long-held beliefs. Davis then described the appeal of Judaism as the emphasis within Reform Judaism on social justice activism: "It teaches justice for everyone." Rather than finding a conflict between being Black and being Jewish, Davis saw these identities as logically compatible: "As a Negro, I felt emotionally tied to Judaism," he told *Ebony* in 1960. Readers of the Black-owned family magazine *Ebony* were likely among Davis's harshest critics, more likely to see his departure from the Black church as an abandonment of African American people.[23]

To the contrary, Davis reiterated, nothing felt so true to his nature as his decision to become a Jew. In Judaism, he explained, he found the affirmative authenticity he lacked, much as Luce found truth in Catholicism. Davis described the late 1950s as a period of self-doubt. He was dating the white actress Kim Novak (and was possibly threatened by studio bosses to cease the relationship) and felt that his performances were flat and fake. At a particularly low moment he returned to the wisdom he found in Jewish teaching: "I unpacked some of my books on Judaism, books I hadn't looked at in almost a year." Davis's spiritual crisis intensified in January 1958 after he married Loray White, an African American dancer, very soon after meeting her. Davis was drunk when they wed, and the relationship may have been a publicity stunt to divert attention from his affair with Novak. White and Davis divorced within a few months. Davis proposed to a white actress a short while later, but they did not marry. Drinking heavily most days, he got into another car accident. When Davis turned to Nussbaum for help, the rabbi warned Davis not to look to Judaism for "a quick cure for your problems." Nussbaum wrote on a piece of paper, "Sammy Davis Jr. is a Jew," and signed it. Nussbaum then described the document as a fake: "I cannot make you a different person merely by signing a piece of paper." Davis could read all the books he wanted, Nussbaum explained, but until he started to live his life as a Jew, he would not become one. Nussbaum again deferred conversion and gave Davis the sole authority for his spiritual transformation: "I can't put religion into you.... I cannot make you a Jew. Only *you* can do that. And you have not yet done it." Although disappointed, Davis apparently appreciated Nussbaum's refusal to convert him on the spot. By spending more time studying and practicing Judaism, Davis would attain the kind of "real" Jewish identity he coveted.[24]

Two additional aspects of Jewish tradition—its heritage of intellectual engagement and its history of struggling against oppression—convinced Davis that Judaism was his faith. In an interview with Mike Wallace (probably in late 1955 or early 1956), he boasted, "I keep the Talmud on my night table—I like to have it there. When friends come up I don't slip

Sammy Davis Jr. and May Britt wed on November 13, 1960, shortly after they each converted to Judaism. Davis's faith and his interracial marriage sparked criticism. (Courtesy Library of Congress, Prints and Photographs Division; New York World-Telegram *LC-DIG-ds-07827)*

it under the pillow." Wil Haygood, whose biography portrays Davis as an insecure, eager-to-please man-child, writes: "He bragged about his newfound reading habits. He walked around proudly carrying a book—*Everyman's Talmud*—under the crook of his arm." *Ebony*'s 1960 profile of Davis of pictures him holding the book. Davis clearly relished the opportunity to talk about Judaism. He told Wallace, "From time to time [my Judaism has] come up in an interview and I'm not about to say 'No comment.'" With a zeal typical of the newly converted, Davis bragged about his new religion, marveling at its heritage of scholarship and wisdom.[25]

Even more than intellectual gravitas, Judaism gave Davis a powerful metaphor about overcoming oppression and succeeding against odds that mirrored the African American struggle for political liberation. Judaism appealed to him, he explained, because of "the affinity between the Jew and the Negro. The Jews had been oppressed for three thousand years instead of three hundred, but the rest was very much the same[,] and I admired how they'd hung on to their beliefs, enduring the intolerance." The prophetic tradition, which Reform Judaism in particular emphasized, stressed the pursuit of justice as the core of Jewish teaching. Invited to perform at hotels that refused him entry to their restaurants or rooms and especially during his ordeal in the army, Davis experienced the indignities of Jim Crow firsthand throughout his life. He identified with the underdog who fought for equal treatment.[26]

Davis's enthusiasm for Jewish chutzpah is clear from a conversation he had during a train ride with Morty Stevens, his arranger and composer. Stevens, who was Jewish, asked Davis if he was becoming a Jew because of what he learned from the books he was reading. Davis tried to persuade Stevens that it was not only Jewish history but Jewish survival that appealed to him. Outliving one oppressor after another made Jews hip: "These are a swinging bunch of people. I mean I've heard of persecution, but what they went through is *ridiculous!*" Reflecting what he learned from his rabbis and from books like Abram L. Sachar's *A History of the Jews*, Davis marveled in his distinctive idiom at the history of Jewish survival across centuries of persecution: "They'd get kicked out of one place, so they'd just go on to the next one and keep swinging like they wanted to, believing in themselves and in their right to have rights, asking nothing but for people to leave 'em alone and get off their backs, and having the guts to fight to get themselves a little peace." This sense of Jewishness—as a heritage of asserting the "right to have rights"—encapsulated Davis's understanding of Judaism as a fundamentally democratic faith from which African Americans and others could draw inspiration.[27]

The Jewish emphasis on "justice" stood out for Davis on one particularly bleak Christmas morning in 1955, when he discovered "Merry Christmas Nigger!" painted on his garage door. Retreating to his bedroom, Davis picked up his copy of Sachar's tome, from which he drew the lesson that Jews' faith and pride in being "different" sustained them through centuries of persecution. The idea that African Americans and Jews held much in common, an idea that Davis studied in Jewish texts ranging from Sachar's *History* to the *Everyman's Talmud*, enabled him to interpret his faith as logical rather than discordant with the freedoms he sought as an African American.[28]

Davis was hardly the first African American to compare the experiences of ancient Israelites and African Americans or to gravitate toward certain Jewish narratives, rituals, or texts. Enslaved African Americans drew upon the Hebrew Bible (Old Testament) story of the Exodus as an inspiring and parallel narrative of slavery and redemption. They retold "prophecies of the destruction of Israel's enemies" as metaphors for the suffering they believed would eventually befall their enslavers. By the early twentieth century, analogies between contemporary African American Christians and ancient Israelites flourished in Black Israelite congregations. Growing up in Harlem, Davis may have been exposed to any one of several Black Israelite groups. Black Israelites adapted contemporary Jewish practice. They taught that the original Hebrews were Black, and they often incorporated Jewish or early Christian rituals into their practice. More prosaically, perhaps Davis sipped Manischewitz wine, a kosher beverage popular among African Americans and widely advertised in *Ebony*, in Black newspapers, and on the radio. If Davis encountered analogies between Israelite and African American histories of oppression within African American Christianity, he found them unsatisfying and continued his search for a more direct relationship to Jewish history.[29]

American Jewish identity entailed complex and often internally contradictory ideas about Judaism as a faith, an ethnic culture, and an inherited trait. Jews in the early twentieth century U.S. feared total cultural assimilation through marriage at least as much as they worried about being singled out as a distinct quasi-racial group. Fears of anti-Semitic persecution mixed with confusion about whether Jewishness or the "Hebrew race" placed Jews within the boundaries of whiteness. Religion alone seemed inadequate as a means of explaining what made the Jewish people unique and cohesive. Many Jewish leaders instead sustained the idea that the Jewish people constituted a race, one that bequeathed a unique ethnic heritage to successive generations—and that must be sustained through marriage to others within the faith. After World War II, most American Jews came to see themselves as white, but their understanding of themselves as an ethnically distinct people remained. Amid arguments in support of the inherited, even biological, aspects of Jewish identity, conversion to Judaism prompted confusion. Rabbis learned fairly straightforward guidelines about the instruction they should provide to potential converts and the rituals required for a conversion ceremony, but they doubted that a non-Jew could be transformed into the inheritor of Judaism's ethnic heritage. By the 1960s, liberal and conservative Jews increasingly described Judaism as more than a faith, attributing their deeply held political perspectives to a wellspring of ethnic inheritance.[30]

Davis converted formally as he prepared to marry May Britt in 1960. Both Sammy and May converted in October, she at Temple Israel (Nussbaum's congregation) and he at Temple Beth Sholom in Las Vegas. Rabbi William M. Kramer, the associate rabbi at Temple Israel, officiated at the wedding ceremony as the couple stood beneath the chuppah on November 13, 1960, at Davis's home in the Hollywood Hills.[31]

Britt and Davis embraced Reform Judaism's emphasis on knowledge of Jewish history, observance of major Jewish holidays, and support of Jewish organizations. A mélange of ritual practices, cultural heritage, and social justice activism, Reform Judaism in the mid-twentieth century stressed the unique lessons of Jewish history. It ignored the abstruse reasoning of Talmudic scholarship in favor of simpler messages, derived from biblical stories in the Torah, about the importance of social activism, ethical individual behavior, and community survival. Glimpses into Davis's Jewish practice suggest he observed the Jewish high holidays; he enjoyed retelling the story of how he stood up to the [Jewish] movie producer Samuel Goldwyn during the filming of *Porgy and Bess* in 1959 and refused to work on Yom Kippur. May Britt supervised their children's Jewish education, so that their son Mark became a bar mitzvah when he was thirteen. Like many post–World War II Jews who expressed their Jewish identity through commitments to Zionist and charitable organizations, Davis gave generously to Jewish charities and supported the State of Israel. Much less clear is whether Davis felt that his adoption of Judaism involved a reorientation of his relationship to God. In his autobiography he does not discuss his religious views or faith prior to his conversion.[32]

No sooner had Davis displayed his interest in Judaism than he attracted the ire of many African Americans and ridicule from colleagues in the entertainment industry. The most scathing responses came from African Americans who accused Davis of abandoning his Blackness. "The reasons he gave [for his conversion] all add up to nothing," one person wrote in to *Ebony*. "I think what he is really trying to do is get away from being a Negro." Davis's descriptions of the commonalities between African American and Jewish histories of oppression struck another reader as proof of Davis's ignorance of "his own black people": "My estimation of Sammy Davis has dropped to zero.... He must realize that he is a Negro." This critique described racial and religious identity as an either-or proposition: one might be *either* African American *or* Jewish. Davis's friend the Jewish comedian Joey Bishop inverted this criticism with a joke: "I wanted to get Sammy Davis Jr. a Christmas present, but what do you get for the guy who is everything?" These critics considered African American racial identity and Jewish religious identity incompatible, their statements suggesting that Davis must have abandoned one identity in order to embrace the other; to claim both was absurd. Although racial diversity among American Jews has grown substantially more common since the late twentieth century, these suspicions persisted during Davis's lifetime.[33]

Entertainers poked fun at Davis's religious transformation. They often expressed astonishment that someone already on society's margins because of his race elected further alienation as a Jew. Jerry Lewis translated his reaction to Davis's conversion into a punchline: "I said, 'You don't have enough problems already?'" Lewis and Davis were friends, and more than many other comics, Lewis permitted Davis a measure of acceptance, teasingly calling him "Samele." The jokes were often crueler, especially as Jewish and non-Jewish comedians mocked Davis's ethnic heterogeneity.[34]

These allegations of racial betrayal stung not least because of Davis's ongoing fundraising and activism on behalf of the civil rights movement. Davis headlined fundraisers for the NAACP and the Southern Christian Leadership Conference (SCLC) at Carnegie Hall and other major venues, raising tens of thousands of dollars. Those donations represented a significant portion of the funds that enabled the SCLC to launch its 1963 campaign in Birmingham, Alabama. Davis urged his celebrity friends to buy tickets to benefits that raised money for Martin Luther King Jr., and he recorded a benefit album. In 1965 Davis marched from Selma to Montgomery with King, and in 1966 he chartered a plane full of Hollywood stars for the march in support of James Meredith, a young Black activist shot by a white supremacist during his solo march for civil rights. Davis nevertheless remained an easy target for critics. His romantic entanglements with several white women, including his marriage to May Britt, and his willingness to make fun of his Blackness when on stage, challenged expectations for Black leaders in the civil rights movement.[35]

Davis's friends in the entertainment business supported his activism, but they turned his racial and religious identities into punch lines. In one bit from the mid-1960s, Dean Martin picked up Davis (who was diminutive) and said, "I'd like to thank the NAACP for this wonderful trophy." According to Joey Bishop (born Joseph Abraham Gottlieb), who wrote the line, Martin was supposed to say "I'd like to thank B'nai B'rith" but could not pronounce the Jewish organization's name. At a bachelor party the night before Davis's wedding to May Britt, his friends feted him with songs and jokes, many of which mocked him for becoming a Black Jew, something the jokes characterized as ethnically farcical. To the tune of "The Lady Is a Tramp," Peter Lawford sang, "That's Why That Sammy Is a Jew" ("Won't go to Harlem and eat hominy grits"). Later in the evening, Milton Berle (born Milton Berlinger), dressed in drag as May and sang a spoof of "My Yiddishe Ma-Ma" as "My Yiddish Mau-Mau," rhetorically linking Davis to an anti-British military uprising in Kenya and thus to Black African nationalism. The humor of Berle's joke rested on the seeming illogic or incompatibility of Yiddish culture and African heritage. If the men gathered that evening knew of the existence of Ethiopian Jews, their humor suggested they still considered Black Jewishness to be inherently funny. Another set of jokes described Davis's conversion as a way of accumulating categories of oppression, making light of the violence of Jim Crow segregation. At a "roast" of Davis at the Friars Club in 1963, Pat Buttram, a white comedian from Alabama, noted that if Davis came to his home town, "they wouldn't know what to burn on the lawn." These jokes presented Davis's Jewishness as absurd and made light of threats against Black lives.[36]

Davis himself delivered variations on this theme, in which he cast his conversion as a doubling down on social alienation. Other critics and comedians mocked his religious identity as ethnically preposterous, but Davis portrayed his conversion as an affirmation of his status as an outsider. At a sold-out engagement at the Copa, an exclusive New York nightclub, he quipped, "You know, when I get up in the morning I don't know whether to be shiftless and lazy or smart and stingy." He told Jack Benny an oft-repeated joke about his golf game, that his handicap was being "a one-eyed Negro who's Jewish." During one performance in Las Vegas from the mid-1960s, before an audience that likely included many Jews, he joked about his status as a racial, ethnic, and religious outsider: "It is true, that I am an American Negro. . . . I have adopted Judaism as a faith," he told his audience, affirming their awareness of his ethnic difference. That collision of difference was the setup for a punch line: "But

I would also like to let you know something [that] probably you're not aware of: My mother is a Puerto Rican. My mother's maiden name was Elvera Sánchez. This is true—*emes*. And, so that means I'm colored, Jewish, and Puerto Rican. When I move into a neighborhood, I wipe it out!" Elegantly easing the discomfort any members of his audience might have with his constellation of racial, ethnic, and religious affiliations, Davis situated his multiple identities at the crossroads of white flight and ongoing battles over residential integration. He used a Yiddish word—*emes*, which means "truth" or "really"—to signify his connection to Jews (and to Jewish members of the audience). He was "acting Jewish," much the way Jewish-born entertainers did, deploying a sense of Jewishness as a claim on Yiddish culture and group belonging. Like Buttram's joke about cross burnings in the South, Davis's shtick invited audience members to identify with his alienation. Davis claimed socially marginal status based on disability, race, and faith. He marked his distance from the mainstream. Becoming Jewish, it seems, did not give Davis purchase on whiteness so much as it magnified his sense of being on the outside looking in.[37]

Davis insisted on the stability of religious, ethnic, and racial identities at a time when all were in flux. Within the complicated ethnic politics of "Judeo-Christian" ecumenism and interfaith dialogue, many post-Holocaust American Jews were wary of arguments in favor of religious convergence, the idea that all peoples and faiths might become one. They invested in Jewish ethnicity and in political Zionism as ways to define themselves as both nonracial and unassimilated. Many American Jewish leaders adopted "sociological" language to describe Jewishness as an ethnic heritage as much as a set of religious beliefs. These trends spoke to American Jews' desires to reassert historically based group distinctiveness, to claim ethnic difference as a core aspect of Jewish peoplehood.[38]

The politics of racial identity intensified amid the civil rights movement, the nascent Black Power movement, and related movements like Black Arts. Although many liberal Jewish Americans stood shoulder to shoulder with Black people in the civil rights movement, Black leaders often viewed the larger Jewish community and the very notion of "Black-Jewish relations" with suspicion. Southern Jews tended to agree with other southern whites and typically did not support Black demands for equal rights. While many white American Jews prided themselves on their exceptional participation in civil rights causes, such support was far from universal, a point driven home when African Americans boycotted Jewish-owned department stores for practicing employment discrimination or mistreating Black customers. The parallels between Jewish and African American history that Davis so often invoked as proof positive that African Americans and Jews shared common experiences became a point of conflict. A resurgence of "white" ethnic pride in the late 1960s and the 1970s benefited Jews but further denigrated the status of African Americans. This new narrative proposed that noble ethnic inheritances allowed Jews, the Irish, and other whites to overcome the oppression that all ethnic peoples experienced, while culturally impoverished Blacks remained largely disenfranchised. This ethnic logic ignored the legacy of Jim Crow and persistent racial discrimination in all sectors of American life. And it seemingly left no place for a Black Jew like Sammy Davis Jr.[39]

Davis categorically refuted allegations that he converted in a bid to appropriate Jewish ethnic success or to curry favor with Jewish power brokers in the entertainment industry. Jewish Americans retained an outsized influence on American popular culture, and they ascended the ranks in the theater, music, and film industries in part through the appropriation, distribution, and performance of musical forms and dramatic motifs that originated among African Americans. Along the way, they dominated the marketplace for popular music, leaving African American performers with little negotiating power. Davis was almost certainly intimately familiar with the importance of Jewish producers, theater managers, and agents from his earliest days in vaudeville. He may have been grateful to many Jewish people for supporting his career, but he insisted that gratitude had nothing to do with his conversion. Referring to Jewish entertainers Jack Benny (born Benjamin Kubelsky), Eddie Cantor (born Edward Israel Iskowitz), and Jerry Lewis (born Joseph Levitch), he denied that they influenced his religious shift: "Don't get the impression I wanted to become a Jew because these great guys who helped me were Jewish. It was just a coincidence." Indeed, those critiques deny the possibility that Davis found Judaism appealing; they reinforce stereotypes of both Jewish power and African American servility.[40]

The alienation Davis experienced as a Black Jew in the United States made his sense of authentic homecoming in Israel all the sweeter. Enmeshed in a broader American Jewish turn toward enthusiastic Zionism, he experienced a sense of being at home among other outcasts. It was a feeling that many American Jews shared. A surprise attack against Israel by its Arab neighbors in 1967, colloquially known as the Six-Day War due to its short duration, galvanized American Jewish support for the State of

Israel. Israel's victory included the annexation of Egypt's Sinai Peninsula and Gaza, the Golan Heights from Syria, and the West Bank from Jordan. For the first time in Israel's history, the new nation included all of Jerusalem, including sites that are sacred to Jews, Muslims, and Christians. The small nation's military dominance surprised and inspired American Jews, among whom Zionism was far from universally embraced even after Israel's political formation in 1948.[41]

Davis contrasted the homecoming he experienced during a visit to Israel in 1969 with the racial discrimination he endured in the United States. In language redolent of Hollywood romance, he described a profound feeling of inclusion: "I had come to the land of the unwanted as *I* had so often been, and they were reaching out to me." Characterizing Israel as the heart of the Jewish world, he added: "This is my religious home." Davis visited Israel as a proudly Jewish man who identified with Judaism's heritage of overcoming oppression. He did so unironically, unconcerned about how the Israeli occupation of the West Bank and Gaza, or its conquest of East Jerusalem and other territory, set it at odds with that democratic ethos of religious freedom. To the contrary, like many Jews in the United States and Israel, Davis took enormous pride in the Israeli military's dominance. The trip's itinerary combined celebrations of Jewish rituals and traditions with repeated gestures of support for the Israeli military, which had recently become an occupying force.[42]

The Zionism that Davis embraced consisted of not only a defensive claim to the land as a last place of refuge for a suffering people but an assertive military offense that enlarged the nation's borders. Davis's Zionism blended devotion to sacred architecture and holy ground with pride in a military deployed to protect them. Davis met with Israeli troops. He observed the Jewish custom of placing a note with a prayer to God in one of the crevices of the Western Wall, a landmark at the center of territorial disputes in Jerusalem between Jews, for whom the wall signifies what remains of the Second Temple, and Muslims, who worship at the mosque that was built atop the temple's ruins. Davis found that the experience affirmed his Jewishness: "It's a kind of oneness I have with Israel and the Jewish people." That oneness did not just comprise beliefs and rituals; it encompassed a nationalist embrace of Israel as the seat of Jewish identity and the geopolitical proof of chosenness.[43]

This account of Israeli territorial entitlement mirrored the narrative of Jewish belonging that Davis told about himself: both were logical, inevitable, and authentic. He was destined to overcome the indignities of

Jim Crow and find a spiritual home as a Jew; Israel was destined to rise from the ashes of the Holocaust and triumph over its adversaries. Ever the entertainer, Davis cast himself as the quintessential Jew in his performances of exile and return for Israeli audiences. In 1969 he performed at the Mann Auditorium in Tel Aviv for the family members of soldiers who died in the Six-Day War. Seizing the dramatic opportunities of his setting, he concluded his performance with the theme from *Exodus*, the 1960 Otto Preminger film that starred Paul Newman, a Jewish actor whose enormous talent and physical attractiveness made him a Hollywood legend. For Davis, performing the theme song from a blockbuster film about Zionism was a religious experience: "I sang like a cantor in a temple." Backstage, he gave several rhinestone-encrusted eye patches to Moshe Dayan, the one-eyed Israeli general and war hero. In Israel, Davis enjoyed an appreciative audience for his literal and symbolic performances of the similarities between the African American and the Jewish experiences. Tel Aviv and Jerusalem gave him the kind of nationalist welcome he never received in the United States. The politics of Zionism complicated Davis's relationships with a variety of Black leaders. Black nationalists and participants in the Black Power movement in particular viewed the struggle of Palestinians as emblematic of the global fight of Black and brown people against European colonialism and white control.[44]

Back in the United States, nothing undermined Davis's attempt to bridge Black and Jewish identities more than his very public, literal embrace of President Richard Nixon in 1972. Davis was thrilled to headline the entertainment for a Young Republicans event at the Republican National Convention in Miami. "Dig man, I'm on my way to do a show for the President," he told a reporter the day of his performance. Davis was still on stage when Nixon came to the microphone and awkwardly praised Davis: "You aren't going to buy Sammy Davis Jr. by inviting him to the White House. You buy him by doing something for America." Untroubled by Nixon's suggestion that he was a purchasable commodity, Davis was instead overcome with gratitude: "I walked up from behind him and put my arms around him, hugged him, and stepped back." The next morning newspapers across the country printed the image of that hug, and by the evening the television news replayed it. Davis tried to explain this seeming abandonment of his liberal politics by stating that before performing at the event he checked with civil rights leader Jesse Jackson, who assured him that Nixon was "carrying on the civil rights programs." The response from other civil rights allies was less sanguine. Sidney Poitier and Harry

Belafonte stopped returning Davis's phone calls. His new friendship with conservative icon John Wayne only augmented the perception that Davis sold out to the Right.[45]

To the end of his life, Davis defended his relationship with Nixon. From his hotel room in Reno in 1986, speaking with the husband-wife team who cowrote his memoirs, Davis grew agitated trying to explain that he did not betray the civil rights movement. He embraced Nixon, he said, *because* he loved his Black brothers and sisters. Remember, Davis told his coauthors, Nixon invited Davis and his third wife, Altovise, to dinner and an overnight stay at the White House. Not lost on Davis was the fact that he was disinvited from performing at John F. Kennedy's inaugural ball in 1960 when word reached the Kennedy people that Davis was engaged to the white actress May Britt. During his White House visit with Nixon, Davis spoke with the president for over an hour, the president listening attentively to Davis's policy suggestions: "We sat and talked about the disenfranchisement of Blacks in America, the unemployment of Black teenagers. We talked about the drug problem." They discussed the discriminatory treatment of Blacks and Hispanics by police and the courts. Nixon's views on these subjects changed with his political fortunes. Earlier in his political career, Nixon supported civil rights. Calculating his odds of winning the 1968 presidential election, he embraced the politics of white grievance. His advisors developed what they termed the "southern strategy," a coordinated effort to woo white voters away from the Democratic Party with promises of "law and order" against student protestors and Black radicals. By 1972 Nixon spoke about "the silent majority" of Americans who held the line against more expansive rights for people of color and other liberal causes. Perhaps Davis was unfamiliar with the deals Nixon cut with segregationists. He likely did not know that Nixon's campaign advisor, Roger Ailes, transformed Nixon's love for Hollywood into a strategy of using celebrities like Davis to win votes from what the president called "the blacks." Davis was won over by Nixon's commitment of $100 million in contracts to minority-owned businesses and over $1 billion directed to minority-owned banks. As someone whose personal experiences convinced him of capitalism's benefits, Davis believed every word Nixon said in 1972 about improving conditions for African Americans.[46]

Historians today debate whether there ever existed an "alliance" between Blacks and Jews outside of select circles of radical politics, but certainly by the late 1960s, the relationship was at a low ebb. At a time of intensifying ethnic nationalism in the United States, with the rise of Black Power and of a "white ethnic revival" that praised Irish, Italian, Jewish, and other European ancestries, Davis's Black Judaism was unusual and complicated. When he embraced Richard Nixon during a reelection campaign event in 1972, he insisted that his support for the president honored what Nixon did for African Americans. His political journey aligned with those of growing numbers of American Jews who affiliated with the Republican Party in the 1970s, including several prominent leftists who became "neoconservative" defenders of both military aggression and cuts to public welfare. At home among Zionists and frustrated by liberals (and, by 1973, employed as a spokesperson for Manischewitz wine), Davis nevertheless insisted that his life story proved the possibility of melding Black identity with Jewish politics.[47]

Celebrity converts to Judaism in the mid-twentieth century represented the quest for spiritual authenticity as an intensely personal choice with immediate political consequences. Unlike Luce, they did not publicly call for global conversions nor did they claim that their religious choices belonged to a national effort to bolster democracy. Their conversions epitomized tensions within the Jewish community (and for Davis, in debates among African Americans) over the meaning and importance of ethnic distinctiveness. For Monroe and Taylor, their status as Jewish wives became something that American Jews appreciated about them but mostly in order to scold other Jewish women into greater devotion to their husbands.

Casual anti-Semitism fueled questions about why any of these famous people wanted to become Jewish. Much as Luce's conversion to Catholicism in 1946 provoked profound anti-Catholicism, conversions to Judaism awakened anti-Jewish animus. As if Judaism itself might offer no redeeming qualities and lacked any intrinsic appeal, a prominent biographer has concluded that Davis wanted to be Jewish because of a "childlike" desire to be white. He misunderstood Davis's interest in Judaism as an attempt to distance himself from Blackness.[48]

The question of *who* could become *what* was never just religious or racial but always intensely political. Those politics never mattered more than they did for the man slowly circling his opponent in the ring on June 18, 1963, at Wembley Stadium in London. Elizabeth Taylor sat ringside with Richard Burton, her frequent costar and, soon, her spouse; she and Eddie Fisher split the year before. Taylor and Burton came to Wembley to see the rising heavyweight star, Cassius Clay, take on Henry Cooper, England's best boxer. Taylor wore a scarf wrapped like a turban, a long coat, and gloves; Clay wore a custom-made red-and-white satin robe. Clay had been praying at mosques affiliated with the Nation of Islam since at least the summer of 1963. He studied the teachings of Elijah Muhammad, the group's leader and prophet, with Malcolm X, the Nation's most prominent minister. The boxing match with Cooper was one of the only professional fights where a competitor knocked Clay to the ground. A dazzling figure inside and outside the ring, Clay was crowned world heavyweight boxing champion within the year. But the notoriety of his religious choice and race pride nearly doomed his career. The freedom of religious self-fashioning, so central to the Cold War defense of American democracy, was more clearly than ever a privilege of whiteness, one that Clay, most familiar as Muhammad Ali, fought against.[49]

Chapter 5 I Know the Truth

The bell rang for the start of the seventh round, but Sonny Liston did not stand up. Slouched on a stool in his corner of the ring, Liston could barely lift his left arm. Blood drained from a cut under one eye. The referee declared that Cassius Clay, the graceful, boastful challenger, won the bout by a technical knockout. Standing in a Miami arena in February 1964, the new world heavyweight boxing champion raised his gloved fists and shouted, "I'm the greatest!"

Reporters, who presumed that Liston would knock down Clay in an early round, gleaned plenty of good copy to send to their editors. The next morning gave them a surprise lede. Clay told a room full of reporters gathered for a press conference that he was a believer in Islam, confirming what many suspected. Answering questions about the sincerity of his beliefs, he retorted: "I know where I'm going and I know the truth and I don't have to be what you want me to be. I'm free to be who I want." He soon clarified that he was a follower of Elijah Muhammad and a member of the Nation of Islam. Within the week, Elijah Muhammad gave him a new name: Muhammad Ali.[1]

Cassius Clay's defiant words encapsulated a powerful defense of his Black manhood. They expressed his freedom of conscience—his freedom to be who *he* wanted to be. When Cassius Clay became Muhammad Ali, he did not simply proclaim a new religious identity; he defied a white establishment that felt entitled to curtail his freedom. He also turned his back on a Black civil rights establishment, rooted in African American churches, that was appalled by the Nation's emphasis on racial separatism and its antipathy to Christianity. To paraphrase Clay, the announcement of his religious conversion "shook up the world."

Rumors flew that Elijah Muhammad or the Nation's minister Malcolm X "brainwashed" Cassius Clay in the weeks just before and immediately after Clay pronounced those famous words. The accusation that other people controlled Clay's thoughts combined widespread fears of mass mind control, antagonism toward the Nation of Islam, and skepticism about a Black man's power of self-creation. The boxer's critics retooled the political theory of "brainwashing," previously employed to explain why a patriotic American might agree with his Communist captors, to discredit religious confessions that defied the Protestant, Catholic, or Jewish norm.

The Nation of Islam taught its members a history of racial difference that cast European whites as morally depraved oppressors. In response to the entrenched white supremacy of the United States, they sought not inclusion but complete racial separation. This unsparing assessment of American racial animosity set members of the Nation apart from the religious faiths that celebrated American democracy. The Nation additionally rejected the nonviolent civil rights movement that the liberal establishment endorsed. Critics in turn cast Clay/Ali as a case study in mind-control tactics, undercutting his assertions of spiritual liberty and excluding him from the ideal of freedom of conscience. The brainwashing explanation simultaneously insulted Ali's intelligence and portrayed his chosen faith as dangerous. Throughout it all, Muhammad Ali asserted his freedom to define his identity as a Black man in America and in the world.

The February 1964 heavyweight boxing title match between Sonny Liston and Cassius Clay was the biggest news in sports. Clay was a flamboyant upstart who won a gold medal at the 1960 Olympics in Rome when he was only eighteen. He went on to win all of his fights, while infuriating his opponents with his flippant aphorisms and wild publicity stunts. With backing from a cohort of white businessmen in his hometown of Louisville, Kentucky, Clay trounced his opponents and displayed an extraordinary flair for generating attention. He drove Cadillacs, recited poetry in the ring, razzed his opponents, and earned a reputation as the "Louisville Lip." That mouth in motion seemed to startle reporters even more than his darting feet or dancing body. Clay was a conundrum, successful as much for the punches he dodged as the hooks he landed and eager to make a name for himself outside as well as inside the ring. Sports reporters wondered if his showboating signaled the end of boxing as a serious sport. His opponent for the heavyweight title, Sonny Liston, seemed humorless by contrast. An ex-con in his early thirties, Liston was feared by opponents for his awesome physical power and his ruthless determination to win. Clay was photogenic and self-congratulatory, telling reporters how beautiful he was. Liston was taciturn. Clay taunted Liston by calling him a "big ugly bear." The odds were eight to one that Liston would defeat Clay when they met in Miami; many sports fans wondered if Clay would survive.[2]

Cassius Clay's stunning announcement about his faith the morning after he defeated Liston eclipsed news about the remarkable title bout. In declaring that he was a member of the Nation of Islam he made a bold statement about his religious and racial identities. The Nation of Islam that Cassius Clay joined, and that renamed him Muhammad Ali, was explicitly opposed to nonviolence and to integration. Only separation from white people and faith in the teachings of the Honorable Elijah Muhammad could save them. The Nation's fiery orator Malcolm X preached against the complacency of Blacks and whites who trusted in the American political system. Like Sammy Davis Jr., Clay was raised within Black Protestantism (his parents were Baptists), and like Davis, he found his parents' faith lacking. Unlike the Judaism with which Davis aligned, the Nation of Islam explicitly incorporated a theory of Black racial origins and distinctiveness. For Cassius Clay as for other followers of Elijah Muhammad, to be in the Nation was to be the strongest, proudest version of a Black man.

The wider American public learned in the last week of February 1964 about Cassius Clay's new faith but knew very little about orthodox Islam or the Nation. If they had heard of the latter, they likely understood it to be a hate-filled Black supremacist group, rumored to be intent on killing white people. No report was more influential in this regard than a 1959 television program, *The Hate That Hate Produced*, a sensationalist documentary coproduced by Louis Lomax, an African American journalist who filmed Malcolm X speaking at a rally, and Mike Wallace, the white television journalist. Wallace worked from a white liberal thesis that years of mistreatment explained an explosion of Black "hate." He transformed Lomax's footage of the Nation of Islam into a warning about a Black supremacist movement. This interpretation stuck. Several years later, an article in the January 1963 issue of the *Saturday Evening Post*, a popular family magazine, portrayed the Nation as a cult-like faith based on antiwhite animus. Cowritten by Alex Haley, who in 1965 published his *Autobiography of Malcolm X*, the article featured photographs of Elijah Muhammad, Malcolm X, and other members of the Nation at prayer and emphasized the interconnections between their religious and racial views. Importantly, the article described the Nation as not only "anti-white, [and] anti-Christian" but also aggressively convert-seeking: "Another major Muslim goal is to turn Negroes away from Christianity, which they call 'a white man's religion used to enslave the black man.' In at least two cases, in Arizona and New Jersey, Muslims have recruited entire congregations of Christian sects by converting the minister." The article amplified the threat that this numerically tiny group posed to Black Christianity when it quoted Elijah Muhammad characterizing Christianity as a white religion: "I'm doing all I can to make the so-called Negroes see that the white race and its religion, Christianity, are their open enemies." These journalists portrayed the Nation as a dangerous combination of zealotry, military-like discipline, and rage against white Christian America.[3]

Most readers of white and African American papers learned little about the Nation of Islam's relentless critique of white supremacy. They read only that "the Muslims have drawn attention to themselves by their avowed dislike of white people." A photographic essay about the group in *Esquire* in the spring of 1963 directly evoked fears of reeducating Black children for lives of militancy and power. One image showed a young Black boy looking intensely at a statue of an Egyptian god; above the image, the magazine's designers superimposed a quotation from Elijah Muhammad about Black people's origins along the Nile, where they once held great power. Long-standing American stereotypes about Muslims amplified this animus toward the racial philosophy of the Nation.[4]

Europeans and their North American descendants did not immediately associate Islam with heathen primitivism. In the seventeenth and eighteenth centuries, they held enslaved people who were Muslim in higher regard than enslaved Africans who practiced one of the many animist traditions. To justify their brutal enslavement of millions of Africans, Europeans and Americans constructed a hierarchy of racial civilization; they ranked Muslims above pagans. These relatively positive impressions of Islam changed in the early nineteenth century. Protestant missionaries who traveled and lived among Muslims in regions of the Ottoman Empire sent back reports of Muslims as outlandish, lascivious, predatory practitioners of a violent faith. Some of the missionaries came to recognize in Islam a complex religious, literary, and ethical Abrahamic tradition that shared much in common with the nobler aspects of Christianity. Theirs were minority voices. By the mid-nineteenth century, non-Muslim Americans treated Islam as a scapegoat, the antithesis of both democracy and morality. American political theorists argued that the nation was a family that grew from a consensual union between husband and wife, enshrining monogamy within republican ideology. Polygamy among high-ranking men in many Muslim countries struck these Americans as sexually scandalous and coercive. Such associations between polygamy, tyranny, and immorality even shaded the Protestant majority's response to other faiths. In the 1840s and 1850s, when the Protestant majority was seeking ways to denigrate the Church of Jesus Christ of Latter-day Saints, they compared the new faith to "the imperial harems of the modern Sultan."[5]

The reality, of course, was more complicated. The Nation emerged in the 1930s under the leadership of its prophet Elijah Muhammad, whose philosophy Malcolm X and other ministers imparted to Cassius Clay and his brother Rudy. Its teachings reflected the influence of some of the first Muslim communities in the United States. Muslims numbered prominently among seventeenth- and eighteenth-century enslaved arrivals in North America, but with the end of the Atlantic slave trade, and as slave traders forced families and language communities apart, their numbers declined. Discernible groups of Muslims arrived amid the waves of new immigrants in the early twentieth century, principally from the collapsing Ottoman Empire, the Caucasus, the Balkans, and Albania. Among these arrivals were adherents of Ahmadiyya, a movement founded in the Punjab in 1889, which sent missionaries throughout the United States to preach the connections between Islam and racial equality. By the 1920s, the Ahmadiyya movement operated small outposts in Chicago, Detroit, Kansas City, and Cincinnati, and it likely found allies within Marcus Garvey's Universal Negro Improvement Association. Ahmadiyya missionaries taught African Americans that Islam offered an interracial alternative to their status as "Negroes."[6]

Another group that influenced the Nation's founding was the Moorish Science Temple. The first Moorish Science Temple opened in Newark, New Jersey, in 1913. By the mid-1920s the Moorish Science Temple of America (MSTA) opened worship centers in Chicago, Detroit, and Harlem. A man named Noble Drew Ali founded the Moorish Science Temple in Chicago and became one of the group's most visible leaders. MSTA followers learned that they were "Moorish Americans," according to a theology that combined the Black nationalist ideas of the Garveyite movement, the Islamic teachings of the Ahmadiyya, spiritualism, and rituals gleaned from Freemasonry and the Shriners. By 1929, the MSTA comprised perhaps 30,000 members, all African American.[7]

Hundreds of miles from the nearest MSTA temple, a man who soon declared himself God incarnate was released from San Quentin prison after serving six months for selling narcotics. Wallace D. Fard drove east. He stopped in Chicago, where he encountered Ahmadiyya participants, Garveyites, and followers of Noble Drew Ali. By 1930, Fard was settled in Detroit. He gathered a small group of followers in his home, proclaimed his divinity, and created the Lost-Found Nation of Islam in the Wilderness of North America. Fard told his congregation that he was born in the holy city of Mecca. Light skinned with an ambiguous accent, Fard may have been David Ford or Fred Dodd, and scholars additionally debate whether he may have been from Turkey, New Zealand, or Portland, Oregon, rather than from Mecca. He explained that Black people were authentically Muslim, that slave traders stole their original Arabic language from them, and that they could now reclaim their racial inheritance by joining the Nation of Islam.[8]

Fard developed a distinctive synthesis of Ahmadiyya Islam, the occult, Black nationalism, and Moorish ancestry. The "Asiatic black man," he explained, was the original practitioner of Islam, a religion that existed since the dawn of humankind. The Nation of Islam's theology rooted Black people in the first faith, the first civilization, and the original revelation from God. It insisted that Islam was the "natural faith of African-Americans." Fard also taught that white people were "devils" whose destruction was destined in order for Black people to regain their dominion over the earth. Fard's gatherings in basements and living rooms soon overflowed as Black Detroiters flocked to hear his message of redemption. He renamed himself Fard Muhammad. Detroit police banned Fard Muhammad from the city in 1933, and he disappeared from the historical record amid a criminal investigation in 1934. By then, the Detroit headquarters of the Nation of Islam counted 8,000 followers, with thousands of others in Chicago and New York. Fard's trusted minister Elijah Muhammad (born Elijah Poole) seized leadership of the group after Fard's death. Elijah Muhammad led the Nation of Islam from his headquarters in Chicago as the messenger of Fard Muhammad.[9]

Fard's message of Islamic-racial redemption reached Malcolm Little as he served out an eight-to-ten-year sentence in Massachusetts. Little was just twenty years old when Boston police arrested him in 1945 for burglary and illegal firearm possession. Several of his siblings had recently converted to the Nation of Islam. They urged Malcolm to pray to Allah and to follow the Nation's dietary laws, based in Islamic law. He joined the Nation and took the name Malcolm X. By early 1950, Malcolm was teaching other inmates about the Nation of Islam. Released on parole in August 1952, he headed to Detroit. Over the next ten years Malcolm X became Elijah Muhammad's trusted minister, a sought-after orator, and a renowned convert seeker.[10]

The Nation of Islam that Cassius Clay joined in the early 1960s bore the unmistakable imprint of Malcolm X's impassioned demands for racial separation and Black empowerment. Malcolm's orations against white supremacy reached hundreds of thousands of African Americans. In 1963, *Newsweek* magazine chronicled the "increasingly restless and militant mood of the American Negro." Even the left-wing publication the *Nation* described Elijah Muhammad and Malcolm X as "Negro militants" committed to "Negro racist-nationalism" in their desire for a distinct African nation apart from the white United States. Elijah Muhammad's outreach to Ku Klux Klan leaders, who shared his vision of racial separation, lent credence to these critiques of the Nation's racial politics. The conservative magazine *National Review* offered a more sanguine interpretation because it agreed with Elijah Muhammad's goal of racial separation: "Behind the flummery of the Black Muslim movement is a serious idea: the alternative of an accommodation between the two communities, rather than a fusion between them." American papers and magazines portrayed the "Black Muslims," as the press called the Nation's members, as a hate group intent on violence against whites. White liberals and conservatives struggled to take seriously the religious worldview of the Nation of Islam or its members, but they more readily grasped the possible consequences of politically mobilized African Americans.[11]

The Nation's message of Black pride, self-defense, and antiwhite protest inspired a teenager named Cassius Clay as he struggled through high school in Louisville in the late 1950s. Already training for a career in boxing, he spent evenings in his parents' home listening to a recording of Louis X's song "A White Man's Heaven Is a Black Man's Hell." (Louis Wolcott gave up a career as a calypso musician to become a loyal minister of Elijah Muhammad's Lost-Found Nation of Islam; he later took the last name Farrakhan.) Louis X's song inspired the teen to write an essay about the Nation for a high school writing assignment. Cassius Clay's alarmed teacher threatened to fail him. Clay likely struggled with undiagnosed dyslexia; the teacher's disdain for his essay may have reflected both her low opinion of her student's intellectual abilities and her outrage at the essay's subject. The poor grade did not diminish Clay's fascination with the Nation of Islam. Shortly before he left for the Olympics in 1960, he listened to a minister for the Nation preach on a street corner in Harlem. Out one evening with friends in Louisville, he bought a copy of *Muhammad Speaks*, the Nation's newsletter. At his side was his younger brother, Rudy, who followed his brother into boxing and may have led him into the Nation of Islam. In Miami, where they trained, they met ministers of the Nation. Sometime in late 1961 or early 1962 they started attending Nation of Islam rallies and services at Miami's Temple No. 29. As Clay's biographer Jonathan Eig notes, "If you were a black man in an American prison, or in a major American city, the Nation of Islam was becoming all but unavoidable." Cassius dropped his last name when among members of the Nation, replacing it with an X to mark his rejection of the "slave name" that his family carried. In 1962, Clay met Malcolm X at a restaurant in Detroit, where Clay introduced himself as a loyal follower of Elijah Muhammad. It was the start of an intense mentoring relationship that lasted until shortly after the 1964 fight against Liston in Miami.[12]

Cassius Clay soaked up the Nation's racial philosophy. He answered reporters' questions about the civil rights movement with answers he learned through intensive study of the Nation's doctrine. He declared that the Nation of Islam was the group that defended and protected the rights of the Black man. Clay told reporters that he attended a Nation of Islam rally for political reasons: "I'm a race man, and every time I go to a Muslim meeting I get inspired." His statements about African American rights echoed what he might have heard from Malcolm X, who told the journalist Alex Haley in a May 1963 interview in *Playboy*, "A Muslim to us is somebody who is for the black man.... Intelligent black men today are interested in a religious doctrine that offers a solution to their problems right now, right here on earth, while they are alive." A key element in Clay's critique of Sonny Liston was that "Liston mixes," referring to Liston's desire to live in a racially integrated neighborhood. Clay was proud of the fact that he followed the advice of the Black Muslims and stayed among his "own kind," away from white areas. He denigrated the mainstream civil rights movement for pursuing integration. These comments earned him no friends in the African American commercial press, a cohort of journalists who understood their work as intrinsic to the achievement of civil rights but avoided the militancy of alternative Black newspapers.[13]

The Nation's patriarchal ethos appealed to Cassius Clay as well. Expectations for masculine strength and leadership within the Nation of Islam shaped his conversion, much as one element in Sammy Davis Jr.'s conversion was the masculine style he observed in Reform Jewish rabbis. Clay likewise agreed with Elijah Muhammad that dignified Black manhood required women's docility and subordination. Elijah Muhammad taught that the Nation's expectations of female virtue and masculine leadership elevated Black people above the damaging stereotypes that circulated in white society. The white mainstream more often treated Black women as sources of endless and often demeaning labor. Amid white stereotypes of Black women's sexual availability, the Nation honored its women for their purity. This patriarchal system appealed to many women and men. Married women learned to be submissive in exchange for their husbands' protective authority. The Nation's patriarchal gender system carried risks for women, from enduring too-frequent pregnancies (Elijah Muhammad forbade women from using birth control) to lacking options if their husbands abused or betrayed them.[14]

In the months before Clay announced that he was a member of the Nation, he played a game of religious cat and mouse with reporters who tracked his comings and goings. In October 1963, the *Afro-American* reported that despite being seen entering mosques and Nation rallies, Clay "won't say he's turned muslim [*sic*]." A month later, speaking to a reporter from the *Atlanta Daily World*, an African American–owned newspaper, the boxer admitted that he attended meetings of the Nation of Islam. By January 1964, Clay's appearances at Black Muslim events were national news, with the Associated Press circulating reports about his trip from his training center in Miami to a Nation of Islam gathering in New York. In response to white reporters' questions, the young fighter denied that he was a Black Muslim or that he converted. In a remarkable turnaround, reporters covering the title bout in Miami, who previously disparaged Liston for his criminal past, now described him as the "good guy in this fight … since it has been reported that Cassius has joined the Black Muslims."[15]

Fearing a backlash (and diminished earning power), Clay at first tried to dispel rumors about his association with Malcolm X and the Nation. At a press conference carried via closed-circuit television to reporters around the country on February 13, Clay evaded questions about his religious affiliation. A reporter for the *New York Amsterdam News* (and the editor who wrote his headline) saw through this ruse, reporting, "Cassius Clay almost says he's a Muslim." Many of the white reporters who attended the Liston-Clay fight in February 1964 were surprised by the announcement the following day that Clay was a member of the Nation, but the boxer dropped hints for months.[16]

Muhammad Ali credited the Nation's theology of Black racial destiny for drawing him to the faith, but few of his Christian critics took that explanation seriously. Instead, they equated serious interest in the Nation of Islam with a weak sense of self. A sports reporter for the *Los Angeles Times* described Cassius Clay as "very impressionable, as the Black Muslim thing points out," partly because of his youth (he was twenty-two years old in January 1964). Clay's reputation for performative self-regard amplified these impressions of him. Since his return from the Rome Olympics, American newspapers and magazines portrayed Clay as a loudmouthed braggart. A major profile of Clay in *Ebony*, the flagship publication of the Black-owned Johnson publishing empire, ran its headline next to a head-only photograph of Clay with his mouth wide open, naming him the "biggest mouth in boxing." The same profile described him as "a blast furnace of race pride." Photographs in the *Miami Herald* caught him similarly posed in a January 1964 photo, mouth agape at his army preinduction physical and written exam, "assuming the pose that made him famous."[17]

Cassius Clay never joked about his faith, before or after he became Muhammad Ali. He spoke of how the Nation of Islam transformed his place in the cosmos and his sense of worth as a Black man. More so than any American religious convert since Clare Boothe Luce, Ali stood in the spotlight of his renown and declared that his new faith gave his life purpose because it reshaped his identity. While many Protestants criticized Luce for misunderstanding God's revealed truth or being misled by corrupt priests, Ali was not believed to have the mental capacity to weigh one set of options against another. And unlike the ex-Communists, for whom religious conversion offered political legitimacy and lent credibility to assertions of newly normative sexuality, his conversion raised doubts about everything about him: his patriotism, his boxing title, and his masculinity.

The source of the original brainwashing accusation against Cassius Clay was none other than his father, who characterized his son as a weak-willed dupe of the Nation's information campaigns. Pat Putnam, a sports reporter for the *Miami Herald*, found Cassius Clay Sr. in a talkative mood in early February 1964, about two weeks before the Liston fight. The fifty-one-year-old sign painter told Putnam that the leadership of the Nation indoctrinated his son for years, "hammering him and brainwashing him" ever since he returned from the Rome Olympics. Described by biographers as a tough and even cruel parent, Clay Sr. denigrated his son's intelligence: "[The Nation's leaders] deal only with the ignorant colored people." Clay Sr. told reporters that his son Cassius became a Black Muslim when he was eighteen years old. The boxer's father laid most of the blame at the feet of Elijah Muhammad, who was practicing nefarious forms of mind control: "All those Muslims … worship one man: Muhammad … He hypnotizes them and has them so they can't think. All the words that come out of their mouths are his words. He completely dominates them. They might as well be in prison." This association between brainwashing and imprisonment or captivity reflected the era's worst fears about the ability of foreign powers to co-opt the minds of Americans. In a year when *The Manchurian Candidate* played at local movie theaters, reporters seized on the possibility that Cassius Clay Jr. was "brain washed" as a teenager by the mysterious Black Muslims.[18]

Hungry for a story, reporters in Miami cornered Cassius Clay in early February. They demanded that he respond to his father's accusations of brainwashing. Clay refused to answer their queries. "I don't care what my father said. I'm not interested and I'm not talking," he told a reporter for the United Press International. Headline writers forged ahead: "Brainwashing," blazed a headline in the *Washington Post and Times Herald* from the same news report. African American newspapers also took up this narrative of Cassius Clay as Elijah Muhammad's prey.[19]

The allegation that Clay was brainwashed was particularly discomfiting for Cold War Americans fearful of infiltrators in their midst. His insistence on his right to define his faith against the expectations of everyone except himself and his god startled a boxing establishment that consigned African American prizefighters to limited stereotypes—either the cooperative, "unthreatening" integrationist like Joe Louis or Floyd Patterson or the brute beast like Sonny Liston. Rather than indicating independent thought or spiritual self-determination, Clay's conversion became indicative of the susceptibility of Black men to the Nation's controversial message, at once indicating weakness and threat. If even the strongest of Black American men was too weak to resist Black Muslim rhetoric, white Americans had reason to fear the Black men under Elijah Muhammad's control, men who denounced whites and advocated racial separation. To critics, brainwashing offered the only plausible explanation for the Nation's growing popularity or for its successful recruitment of Cassius Clay.[20]

Clay was additionally susceptible to these accusations for the myriad ways in which he ignored normative gender roles. Handsome and physically impressive, Clay preferred to call himself "pretty." He did not drink, smoke, or attend wild parties. Some sportswriters speculated that Clay was gay. As a faithful Muslim, Clay/Ali initially avoided the heterosexual promiscuity more often associated with male celebrities.[21]

It did not take long for Muhammad Ali to more than make up for his youthful purity. His first wife, Sonji Roi, chafed at Ali's expectations that she conform to modesty in dress and submit to him; the marriage ended in divorce after a year. When Ali married for a second time in 1967, he wed a fellow member of the Nation, seventeen-year-old Sister Belinda Boyd, with the expectation that a traditional Muslim wife would provide him with the stable homelife he desired. Ali was almost immediately unfaithful to Boyd. His trainer Ferdie Pacheco called him a "pelvic missionary."[22]

In the spring of 1964, Cassius Clay still hewed closer to the Nation of Islam's doctrine of sexual fidelity. The night of his victory against Liston, he left the stadium and met up with his friends and family. Football star Jim Brown wanted to take him to the elegant Hotel Fontainebleau to party with "chicks," but at the boxer's insistence they instead returned to Malcolm X's room at a motel in Miami's Black neighborhood. Rudy Clay, musician Sam Cooke, and a few other men from the Nation of Islam gathered to celebrate Cassius's victory. "To my surprise," Brown recalled, Clay led him to a back room and spent the next two hours lecturing him about Elijah Muhammad and the Nation of Islam. Clay apparently included in his lecture a description of "The Great Wheel," one of the more esoteric elements in the Nation's cosmology. Wallace Fard and Elijah Muhammad reinterpreted the wheel in the sky from the Book of Ezekiel to describe a device in outer space, loaded with weapon-bearing planes that would one day save Allah's followers and destroy his enemies. Brown was stunned: "He told me about the Mother Ship," Brown said, "how it came out of the sky, gave birth to all the little ships. I'm thinking girls and booze, and girls, and Ali is trying to convert me." Cassius Clay was a true believer, conversant in the Nation's theology and single-minded in his devotion to it.[23]

Cassius Clay learned from Malcolm X and Elijah Muhammad that it was white people who brainwashed Black people for millennia and that the Nation offered Black people their only hope of intellectual or spiritual autonomy. The promises of the integrationist civil rights movement were pablum designed to promote complacency among African Americans, Malcolm taught. Followers of Elijah Muhammad learned a history of racial difference that explained the impossibility of interracial brotherhood. Unlike the submissive civil rights integrationists, Muhammad taught, the Nation's men were free of white society's control. They were the truly independent and powerful men. As Jim Brown discovered, when it came to talking about Islam, Clay was serious and well informed.

Clay's stern erudition at a press conference the morning after the title fight startled reporters who saw him gleefully exult in the ring the night before. Most of the seasoned reporters left the room after Clay answered questions about winning the title. A few younger reporters changed the topic of conversation to the Nation of Islam and its opposition to racial integration. It was at this moment that Clay asserted that he was "free to be who I want." A reporter followed up: "Are you a card-carrying member of the Black Muslims?" Clay was incredulous: "Card-carrying, what does that mean?" He recalled his lessons in racial separation: "In the jungle, lions are with lions and tigers with tigers, and redbirds stay with redbirds and bluebirds with bluebirds. That's human nature, too, to be with your own kind. I don't want to go where I'm not wanted." When a reporter suggested that Malcolm X was a negative influence in the boxer's life, Clay rose to Malcolm's defense. He all but admitted his faith to the world.[24]

Clay reiterated his faith and politics during press conferences in Miami over the next few days. "I am a believer in Islam," he said. "I have seen what the Black Muslims do—they have no narcotics problems, no prostitution, no women scandals, no drinking and they are very righteous." Though baptized at age twelve, "I ain't no Christian now. I believe in Islam, the religion of peace, and there are 750 million others who believe in it all over the world." He critiqued the civil rights bill then pending in Congress as "token integration," a source of "trouble." "I don't want to marry no white women like Chubby Checkers or Sammy Davis," he added. Well versed in the Nation's theology of racial destiny, he spoke about how the realities of white supremacy demanded that Black Americans seek a separatist path to justice. Scenes of white southern police officers turning fire hoses on nonviolent civil rights demonstrators and of attacks against Black churches offered Ali proof that Christianity left African Americans defenseless against white supremacy: "I don't want to be washed down sewers. I just want to be happy with my own kind." Inverting the logic of Christian nonviolence and stereotypes about Nation of Islam militancy, Ali argued that it was the Black church that provoked attacks, while Islam promoted peace: "Followers of Allah are the sweetest people in the world."

His statements reflected his agreement with Elijah Muhammad's belief that total racial separation would forge the path to peace.[25]

Elijah Muhammad made it official, telling reporters in Chicago that Cassius Clay was a member of his organization. Cassius Clay took "X" for a last name at some point during the previous year or two. Fewer than two weeks after the title fight, Elijah Muhammad gave Cassius X a full Arabic name, Muhammad Ali, even as the prophet's closest advisors continued to bear an X in lieu of a surname. Muhammad's embrace of the boxer came as a surprise. Muhammad had spurned Clay in the past because the Nation forbade participation in sports. *Muhammad Speaks*, the Nation's weekly newspaper, entirely ignored the Liston fight. Now the paper began to devote full-page spreads to the converted boxer.[26]

The press castigated Ali during the days and weeks that followed his announcement of his conversion. Descriptions of Malcolm X tended to portray the Nation of Islam as dangerously antiwhite, but articles about Muhammad Ali emphasized the outlandish, even foolish aspects of the Nation's theology and practice. Despite his victory, prize purse, and all the accolades that should have come with the heavyweight title, allegations flew that the title match was faked. In these critiques, the Nation did not materialize as a "real" religion; it was a cult of personality with ideas so strange they strained credulity. It was a sham, a childish kind of make-believe that appealed to simpleminded fools—fools, these reporters implied or said outright, like Muhammad Ali. The foul stench of fraud hung over Ali's title.

Racist scorn filled reporters' discussions of Ali's conversion. Jim Murray, who wrote for the *Los Angeles Times*, disparaged Ali's descriptions of Black Muslims: "To hear Cassius tell it, they come on like 'Amos 'n Andy in Saudi Arabia,' or the Mystic-Knights-of-the-Sea-on-Caravan." The layers of derision ran deep; Murray evoked stereotypes of Black entertainers and of Arabs, merging them into a disdainful caricature of Black stupidity as portrayed in horror films that made a punch line out of Black characters' deaths: "Cassius is like the guy in the movie who has wandered into the haunted house to use the phone and hasn't noticed the butler is a werewolf, that's blood on the floor, and he thinks the suit of armor in the corner is empty and that it's just an optical illusion the eyes in the wall painting are following him.... I expect him to trade in his Cadillac for a camel any day now." These kinds of media portrayals told readers that the champion athlete was far too stupid to think for himself, let alone make a reasoned religious choice.[27]

Another set of critics suggested that Malcolm X co-opted the boxer's thoughts. Within a few days of Liston's defeat, *Philadelphia Tribune* reporter Art Peters described how "the dynamic and sometimes fiery Malcolm had exerted an almost Svengalic influence over the twenty-two-year-old challenger during his training sessions and, in fact, is credited with 'conditioning' the champion's mind for his bout with Liston." As readers of Peters's article might have recognized, Svengali was the hypnotist in George du Maurier's 1895 novel *Trilby*, a story about a working girl in Paris and the various artists and musicians who fell in love with her. Formerly tone-deaf, Trilby becomes a virtuoso singer while under the villainous Svengali's spell. *Harper's* magazine published a serialized version of the novel, and it was adapted many times over for the stage and screen. Invoked to describe the relationship between Malcolm and Ali, Svengali epitomized the threat of a charismatic villain who corrupts innocent minds.[28]

Derision about Ali's name escalated in March 1964 after he failed the written portion of the army's induction exam. It was his second attempt at the aptitude test, which he first failed in January, shortly before the fight against Liston. Ali failed it yet again in mid-March and received a 1-Y classification that made him ineligible for active service. When reporters confronted Ali about the implications of the second test result, Ali defended his name: "Don't call me Cassius Clay," he warned them. "I am Muhammad Ali, heavyweight champion of the whole world. That is a beautiful Arabic name. That's my name now." When Ali attended a fight at Madison Square Garden, fans booed when he was introduced, by his insistent request, as Muhammad Ali. The mockery irked Ali because it second-guessed not only his acuity but his boxing title: "A stung, confused Cassius—'Call me Muhammad Ali'—Clay said today he can't understand the wave of criticism that has followed his rejection by the Army. ... 'I will leave it to a wise and intelligent world to decide what kind of a champion I am.'"[29]

Some reporters suggested that Ali was a malingerer who never intended to pass the army's tests. If so, he was not only intellectually weak and morally suspect but also unpatriotic. Sources within the Nation of Islam told a *Philadelphia Tribune* reporter that Ali wrote "Islam" on his preinduction paperwork, perhaps as a way to identify as a conscientious objector. Both Elijah Muhammad and his son Wallace served time in prison for refusing the drafts for World War II and the Korean War, respectively. Reporters implied (and assumed that their readers understood) that Ali planned all along to evade military service and failed the tests intentionally. As tens of thousands of American men were called up for military service to fight in Vietnam, draft evasion seemed the height of cowardice, a dereliction of duty to the nation and also to one's fellow citizens now headed to dangerous circumstances in a foreign land. Ali's failure of the army's test crystallized the antipathy that many Americans felt toward the Nation of Islam and toward a Black man who dared claim a status that stood defiantly against white supremacy. These events were more than an irritation to many people; they provoked calls for action. Senator Jacob Javits of New York received dozens of letters from constituents demanding to know why Ali wasn't inducted into the army. This outrage expressed anger at the idea of a Black man declaring his freedom of conscience.[30]

Associations between the Nation of Islam and the perpetration of a fraud cast a shadow across Ali's victory over Liston. The same day that newspapers around the country carried the AP story about Ali's announcement of his conversion to Islam, they reported on an investigation into the legitimacy of his heavyweight championship title. Although the Miami Beach Boxing Commission announced its satisfaction with the legitimacy of the title bout, Senator Philip Hart, a Michigan Democrat, harbored sufficient suspicion about Liston's claims of a debilitating shoulder injury to launch an investigation under the Senate's antitrust jurisdiction. Word reached Senator Hart that Liston's promoters, Inter-Continental Promotions Incorporated, entered discussions with Ali's management about promotion rights for a rematch to challenge Ali's title even before the first fight with Liston began. Liston held a 22 percent share of Inter-Continental stock. Liston's promoters were unapologetic, describing their deal not as proof that Liston threw the match but rather as evidence that they were savvy operators, preparing for their next set of profits in the event that Ali became the champion. Newspaper reports linked the allegedly fraudulent fight to the illegitimacy of Ali's new faith. An article about the boxers' promoters concluded by switching subjects, devoting five paragraphs to Ali's "membership of the Black Muslims [sic] Negro supremacy sect." Before March 1964 was out, the president of the World Boxing Association threatened to strip Ali of his title because of his association with the Nation.[31]

Rejecting the boxer's new name became a snide way for reporters to denigrate Ali's claims of independence. They saw Ali's conversion as a childish tantrum, failing to recognize the intensity of his beliefs. In March

1964, a reporter described Ali's arrival in Chicago to meet with "Elijah Muhammad (Poole)"; the headline writer added a parenthetical "Cassius Clay" after Ali's name. Speaking to reporters at one of the city's airports, Ali held a large wooden cane, which he compared to Moses's staff. "I'm a prophet, like Moses," he told the bemused reporters. "My predictions come true." The rest of what he said was less sensational. He emphasized that he accepted his Muslim name, prayed facing east five times a day, and wanted to pursue peace, not armed conflict. His bearing and attire attested to his new religious identity. On the lapel of his overcoat he wore "a red and white Muslim pin." Reporters ridiculed Ali's confidence and mocked his declaration of a new name, faith, and culture. When Ali defended his title in October 1964 against challenger Floyd Patterson, the press (and Patterson, a Roman Catholic) portrayed the matchup as a confrontation between the cross and the crescent, between an American Christian devoted to civil rights and a Black Muslim who hated America. Ali took the bait, telling reporters that his victory would be a victory for all Muslims.[32]

Leadership fractures and political controversies within the Nation of Islam forced Muhammad Ali to take sides. For months, Elijah Muhammad and Malcolm X argued over the Nation's engagement with American politics. Elijah Muhammad and Malcolm X already had a tense relationship. Muhammad was jealous of the attention his most famous minister received and concerned about a challenge to his leadership. His own indiscretions ultimately caused the rift. Rumors that Muhammad carried on extramarital affairs and neglected his out-of-wedlock children circulated within the Nation's inner circle as early as 1962. Although Malcolm at first tried to ignore the ugly gossip about his spiritual mentor, he eventually assented to Muhammad's request to conduct an internal investigation. Muhammad wanted Malcolm's investigation to put the matter to rest, but it instead led Malcolm to sympathize with the women Muhammad had sex with. Many of the women were Muhammad's secretaries, whom Muhammad subsequently banished from the Nation. Tension between Elijah Muhammad and Malcolm X intensified throughout 1963, the combined result of Malcolm X's disillusionment with his mentor, Elijah Muhammad's suspicions that Malcolm was trying to depose him, and paranoia within Muhammad's inner circle about whether Malcolm would expose what he knew about the prophet's illicit sex life.[33]

A persistent point of contention was the political content of Malcolm's speeches, something that Elijah Muhammad criticized for years. Malcolm's far-ranging lectures deftly combined the Nation's theology with Black nationalist politics. In November of 1963, Malcolm X made his infamous statement that the assassination of John F. Kennedy was evidence of "chickens coming home to roost" after decades of U.S. imperialism. Elijah Muhammad seized the opportunity to silence his most popular but also least controllable minister. By the time of the Clay-Liston fight in Miami in February 1964, Elijah Muhammad suspended Malcolm indefinitely from the Nation of Islam.

The bond between Malcolm X and Muhammad Ali did not survive these fissures within the Nation. Malcolm and Ali traveled to New York City together in early March 1964, a trip that included a visit to the United Nations and meetings with African diplomats. The following week, Malcolm X announced that he had broken with Elijah Muhammad and was forming Muslim Mosque, Inc. His organization combined faith and politics in the pursuit of "black nationalism and self-defense." Thereafter, Muhammad Ali no longer met with Malcolm X in the evenings at his hotel or watched newsreel films with him. In the summer of 1964, Malcolm X joined the hajj to Mecca and experienced a religious and political epiphany that dispelled his former faith in racial separation. He tried to build Muslim Mosque, Inc., into a new Black Muslim organization committed to internationalism, Black power, and peace, but he knew that Elijah Muhammad viewed him as an existential threat to the Nation of Islam. In February 1965, members of the Nation of Islam killed Malcolm at the Audubon Ballroom in Harlem. Over the next decade, Malcolm's former followers and even Elijah Muhammad's son Wallace led other members of the Nation of Islam into Sunni Islam. Louis X, by then Louis Farrakhan, took over leadership of the Nation of Islam after Elijah Muhammad's death, doubling down on its Black separatist ideology and adding a new strain of anti-Semitism.[34]

Ali learned from his mentors in the Nation of Islam to see connections among African nationalism, Islamic identity, and resistance to white supremacy. He spent a month in Africa soon after he publicly announced his membership in the Nation of Islam. While in Egypt, he proclaimed a desire to fight with Egyptians against any future Israeli military assault. In 1967, the Student Nonviolent Coordinating Committee likewise stood with other Black Power organizations in solidarity with Palestinians and other Arabs in their ongoing military confrontations with the Jewish state. Ali's global consciousness similarly led him to oppose the American war in Vietnam. The army revised Ali's draft status to 1-A in 1966, making it likely that he would be called up to serve. Ali was not drafted in 1964 because he failed the army's tests; now he made a principled stand against the Selective Service process. In April 1967 he answered a summons for induction but refused to comply, claiming exemption as a minister of the Nation of Islam. In June, he was convicted of draft evasion, stripped of his title and passport, and banned from boxing in every state in the United States. American foreign relations again served as a stage upon which converts enacted their religious and political legitimacy and declared their relationship to Americanism.

Muhammad Ali and Sammy Davis Jr. approached questions of civil rights and global identity in ways that exemplify the political implications of their religious conversions. Like many other people who engaged in the politics of the Arab-Israeli conflict, they developed their understandings of Zionism, Arab nationalism, and anticolonialism in response to travel abroad. While Ali's identification with a global Muslim and pan-African people inspired him to oppose the American war in Vietnam, Davis interpreted his encounters in Israel as a validation of his patriotic American Jewishness. Davis remained committed to the integrationist strain of the American civil rights movement (even if he failed that movement by supporting Nixon); through Judaism, he felt connected to a diasporic Jewish peoplehood and a nationalist pride in the State of Israel. As a Zionist, he identified with a transnational Jewish experience of expulsion, survival, and migration. What he learned about Jewish history and Israeli strength validated his confidence in a civil rights strategy premised on state power. As Jews gained strength through the success of Israel, so too would African Americans achieve their goals through traditional avenues of power in the United States. Ali identified with the anticolonial struggles of brown and Black people around the world. Both men understood their chosen faiths as affirmations of their racial identities, connecting them to a politically powerful global community.[35]

Ali became a vociferous critic of the American war in Vietnam and of American militarism in general. An adept student of his teachers within the Nation, Ali joined them in refusing to enlist in the military. Like others in the Nation, Ali saw his Muslim identity as a critique of the American state. His faith required a nationalism unbounded by international borders, one that extended across oceans to embrace a "Moorish" ancestry and pan-African brotherhood. Scholar Judith Weisenfeld calls this combination a "religio-racial" nationalism that transcended histori-

Muhammad Ali announced his membership in the Nation of Islam to the world in 1964 and remained a devoted Muslim for the rest of his life. He is pictured here in Chicago in March 1974 at a gathering to hear Elijah Muhammad's annual Saviour's Day message. (Courtesy National Archives, photo no. 412-DA-13795)

cal time and geography. Banned from professional boxing, Ali forged an alternative career as a minister and lecturer for the Nation, appearing on college campuses much as his late mentor Malcolm once had.[36]

Ali did not fight another professional match until 1970, when the Supreme Court threw out the draft conviction. Once again able to box and compete for the title, Ali took on Joe Frazier and George Foreman in increasingly brutal matches, regaining the heavyweight title from Foreman in 1974 in Zaire. These fights exacted an awful toll. By the decade's end Ali's hands had tremors and his speech had slowed, early indications of the brain injuries that presaged Parkinson's disease. Like his late mentor Malcolm, Ali was suspended from the Nation—in Ali's case, after defying

Elijah Muhammad's command that he cease boxing. He moved toward Sunni Islam in the 1970s under the guidance of Wallace Muhammad, Elijah's son who rejected his father's organization, and remained devoted to his faith for the rest of his life. His health declined, forcing an end to his boxing career. A man who made a career as a fearless fighter in the ring, he never wavered from his devotion to a faith that he understood to be the epitome of peace.[37]

The reactions to Ali's conversion bring to light a moment when Americans looked fearfully at religious conversion as a dangerous wedge in the nation's racial politics and military engagements. Like a true inheritor of the Enlightenment, Ali insisted that he was empowered to choose his faith. His freedom to be who he wanted to be was precisely what the accusation of brainwashing denied him. Conversion to Islam had a delegitimating effect, leading to the loss of his boxing title. While many African American writers and political organizers rallied to Ali's side in 1967 when he refused to be drafted to fight in Vietnam, in 1964 he was pilloried for adopting a faith that rejected the mainstream civil rights movement. The insinuation lingered that he was either too dumb or too duped to choose his faith for himself.

The implications of that response are especially notable in comparison to the way Americans responded to the dramatic conversions of ex-Communists. Many former Communists and leftists experienced highly public conversions to Christianity that helped them gain credibility as patriotic Americans. If anyone should have been accused of susceptibility to mind control, it should have been former spies for the Soviet Union and operatives in the Communist underground. Instead, conversion to Protestantism and Catholicism served as a kind of ideological antiseptic for white ex-Communists, credentialing them as soldiers of the American Cold War.

The response to Ali established brainwashing as a default explanation for conversions to religious sects that challenged political and religious norms. Like the soldiers in *The Manchurian Candidate*, men who were supposed to be among America's bravest and strongest but succumbed to the mind-control methods of their Communist captors, Ali signified an awesomely strong body crowned by a feeble mind. Brainwashing was a process that resulted in a confession of what seemed a genuine conversion but in which a nefarious power co-opted the individual's identity. Ali's racial, religious, and political identifications validated brainwashing as a

theory of coercive co-optation of American men. "Brainwashing" struck
Cassius Clay Sr.—and many others—as just as well suited to the educational strategies of the Nation of Islam as to Communist techniques for
mental control.

Muhammad Ali's statement of self-determination the morning after
he defeated Liston was more than an attempt to get reporters to leave
him alone: he declared his power to (re-)create himself. "I'm free to be
who I want to be" spoke for a generation of identity seekers. Within ten
years of that famous press conference, more Americans than ever before changed religions, incorporated unconventional practices into established faiths, and joined esoteric groups. Muhammad Ali—speaking then
as Cassius Clay—could foresee none of this, nor were those other faiths
what concerned him. He spoke from his subjective experience as an African American man defending his power to define his own life's course.
His words reflected his immersion in the theology of race, nation, and
Islam that he learned from his teachers in the Nation of Islam. In making
those arguments, he drew upon his own experiences of white racial animosity. Accusations that Elijah Muhammad and Malcolm X brainwashed
him were attempts to undercut that authorship of self. Denigrated all his
life for being stupid, Muhammad Ali no sooner claimed his title as a mar-
vel of physical strength and agility than he declared his membership in a
group devoted to praising his intelligent, Black manhood.

Chapter 6 Redemption

Susan Atkins was twenty-one years old in the summer of 1969, living with other followers of Charles Manson on a remote ranch in Southern California, when she participated in a ghoulish, drug-fueled murder spree that left eight people dead. Arrested and imprisoned, Atkins lost custody of her infant son but displayed no hint of remorse. She gleefully regaled another inmate with the horrific details of how she killed Sharon Tate, an eight-months-pregnant actor; she said that "Charlie" was Jesus Christ. Atkins seemed to relish the idea that she was depraved. According to women who met Atkins at a Los Angeles jail, she "bragged that she had done everything sexual that could be done, and on more than one occasion propositioned other inmates." A jury found Atkins guilty of murder, and the judge sentenced her to life in prison at the California Institute for Women.[1]

When redemption found Susan Atkins, it arrived not as the pardon or commuted sentence she and her lawyers sought but sotto voce from Jesus. One evening in September 1974, she later wrote, Jesus spoke to her in that prison cell. He forgave her sins, and she accepted him into her heart. Soon, she started a prison ministry to lead other inmates to Christ. The publication of her memoir, *Child of Satan, Child of God* (1977), renewed public interest in her harrowing story. Promoted by evangelical Protestant publishing houses, Atkins's life offered both a warning against dangerous cults such as Manson's and the promise that Jesus's love was available to all.[2]

America's young people appeared to be in crisis. In the 1960s and 1970s, new "cults" seemed to feed upon youthful innocence and end in bloodshed. News reports described the murderous rampages of the Manson gang in 1969, Patricia Hearst's kidnapping and claims of brainwashing, the Jonestown massacre in 1978, and sexual abuses carried out by members of the "Children of God." Each of these stories described authoritarian, secretive, and immoral communities that co-opted vulner-

In 1969, Susan Atkins was arrested for her role in the Manson murders. Pictured here at her trial, she received a life sentence, during which she was born again in prison. (Courtesy AP Images, ID 7003060105)

able young people, depriving them of the ability to think clearly. Experts advised parents to rescue and "deprogram" children who joined the Hare Krishna or a similar group. Although scholars debated the very meaning of a "cult" (a term that most scholars of religion now reject) and the mechanisms of brainwashing (another much-disputed idea), both terms became essential to vernacular explanations of an individual's otherwise incomprehensible choice. Stories similar to the one Atkins told captivated evangelicals at a time when a youth-driven counterculture and the seeming ubiquity of "cults" raised serious doubts about Christianity's grip on the nation's morals.[3]

Making matters worse for evangelicals, the secular news media and academics occasionally failed to distinguish between joining a cult and being born again. Decades after Sinclair Lewis skewered fundamentalist Protestant preachers as media-savvy hucksters in his novel *Elmer Gantry* (1926), allegations of fraud and opportunism persisted. The film *Marjoe* (1972), an insider's account of false evangelism, exposed the money-making manipulation of the born-again experience that Marjoe Gortner learned from his days as a four-year-old child prodigy who preached and collected cash in the aisles of his parents' church. The film won the Academy Award for Best Documentary Feature in 1973. Far from the presumptive standard-bearers of American religious values, evangelical Protestants had to defend themselves from journalists and even presidential campaign strategists who in 1976 referred to Jimmy Carter's faith as contributing to a "weirdo factor" that might harm his election chances.[4]

Evangelical leaders responded, in part, by promoting astonishing stories of people who were born again. In addition to Atkins, a growing, eclectic cohort of famous evangelical converts included ex–Nixon aide Charles ("Chuck") Colson (1973) and former Black Panther Eldridge Cleaver (1976), among dozens of others. The more abject the sinner, the more newsworthy the discovery of faith in Jesus Christ. The same individuals who became case studies of mental instability in the secular press became heroes within conservative evangelicalism. Journalists described an epidemic of "snapping," a "sudden personality change" that occurred among increasing numbers of young people drawn to new religious movements. Authors of a study of "snapping" listed Colson and Cleaver as paradigmatic examples of sudden "transformations" when they became evangelical Protestants. *Christianity Today* and other evangelical publications applauded the born-again conversions in the 1970s of folk singer Noel Paul Stookey, Bob Dylan, country singer Richie Furay, and Barry McGuire of the Mamas and the Papas, among other celebrities. (Stookey, who left the folk group Peter, Paul and Mary to embrace evangelical Christianity, credited Dylan with inspiring his Bible reading following a conversation the two had in 1968.)[5]

Conservative evangelicals harnessed the cultural power of born-again conversions to redirect a national conversation about youth, choice, and authentic faith. They circulated stories of especially shocking conversions with the help of conservative evangelical culture industries, which included the Christian Booksellers Association, the National Religious Broadcasters, Pat Robertson's Christian Broadcasting Network, Jim and Tammy Faye Bakker's PTL network, magazines such as *Christianity Today*, the Billy Graham crusades, Christian film companies, and a host of other groups, many of which received significant funding from "free enterprise"–loving Christian businessmen and their private foundations. On Sunday mornings, approximately 130 million Americans tuned their radios or television dials to a broadcast of a Christian worship service. Colson's conversion narrative, *Born Again* (1976), was an international best seller. The proliferation of these stories, coupled with the presidential campaign of the openly born-again Jimmy Carter, inspired editors at *Newsweek* and *Christianity Today* to declare 1976 the "Year of the Evangelical." Republican presidential candidate Gerald Ford announced that he, too, had been born again. Books by white evangelical authors about suffering, grace, and redemption sold millions of copies, including *The Total Woman* (1973), Marabel Morgan's advice book for Christian wives; *Joni* (1976), Joni Eareckson Tada's memoir of surviving a spinal cord injury that paralyzed her legs and hands; and Billy Graham's spiritual guide *Angels: God's Secret Agents* (1975). As religion scholar Daniel Vaca explains, Christian bookstores located in predominantly white suburbs helped publishers target their ideal consumer market. Seemingly trying to keep pace with the born-again boom, Billy Graham published *How to Be Born Again* in 1977, noting in the book's preface that "today being 'born again' is big news." A key selling point of all of these books—and of television ministries, too—was that each person could make choices, about what to buy and about what to believe, as a self-actualized subject. Far from constrained by external forces or systems, the believer was free to choose his or her path of salvation. Religious conversion, of the appropriate kind, was liberation.[6]

The story of how white evangelicals mobilized their cultural resources to distinguish being born again from joining a cult helps explain how and why arguments about freedom and sexual morality shaped the "New Christian Right." While some evangelical Protestants continued to align with the political Left, a growing body of conservatives saw the rise of Black Power, feminism, abortion rights, and gay liberation as ominous signs of cultural decline. By the late 1970s, those social forces, and the fight over abortion rights in particular, helped a new "religious Right" cohere and inspire candidates and voters alike. But in the early 1970s, when Susan Atkins found Jesus in her prison cell, none of that was fore-ordained. White evangelicals were not yet mobilized into a politically powerful voting bloc nor assured of their cultural sway. Some navigated debates over identity and religion in the 1970s by arguing for their faith as a pathway to freedom and contrasting it to the coercive practices of cults. Imprisonment, both literal and metaphorical, figured centrally in their narratives of born-again conversion. Prison ministries proliferated, promising not an end to incarceration but the spiritual liberation of God's grace. Those promises flowed in exhortations about the contrast between the libidinous excesses within cults and the monogamous heterosexual rectitude believers found within evangelical Protestantism.

The association between evangelicalism and "morality" seemed surer in earlier decades, when "religious" usually meant Christian and "Christian" still implied Protestant. The evangelical Protestants who championed Atkins, Colson, and Cleaver sought to reclaim an older tradition of Protestant moral leadership that drove movements from the abolition of slavery in the mid-nineteenth century to the prohibition of alcohol in the early twentieth. In doing so they argued that a radical interior change rendered obsolete the very movements for social transformation—from reproductive justice to gay liberation to Black Power—that threatened white Christian men's grip on cultural and political power.

Detailed accounts of the sexual abuse of women recur in several of these stories. These descriptions appear not so much as calls for remorse on the part of the perpetrators of violence as plot devices that enable the individual at the story's center to find redemption. These stories culminated in spiritual conversions that reified heterosexual patriarchy and masculine dominance. African American converts similarly operated in these stories as props of white Christian affirmation, their own discoveries of Jesus's redeeming love proof that white evangelicals could not be racist, even those, like Colson, who were architects of white supremacist political strategy at the highest levels of government. A public confession of "Christian" faith came to imply the acceptance of this white, hetero-sexual ideal.

Religious experimentation recurs throughout U.S. history, but contemporaries tend to meet new spiritual movements as frightening ruptures in the fabric of American religious life. In the 1960s, young people seemed drawn to new religious movements at an accelerating rate. High-profile lawsuits followed, as parents, attorneys, and brainwashing experts accused these groups of enslaving young minds.

Lawsuits targeting the International Society for Krishna Consciousness (ISKCON), or Hare Krishna, focused on the group's intensive recruitment techniques. Swami Prabhupada founded ISKCON in New York City in 1966, the same year he arrived in the United States from the Bengali region of India. He led a movement that combined sacred Hindu texts, recurrent chanting (*kirtan*), and an anti-capitalist aesthetic that appealed to the 1960s and 1970s counterculture. Prabhupada taught his followers that chanting a simple "Hare Krishna" mantra induced spiritual liberation and union with God.

Robin George was fourteen years old when she first visited an ISKCON temple in Southern California. George ran away from home soon after that first visit and resided at Hare Krishna centers throughout North America. Her parents eventually located her and brought her home with them. They sued ISKCON "for false imprisonment and emotional distress." Their lawyer hired psychologist Margaret Singer, known for her theories about cults and their strategies, as an expert witness. Singer drew a straight line between the brainwashing methods of Chinese Communists and those of new religious movements. Although the Orange County, California, jury initially awarded a huge settlement to Robin George's parents, the award decreased in amount with each defendant's appeal. The very legitimacy of the concept of brainwashing was at issue; the state court removed all references to brainwashing from its decision. Robin's parents eventually reached an out-of-court settlement with ISKCON. Despite these court challenges, Margaret Singer remained an in-demand expert, hired by the court to evaluate Patricia Hearst for evidence of brainwashing during her 1976 trial.[7]

These stories about ISKCON became especially poignant when they involved minors. Jerome Yanoff went in search of his twelve-year-old son, David, who disappeared from their home in Chicago after visiting his mother in California, where she joined a Krishna commune. After a month living with his mother, David informed his aunt and uncle, who came to visit him, that he did not want to return to his father. Jerome hurried back from a vacation in Europe and found David at the Krishna temple. Jerome describe their harrowing reunion: "We hugged and I picked him up.... I carried him out of the temple. All of a sudden I was completely surrounded by 10 of them. They grabbed him and pulled my arms back and threw me to the ground." David screamed, and then he was gone. "By the time I got to my feet," Jerome continued, "they'd taken him away ... and that's the last I ever saw of him." A Chicago court awarded Jerome full custody of David. Jerome obtained a writ of habeas corpus in California and a warrant for David. When the court date arrived, David and his mother were no-shows; other Hare Krishna members "took the stand to say that David and his mother had disappeared." Stories like David's proliferated across the country; no one's child seemed safe.[8]

Parents of adult children risked kidnapping charges when they hired "deprogrammers" to seize their children from these groups and return them to their prior religious commitments. (Therapeutically oriented "exit counselors" marketed themselves as a less violent alternative to deprogrammers.) The New York Civil Liberties Union represented Vasu Gopal, called Edward Shapiro by his parents, a twenty-two-year-old who joined Krishna and found that it superseded his earlier Jewish faith. Dr. Elia and Barbara Shapiro subjected their son to "deprogramming" and sent him to Canada with a group that aimed to convince him that ISKCON was a cult. Gopal rejoined a Krishna temple as soon as he was released. When he tried to access the $20,000 he held in a trust, his parents went to court to stop him on the grounds that he was not mentally competent to make sound financial decisions. They tried to have their son involuntarily committed to "a Long Island mental hospital," based on two physicians' statements about his mental health. The New York district attorney's office meanwhile indicted two Krishna officials for unlawful imprisonment and demanded that Gopal appear in court as a material witness. The family drama centered on the question of what made a group a religion or a cult, with religion scholar Diana Eck speaking out on behalf of ISKCON's legitimacy. The state supreme court in Queens, New York, ruled in 1977 that Hare Krishna was a "bona fide religion" and had not "brainwashed" its followers, ending the Shapiros' attempts to separate their son from the movement.[9]

Exposés by former "cult" members amplified parents' fears that their children were captives to autocratic gurus. "I was at one time a member of a so-called religious cult," one man wrote in to the *Chicago Tribune* about his years with ISKCON. He described the experience as being held "mentally captive" by leaders who emulated the Communists in China who indoctrinated American soldiers: "People are brainwashed into belief by Korean [*sic*] brainwashing tactics, consisting of fatigue, improper diet, lack of sleep, forgetting the past, repetition, and the message that no one cares except members of the group." This ex-Krishna follower mentioned the hours each day he spent chanting, the Indian-style dress ISKCON members wore, and the fact that the group sold incense and other goods while maintaining its tax-exempt status as a religious organization.[10]

Patricia Hearst's 1976 trial for the crimes she committed as a member of the tiny but notorious Symbionese Liberation Front (SLA) revolved around these questions of whether she acted of her own free will. The state argued that the twenty-year-old newspaper-family heiress knew what she was doing, chose to spout the group's incendiary communiqués, and gladly fired off guns from the SLA's huge stash of semiautomatic rifles. Her defense team insisted, to the contrary, that she participated in bank robberies under duress; she suffered from Stockholm syndrome, which made prisoners sympathize with their captors. Psychiatrists testified about how Hearst's brainwashing compared to that of the unrepatriated American soldiers from the Korean War. As proof they described how two men in the SLA raped her repeatedly and noted that leaders of the group told her that any attempt to escape or to contact her parents would lead to mass bloodshed. Perhaps, some trial experts suggested, she experienced a kind of religious conversion. The question at hand was not simply Hearst's guilt or innocence but whether she was a victim, a survivor, or a con artist. The very idea of the modern, unitary self was on trial. Did she creatively compile interchanging aspects of multiple identities, or had her captors manipulated her inherently unstable identity for their own purposes?[11]

Perhaps the self was becoming more fragile or more susceptible to influence. Perhaps Patricia was in search of an identity and gladly adopted the one the SLA gave her. Perhaps she was a convert to the SLA's "cult," brainwashed into their belief system as thousands of other young people in the 1970s seemingly were to radical, sometimes violent, groups. The most important cultural consequence of Hearst's strange story of captivity, crime, and prosecution may be that it undermined the idea that one could ever know for certain who a person was or what he or she believed. Hearst was as unreliable a witness of her experiences as Harvey Matusow was of his. She changed her story often and profoundly. Observers then and since puzzled over when was she telling the truth, and which of her identities was authentic. Echoing fears from the 1950s of brainwashed prisoners of war and "authoritarian personalities," the Patricia Hearst case revived the dread of mass mind control and attached those anxieties to the fragile identities of young (white) women and men.

The activities of the secretive organization called the Children of God (also called "The Family" or "The Family of Love") especially troubled evangelicals because the group emerged in the late 1960s among followers of the Jesus People movement, a youth-driven evangelical effort that embraced countercultural styles (what historian Steven P. Miller calls a "fundamentalist-hippie brew"). Some Jesus People took their unconventional and charismatic faith and successfully channeled it into Christian organizations such as Calvary Church and the Vineyard churches, new centers for evangelical worship that embraced guitar music and a countercultural aesthetic. The Children of God showed that the movement's impulses might produce authoritarian religious groups with social values that conflicted with those of conservative Protestantism. The founder, David Berg, said he was a "revolutionary for Christ" and preached the imminent arrival of the millennium, the unredeemed evil of the secular world, and the necessity of perpetual evangelism. His followers numbered in the thousands and lived in communes in the United States and Europe.[12]

Berg's exploitation of girls and women made him and his group notorious. Under his leadership the Children of God developed recruitment practices known as "'flirty fishing' expeditions, in which female members tried to seduce potential recruits." In the 1970s, Berg published "Mo Letters," which provided a biblical justification for male followers having more than one wife. Some of the wives were underage. A report by the New York attorney general in 1974 accused Berg of commissioning sexual crimes, including public sexual intercourse with a "young girl" moments after declaring her to be his new wife. (The Children of God denied these allegations.) The group's appeal to young people was alarming. As one historian of the movement notes, the "first anticult organization in America" was organized in 1971 by the parents of young people who joined the Children of God.[13]

Evangelicals produced memoirs and other media to explain that a born-again conversion, rather than secular "deprogramming," could bring young people out of cults. Zondervan, an evangelical publishing house, published *The Children of God: The Inside Story* (1984), a tell-all book by a former member named Deborah Davis, David Berg's daughter. She wrote the book with her husband, Bill, who also belonged to the group: "The couple acknowledge that they were indeed 'brainwashed' while members of the Children of God, but they contend that they were willing prey." Filled with remorse and anxiety, Deborah Davis thought of ending her life. Like many religious seekers before her, from Clare Boothe Luce and Whittaker Chambers to Sammy Davis Jr., she found a religious faith that saved her from suicidal intentions. Deborah Davis left the Children of God and became a born-again Christian. She told her story as one of corruption and redemption, in which God's power and love saved her from the depravity of an immoral cult. Conservative Protestant publishing houses promoted narratives like this one, which told of journeys away from sexual sin and corrupt belief to the purer light of Christian faith.[14]

The people who disparaged "cults" made little distinction between new religions with peaceful practices and secretive, socially coercive groups that embraced violence and sexual abuse. Certainly, several of these groups engaged in criminal behavior. Even before the ultimate horrors of Jim Jones's People's Temple emerged in 1978 with mass death by poisoning in Guyana, anyone following the news about Patricia Hearst's kidnapping could compare her vulnerability and alleged brainwashing to the murderous behaviors of Susan Atkins or to the sexual violence within the Children of God. Stories about evangelical Protestants' born-again conversions contrasted the Christian believer's freedom with the cult follower's co-opted self. This contrast proved essential to the cultural ascent of American evangelicals.

Washington, D.C., reporters' discovery in December 1973 that Chuck Colson, President Nixon's former "hatchet man," was attending prayer breakfasts at the White House seemed utterly at odds with what the public knew about him. Little about Colson was appealing. Beneath his immovable hair and thick black-framed glasses, he had an amphibian mien that exuded the unearned self-confidence of a white man accustomed to power. At Nixon's right hand, he helped orchestrate a "white ethnic strategy" that drew support from blue-collar whites by praising them as hardworking Americans while denigrating "forced busing" and other programs that benefited African Americans, a racist dog whistle audible in a traffic jam. In an August 1972 memo to White House staff members, Colson instructed them to devote themselves entirely to Nixon's reelection campaign until Election Day: "Just so you understand me, let me point out that the statement in last week's UPI story that I was once reported to have said that 'I would walk over my grandmother if necessary' is absolutely accurate." The man responsible for smearing the president's opponents by leaking false allegations, and now implicated in the ongoing Watergate investigation, seemed an unlikely exemplar of religious piety. Nominally Episcopalian, Colson had "turned religious." Reporters scoffed at the idea that a "tough guy" such as Colson now embraced the gentle love of Christ. They wondered whether it was a publicity stunt or evidence of a mental breakdown. Thanks to the success of his carefully crafted conversion narrative, *Born Again* (1976), which was adapted into a major motion picture in 1978, Colson became a media star and major political force among evangelicals. As he toured the country to share his testimony and promote his book and film, he launched the Prison Fellowship Ministries, which sought to convert convicted felons.[15]

What the American public knew about Chuck Colson in 1973 was that he did the president's bidding—and that his name was all over the Watergate investigators' notes about criminal behavior orchestrated by the White House. From 1968 to early 1973, Colson belonged to a small but passionate group of aides who executed President Nixon's orders. H. R. Haldeman, the chief of staff, controlled access to Nixon, with Colson, a special assistant, there to carry out the president's dirty work. When the president sought revenge on his opponents, it was Colson and John Dean, the White House counsel, who drafted the "enemies list." Colson later said he knew nothing about the list, despite evidence that he added at least twenty names to it. (Haldeman persuaded the Internal Revenue Service to audit many of the liberals and left-leaning lobbying groups on the list.) The results could be violent; in May of 1971, according to Watergate historian Stanley Kutler, "Haldeman told the President that Charles Colson would use his connections with the Teamsters' Union and hire some 'thugs' to attack [antiwar] protestors." Colson was a prolific hatchet man. Arthur Burns, chairman of the Federal Reserve Board, favored legislation that would increase the salary of Federal Reserve employees, taking effect only after he retired from his role. After Burns testified before Congress in 1971 that Nixon had not done enough to control inflation, Colson spread false rumors that Burns was seeking a raise for himself even as he urged wage and price controls for others.[16]

Colson's legal trouble began after he hired Howard Hunt and G. Gordon Liddy for Nixon's notorious "Plumbers," a secretive cohort empowered to combat damaging leaks about the president. The Plumbers targeted not only people working within the administration who disclosed classified information to the press but also individuals on the "enemies list." Hunt and Liddy came on board in 1971 to orchestrate Nixon's retaliation after a foreign policy breach. Earlier that year, the *New York Times* published the *Pentagon Papers*, a classified report by the RAND Corporation that detailed American policy in Vietnam. Even though the report primarily implicated Nixon's Democratic predecessors in the White House, Nixon considered it a dangerous precedent for undermining the secrecy he demanded about his own foreign policy operations. A former RAND employee named Daniel Ellsberg was quickly identified as the person who gave a copy of the report to a *New York Times* reporter. Colson wrote to John Ehrlichman, one of Nixon's principal advisors, that they should "paint Ellsberg black" as part of a broader strategy of discrediting the president's critics. The Plumbers had their orders: they broke into the offices of Daniel Ellsberg's psychiatrist in search of embarrassing evidence of poor mental health. Colson also backed a plan "either to raid or firebomb the Brookings Institution" to access an analogous report about the Nixon administration's Vietnam policy. Even worse, perhaps, Colson played a central role in the cover-ups of the break-ins at Ellsberg's psychiatrist's office and the Democratic National Committee's headquarters at the Watergate Hotel. Colson paid Hunt hush money and promised him clemency if he lied to prosecutors about the White House's role in the crimes.[17]

Colson was awaiting a judge's decision about the extent of his legal jeopardy when the news of his conversion spread in the early months of 1974. He was under two federal indictments: a conspiracy charge for his part in orchestrating and covering up the June 1972 Watergate break-in and an obstruction charge in the criminal case against Daniel Ellsberg. Colson pleaded not guilty to the conspiracy charge. He was so confident that he would avoid prison time that he pleaded to the obstruction charge, admitting his participation in the attempt to defame Ellsberg and thereby shape the outcome of Ellsberg's prosecution. The judge in Colson's case agreed to drop the conspiracy charges. White evangelical power brokers in D.C. rallied around Colson, offering him spiritual and legal advice. Here was a story of redemption to convince even the most stalwart skeptic that God's grace was available to all.[18]

Colson's conversion and the support he found from evangelical Christians originated with a group called "The Family" or "the Fellowship," a secretive, international network of powerful Christian men. (Here I'll refer to it as "the Fellowship" so as not to confuse it with the "The Family" of the Children of God.) Tom Phillips, the CEO of Raytheon who inspired Colson to convert in the summer of 1973, introduced Colson to Doug Coe, the leader of the Fellowship. Through Coe, Colson entered the elite prayer "cells" that united an off-the-books network of politically and financially well-connected men. Founded in the 1950s by Abraham Vereide and best known for its sponsorship of the National Prayer Breakfast, the Fellowship aimed to integrate conservative expressions of Christianity into national political life, with the goal of making the United States a more Christian nation (as the group understood and defined "Christian"). The Fellowship intentionally obscured its importance, but it was essential to the ways Colson found and described his new faith.[19]

Colson explained to his friends that he entered a guilty plea not because he had done anything illegal but because his guilt about all the unkind things he had said and done weighed heavily on his conscience. He was guilty of pride but not of perjury. The idea that one of the most loathed figures from the Nixon White House claimed not only innocence but spiritual truth created a media storm. In late May 1974, as Colson awaited sentencing, he appeared on *60 Minutes* for an interview with Mike Wallace. The promotional tag line for the segment underscored the improbability of Colson's new identity: "Charles Colson, who used to be known as the White House hatchet man, Charles Colson has come to Christ." Viewers learned that although Colson's prior loyalties attached to President Nixon, he now found common cause with former political adversaries who shared a love for Jesus. The producers staged the interview in the home of Harold Hughes, a "liberal Democrat" senator from Iowa, with whom Colson now met for weekly prayer. Colson and Hughes met and formed a bond at gatherings of the Fellowship. Mike Wallace likely thought that a shared Christian faith united Colson and Hughes, not a global network of faith-based political influence.[20]

Colson explained that his conversion meant he was "going to live a Christian life and [he was] going to live by the teachings of Christ," but Wallace pressed him to explain whether he repented for his past sins. In particular, Wallace wanted to know whether Colson had apologized to Fed chair Arthur Burns: "Have you made a palpable witness? Have you tried to make it up to those you've hurt?" Colson replied, "In my own heart, yes." Wallace was unsatisfied. "In your own heart. But ... have you apologized to anybody for some of the tactics that you used?" Colson said that in "a couple of instances ... where it came very naturally," he did so. Colson conceded that he wished that he wished he had put his "faith in the Lord" to advance the White House's objectives, rather than trusting his "own wits." (In *Born Again*, Colson's smearing of Burns is the only misdeed to which he admits.) He insisted that he "never had anything to do with the enemies list."[21]

The interview highlighted a contrast between the way that Mike Wallace interpreted guilt and innocence and the evangelical Christian perspective Colson was absorbing alongside his new brothers in the Fellowship. Wallace brought up other instances of Colson's notorious meanness, such as threatening Frank Stanton while he was president of CBS. Colson denied that he ever spoke to Stanton. Wallace persisted: "He has put in an affidavit. And Frank Stanton says that Colson threatened that the White House would bring CBS to its knees in Wall Street and Madison Avenue. What I'm saying is ... a new Christian, beside talking to his God, does he do penance for deeds like that?" At times seeming to reference a Roman Catholic rather than an evangelical Protestant response to sin, Wallace pressed Colson to judge whether the newly released transcripts of Oval Office recordings indicated "amorality." Hughes interjected with a phrase evangelicals used for new converts, telling Wallace that Colson was still "a baby in Christ, not full maturity, not full understanding," and therefore seemingly unable to judge whether the Nixon White House acted immorally. His composure regained, Colson interjected, "I don't believe that when you accept Christ in your life ... that you necessarily should set yourself up as a judge of others. As a matter of fact, Christ teaches us exactly the opposite." Of course, Wallace did not ask Colson to judge others; he asked him to judge himself. Presented with a convert seemingly inured to repentance, Wallace was befuddled: "Well, I—I confess you leave me somewhat bewildered, then, as to the meaning of your faith." That awkward disconnect came to define the reception that Colson and other born-again converts received as they told their stories: admiration from other evangelical Christians on the one hand and confusion or even derision from people who did not have ties to evangelicalism on the other.[22]

The language of born-again conversion that Colson and others employed was indebted to the theological and cultural revolution launched by the Reverend Billy Graham in the late 1940s. At his massive revivals in football arenas and on radio and television broadcasts, Graham took his "plain-folk preaching" style to the masses. In Graham's magazine *De-*

cision, in best-selling books like *Peace with God* (1953), and especially in his televised preaching, he convinced hundreds of thousands of people to make a "decision for Christ." As Graham biographer Grant Wacker notes, "he made clear—repeatedly—that he saw himself as an evangelist with one purpose: to win people to Christ." Graham did so by preaching the authority of the Bible, the redeeming love of Jesus Christ, and the certainty that the end times (the millennium) would soon arrive. Christians could be confident that Christ would return at the end of human history. As Wacker summarizes, "after death, believers would enter into the everlasting joys of heaven and nonbelievers the everlasting sorrows of hell. Believers were obliged to share this good news—the gospel of salvation—with others." The "new birth" of the believer was the centerpiece of this ministry. In its theology, if not in its style, Graham's evangelicalism sustained the core features of militant fundamentalist Protestantism. As historian Matthew Sutton demonstrates, Graham repackaged fundamentalism as a more genial "evangelicalism," but the faith's attention to sin, salvation, and apocalypse endured.[23]

Graham's savvy combination of proselytizing and mass communication had precedent among American evangelicals and fundamentalists. Charles Grandison Finney, a northern Presbyterian preacher, held popular tent revivals in the early nineteenth century. He scandalized southern evangelicals by describing conversion as a rational and fairly instantaneous experience, which might occur over the course of a single prayer service. Evangelical revivals led by Dwight Moody in the late nineteenth century and Billy Sunday in the early twentieth encouraged individuals to experience ecstatic conversions and give their lives over to Christ. Moody built a global evangelical communications network, while the impassioned urban revivalism of Billy Sunday in the 1910s and 1920s captivated millions of people. Over the course of Sunday's 1917 revival in Boston, approximately 1.3 million people gathered in his custom-built tabernacle, and 60,000 "walked the sawdust trail" to shake the preacher's hand and declare that they were born again. Pentecostal evangelist Aimee Semple McPherson achieved even greater fame, becoming the first woman in the United States to own her own radio signal, which she used to broadcast her sermons. With her massive Angelus Temple situated a few miles from Hollywood, McPherson delivered fervent prayers assisted by professional costumes, lighting, and props. Finney, Moody, Sunday, and McPherson were innovators, bringing steadily higher production values to American evangelicalism. Graham launched a film company, World Wide Pictures, whose first two films, *Mr. Texas* (1951) and *Oiltown, USA* (1953), focused on the evangelical foundations of "free enterprise" set against the booming Texas oil industry. Screenings of the latter film in the Sam Houston arena were combined with prayer meetings designed to elicit mass conversions.[24]

Graham was not alone in these efforts. By the 1970s, the Christian Broadcasting Network hosted television programs by Oral Roberts, Jimmy Swaggart, George Otis, Pat Robertson, and Jerry Falwell. The conservative Protestant media landscape had expanded monumentally beginning in the 1930s and 1940s, when fundamentalists and others established new print, radio, and eventually television networks devoted to circulating their messages. The Christian Booksellers Association brought together Christian publishers at annual conventions and supported an international network of Christian bookstores, authors, and editors. Christian record labels grew, with evangelical rock and roll joining gospel and choral music as a route to spiritual expression. From the "evangelical left" and "right," the Christian presence in radio, television, film, family magazines, music, and other culture industries flourished on an unprecedented scale. The message broadcast from these media beckoned new Christians and old to commit (or recommit) their lives to Christ and redeem themselves and the world.[25]

For Americans who were not evangelical Protestants or engaged with these subcultural networks, the publicity surrounding Colson's conversion was surprising and confounding. Chuck Colson became a famous convert of this evangelical age in part because the culture industries of American evangelicalism saw how much his story could do for their cause. His notoriety also grew because mainstream media outlets promoted the seeming incompatibility of an amoral political hatchet man finding Jesus.

Colson survived his *60 Minutes* interview, but to his dismay, he was sentenced to one to three years in prison. In July 1974 he began what became a seven-month stretch, with his time split between Fort Holabird in Maryland (chosen because its location near Washington enabled him to appear as a witness in ongoing criminal cases against other Nixon aides and cabinet members) and the prison camp at Maxwell Air Force Base in Alabama. While in prison, he took notes for a political memoir, but his editors encouraged him to set it aside and write about his new faith instead. The result was *Born Again*, first published in February 1976. Rejected by secular publishers, Colson and his manuscript had better luck with Chosen Books, which gave him a $25,000 advance. Colson's editor at

Chosen, Leonard LeSourd, was a respected figure among establishment evangelicals, having served as the editor at *Guideposts* magazine for Billy Graham. His wife, Catherine Marshall, was a successful author of popular evangelical books. With help from LeSourd, Colson's book sold half a million hardback copies by the fall of 1976. Evangelicals named it the "most significant" book of the year. Colson wrote several other books during his lifetime, but none made the impact of *Born Again*. A version of the book appeared as a major motion picture in 1978, starring Hollywood actor Dean Jones as Colson and produced by Frank Capra. Better known for roles in the Disney films *That Darn Cat!* and *The Love Bug*, Jones brought sincerity to his role as Colson; in the early 1970s, he, too, was born again. He self-described as a womanizing "predator" whose life transformed when he dedicated his life to Christ. Zondervan published Jones's memoir, *Under Running Laughter*, in 1982. The *Born Again* movie adaptation fared poorly at the box office, but Colson's Prison Fellowship Ministries promoted it widely to church groups.[26]

Born Again showcased the theme of the debased white man, spectacularly redeemed when he accepted Christ. Never more than mildly contrite, Colson confessed to sins of pride and blamed his reputation as an unrepentant jackass on false rumors and misunderstandings. He suffered from the sin of pride and because of the moral corruption surrounding him in Washington; he pleaded guilty to something he did not do in order to expiate his other sins. (Like a Christ figure, he went to prison for the sins of others.) Colson and his editors glossed over his graver misdeeds. Although the film version of *Born Again* flopped, no conversion elicited quite as much mail since Clare Boothe Luce's announcement nearly thirty years earlier.

Born Again tells the story of an ecstatic romance between white men beckoning one another into submission to Christ. Their conversions ultimately affirmed their heterosexual masculinity. All of the people who guided Colson to Christ were wealthy, powerful white men. He described his interactions with them in ways that emphasized their emotional and physical proximity. By the summer of 1973, he wrote, he was making good money as a lawyer in private practice but remained despondent about the escalating crises in the Nixon presidency. His description of a business meeting in Boston with Tom Phillips, the Raytheon CEO, invoked the allure of Phillips's tender masculinity. Colson went into their meeting looking sufficiently miserable that Phillips asked him if he was getting sleep and otherwise coping with "this Watergate business." Defensive, Colson insisted that he had "no direct or indirect involvement in the burglary." As they spoke, Colson wrote, he noticed something different about Phillips: "There was a new compassion in his eyes and a gentleness in his voice." Colson had heard that Phillips recently went through "some kind of a religious experience" and asked Phillips about the rumors of a new religious faith. The book and film recreate Phillips's response using the stock phrases of evangelical witness: "Yes, that's true, Chuck. I have accepted Jesus Christ. I have committed my life to Him and it has been the most marvelous experience of my whole life." In the book and film, this conversation serves as the initiating event that sparked Colson's eventual conversion.[27]

The manly allure of Christian vulnerability shaped the way Colson described the spiritual crisis that gripped him that summer, but Colson's fascination with Tom Phillips created challenges for the film adaptation of his book. Both the book and film versions of *Born Again* explain that in August 1973, Colson and his wife, Patty, embarked on a trip to Maine, a reprieve from weeks of congressional investigations and testimony. One night, while they were en route to their vacation spot, Colson left Patty at her parents' home outside of Boston and drove to Tom Phillips's home in the suburbs. The book described the meeting as taking place at night, Colson arriving as Phillips toweled the sweat off his body after playing tennis with his teenage children on a humid New England evening. Perhaps the screenwriters or director of the film version worried about the homoerotic possibilities of those visual cues. In the movie, the setting is afternoon, and the actor playing Phillips wears a suit.

In that pivotal scene, Phillips urged Colson to admit that the Nixon White House brought about its own downfall by dragging its enemies through the mud. Then Phillips loaned Colson a copy of C. S. Lewis's *Mere Christianity* and urged him to be born again. Colson was incredulous at the simplicity of this description of conversion: "That's what you mean by accepting Christ—you just ask?" That effortlessness, and the confidence that Phillips exuded, drew Colson in. He juxtaposed the contented Christian manhood that Phillips embodied with the overwhelming shame that he felt as he confronted the sin of his pride: "Suddenly I felt naked and unclean, my bravado and defenses gone. I was exposed, unprotected." Both in print and on film, Colson and Phillips moved closer to each other as they discussed Christ; Phillips leaned in toward Colson as he read aloud from a discussion of pride in *Mere Christianity*.[28]

Confessing the sin of pride—of masculinity gone wild—became the act of repentance that initiated Colson's conversion. Recalling the time that he "joked" with a reporter that the reporter might get in the good graces of the Nixon administration by "slashing his wrists," Colson judged himself arrogant—but not, say, cruel or vindictive—for having thought the comment funny. He felt no remorse for the harms he caused other people, only for the deficits of character they revealed: "My self-centered past was washing over me in waves. It was painful. Agony." He and Phillips prayed together, and then they said their good-nights. In a memorable scene from both the book and film versions of *Born Again*, Colson cried as he drove away, quickly pulling over to the side of the road: "With my face cupped in my hands, head leaning forward against the wheel, I forgot about machismo, about pretenses, about fears of being weak. And as I did, I began to experience a wonderful feeling of being released.... And then I said my first real prayer.... I didn't know how to say more, so I repeated over and over the words: *Take me.*" It was an ecstatic outpouring of emotions, an opening up of the vulnerable self to a dominating faith. For Colson, the manliness of mentors like Tom Phillips made his own submission to Christ a way to affirm rather than question his masculinity.[29]

The book *Born Again* jumped between scenes of emotional vulnerability with reminders to readers and viewers that Colson was a man of intellectual seriousness and great professional accomplishment. With help from his editor, LeSourd, Colson conveyed both the spiritual power of his conversion and the availability of Christ's love to all. His religious transformation continued with a lawyerly study of *Mere Christianity* during his week-long vacation in Maine. Reading and taking notes, Colson wrote "Is there a God?" at the top of a legal pad and proceeded to take notes in "pro" and "con" columns. At the end of the week, he wrote, "I sat alone staring at the sea I love, words I had not been certain I could understand or say fell naturally from my lips: 'Lord Jesus, I believe You. I accept You. Please come into my life. I commit it to You.'" Following the advice of Phillips, Colson adopted a simplistic, if heavily patriarchal, understanding of evangelical Protestantism, in which faith in Jesus and the truth of his teachings was the sum total of what made one a Christian.[30]

White evangelical power brokers enabled and supported Colson's conversion. Although Colson was accustomed to spending his days with formidable men, the people he met through the Fellowship presumed a spiritual intimacy that transcended the Republican-Democratic divide. In *Born Again*, he described the new friends he made in the Fellowship, including its leader Doug Coe, in the weeks leading up to his *60 Minutes* interview. Colson was unnerved when Coe showed up at his office within days of his return from Maine, acting like an old friend. He was especially annoyed when Coe described a Democratic senator, Harold Hughes, according to Colson's retelling, as "a tremendous Christian." The meeting with Coe was emotionally and physically proximate. "Doug ... gripped my hand, stared knowingly into my eyes for a long moment and then, as quickly as he had come, with a cheery 'Bye, brother,' was gone."[31]

Coe soon introduced Colson to the Fellowship Foundation. Colson began to meet with a small group of Christian men at a town house in Embassy Row for breakfast and prayer each Monday morning. At one memorable breakfast Colson walked in to discover that Arthur Burns (who was Jewish) was there. In the book, Colson lingered over the men's affection as they joined hands and prayed: "I felt Burns's grip tighten. As many of the men left, they either embraced the senator [Hughes] or gripped his hand warmly." Although Colson was reluctant to talk about Burns when Mike Wallace asked him about an apology in 1973, Colson called attention to it in *Born Again*, the squeeze of Burns's hand providing an invitation to brotherhood. Colson asserted that after the meeting ended, he approached Burns and apologized to him for planting the false story that Burns sought a pay raise for himself rather than for future Fed employees. The emotional and physical intensity between these men was significant enough that the writers and directors of the film version of *Born Again* intercut scenes of Colson with Phillips, Coe, and others in the Fellowship with scenes of Colson in bed with Patty, seemingly lest viewers misinterpret him as anything other than heterosexual.[32]

The publication of *Born Again* in 1976 inspired Colson to create Prison Fellowship Ministries (PFM), a national organization that sought to convert federal prison inmates to Christianity. PFM works from the premise that Jesus Christ provides the only path to redemption and thus the only hope for men and women who have sinned their way to imprisonment. Colson launched PFM with substantial funding from men he knew from the Fellowship and other evangelical organizations. PFM hosted Bible study for prisoners, brought in visitors who could testify to prisoners, and organized week-long seminars in which prisoners were granted a furlough, then returned to prison in order to serve as lay preachers to their fellow inmates. In a form of what religion scholar Tanya Erzen calls "testimonial politics," PFM and similar groups argue that only salvation through Christ, and not social programs that address economic issues, solved the prisoner's problems. Faith alone offered a complete transformation of the individual. As Erzen observers, these narratives of transformation "place the blame on a person's choices" and deflect attention from drug sentencing laws and racial bias in law enforcement, which contribute to many arrests and convictions.[33]

Essential to the written and visual narrative of Colson's Christian manhood was his assertion of his faith as a choice. He grounded both his religious transformation and his political philosophy, particularly his prison ministry, in neoliberal principles. Although neoliberalism takes many forms, at root it is the idea, as political scientist Lester Spence explains, "that society (and every institution within it) works best when it works according to the principles of the market." Neoliberalism elevates the importance of entrepreneurs and business owners; emphasizes the value of human capital; and, most especially, valorizes choice. Government spending, the neoliberal philosophers explained, begot deficits, which fed inflationary currencies. Uncertain of the future, people lived haphazardly and promiscuously. Dependence on welfare and premarital sex among the affluent represented two variations on the theme of social decay haunting neoliberals' hellish rendering of the welfare state's erosion of social responsibility. The 1970s inaugurated a neoliberal era in which "choice" and "freedom" meant the opportunity to engage in a marketplace in which labor, finance, and power bore no necessary relationship to justice. This emphasis on wage earning as a "choice" carried particular repercussions for women with dependent children. Even as married women's workforce participation became an economic necessity for a growing number of two-parent households in the 1970s and beyond, neoliberal thinkers framed women's decisions about childbearing and wage earning as autonomous "choices" for the "working family." Advocates of this emphasis on choice insisted that women's struggles with such issues as low-wage, low-benefit service jobs and inadequate childcare options were private concerns rather than matters of public policy.[34]

Evangelical defenders of neoliberalism like Colson insisted on the power of human capital (people's own agency and power) to be transformed through faith in God. According to this ideal, believers succeed in business, and they conform to a norm of family life in which men and women marry, become parents, and honor men's leadership. The efforts of neoliberal Christians suggest another element of what historian Daniel Rodgers terms the "age of fracture," his term for the last quarter of the

NOW A MOTION PICTURE

BORN AGAIN

While the White House was being torn apart, one broken man was being put back together.

...the true story of Charles Colson

A ROBERT L. MUNGER production "BORN AGAIN" starring DEAN JONES · ANNE FRANCIS
JAY ROBINSON · DANA ANDREWS · RAYMOND ST. JACQUES · Directed by IRVING RAPPER
Executive Producer ROBERT L. MUNGER · Produced by FRANK CAPRA, Jr.
Screenplay by WALTER BLOCH · Music by LES BAXTER Special screen appearance BILLY GRAHAM
Prints by CFI ◢▪▬ AVCO EMBASSY PICTURES Release
© 1978 BY AVCO EMBASSY PICTURES CORP.

Chuck Colson's best-selling book about his religious conversion inspired a 1978 film adaptation by a commercial production company, with actor Dean Jones starring as Colson. (Reproduction courtesy Wheaton College Billy Graham Center Archives, Wheaton, Illinois; no known license holder)

twentieth century. Market metaphors of choice, agency, and fluidity proliferated across American intellectual life and culture. These metaphors
permeated American religiosity, too.[35]

As a book, film, and even a comic book, *Born Again* made the case
that individual redemption was the key to national renewal. "While the
White House was being torn apart, one broken man was being put back
together," ran the movie's tag line. A poster for the film showed Colson
(as portrayed by the actor Dean Jones) smiling and embracing a female
figure, presumably his wife, whose face the viewer cannot see. One of Colson's hands holds a Bible. Behind him is a circle of images from his past—
protestors outside the Watergate hearings, his suit-and-tie-wearing figure
behind bars, a scene of him playing football with one of his sons, and the
faces of several key figures, including his wife Patty and his law partner
David Shapiro.

Spire Publishers published the comic-book version of *Born Again* in
1978 or 1979. It explained how Colson's experiences led him to create
PFM. In a scene just after Colson's release from prison, a block of narrative text announced, "And of all the men who need Christ—the men
in prison need him most of all!" In the next image Colson tells Patty,
"I believe God wants me in Prisons!" "What???" she responds. Two pages
later, a smiling African American prisoner, his hand on Colson's shoulder, says, "For the first time in a life of HATE—I discovered that someone CARES!" This image of the ecstatic Black prisoner, a man who is
portrayed as having ended up in prison because of his personal failings,
encapsulated the philosophy of criminal justice reform that Colson promoted. Since salvation came only through Christ, Colson wanted to bring
that joy to men behind bars, while doing nothing to change their prison
terms or diminish the effects of mass incarceration. Colson may have
hoped that *Born Again* would cross over to secular audiences as a film.
When that failed, he put most of his energies into building PFM and supporting other evangelical converts.[36]

Colson took a special interest in fellow ex-cons like Eldridge Cleaver,
a former leader of the Black Panther Party for Self-Defense and more recently a political exile. To a certain extent, the news media lumped the
two men together. When the *Los Angeles Times* broke the story in March
1976 that Eldridge Cleaver was born again, it printed his photo alongside
those of Colson and Susan Atkins. Colson and Cleaver shared little in
common personally or otherwise, but the idea of a brotherhood in Christ
convinced each of them that they should make common cause.[37]

Eldridge Cleaver's religious conversion in the mid-1970s accompanied a profound change in his politics. He spent much of his youth and young adulthood in prison for crimes ranging from drug possession to sexual assault. Prison radicalized him. Cleaver was an avid and curious reader, despite his interrupted education, and the California prison system provided him access to books about philosophy, political theory, and history. Inspired by the racial separatist ideals of Malcolm X, he converted to the Nation of Islam in the early 1960s. After Elijah Muhammad expelled Malcolm X, an outraged Cleaver abandoned the Nation. He wrote prolifically about his thoughts on politics, religion, and sex throughout the remainder of his time behind bars. Following his release from prison in late 1965, he compiled many of those essays in *Soul on Ice* (1966), his first book, which established his reputation as a radical thinker and writer. Presenting a Marxist interpretation of sexuality and racial inequality, Cleaver wrote about his former career as a burglar and rapist (for which he expressed regret), his disdain for writer James Baldwin's homosexuality, and his understanding of heterosexual desire—of Black men for white women and of white men for Black women—as an effect of the racial caste system that propped up capitalism.[38]

Cleaver's longing for an assertive Black political masculinity led him to the Oakland-based Black Panthers in the spring of 1967. The Panthers' armed defiance of racist policing practices inspired Cleaver to become their minister of information. The arrests that year of the group's founders, Bobby Seale and Huey Newton, left a leadership gap that Cleaver and his new wife, Kathleen Neal Cleaver, filled. As tensions between the Panthers and the Oakland Police Department intensified in the wake of the assassination of Martin Luther King Jr. in April 1968, Cleaver and a seventeen-year-old Panther named Bobby Hutton found themselves in a residential basement, choking on tear gas and facing a barrage of police bullets. Cleaver survived, but the police officers killed Hutton. The police arrested Cleaver for violating his parole. He managed to get released from jail in June, but when his trial approached that fall, he fled the country.[39]

During seven years of exile, Cleaver lived in Cuba, Algeria, and France, searching socialist and communist nations in vain for the radical racial and economic equality described in books he read. Disillusioned and isolated, he started to plan his return to the United States. He also began to defend American institutions and even the U.S. military. Cleaver flew from Paris to New York City in November 1975, accompanied by two FBI agents. In an opinion piece for the *New York Times*, the man whom younger radicals affectionately nicknamed "Papa Rage"—who once shocked and delighted students at Stanford University by shouting "Fuck Reagan!"—now labeled the American political system as "the freest and most democratic in the world." Perhaps even more startling, by January 1976, Cleaver defined himself as born again.[40]

Cleaver felt that his life affirmed the truth of God's power when he was suddenly released from prison in August 1976. A born-again, white life insurance executive named Art DeMoss paid Cleaver's $100,000 bail in August 1976 after reading about the former Panther's conversion in the newspaper. Wealthy but unpretentious, DeMoss supported Colson's PFM and saw in Eldridge Cleaver another incarcerated cause he could champion. DeMoss was a major financial backer of evangelicalism's recruitment and political engagement efforts; he sat on the boards of Campus Crusade for Christ and the Christian Freedom Foundation. (After De-Moss's death in 1979, his family created the Arthur S. DeMoss Foundation. The publicity-shunning foundation contributed millions of dollars to groups such as Campus Crusade for Christ and Walk Thru the Bible Ministries. Most controversially, the foundation paid for television ads in the early 1990s with the tag line "Life. What a Choice," which purported to feature children whose mothers placed their newborns up for adoption rather than have abortions.)[41]

Cleaver's Blackness and past radicalism made him a curiosity on the evangelical culture circuit and in mainstream media. He was interviewed on *Meet the Press* and profiled in *Reader's Digest*. His antipolice, anti-authoritarian days as a Panther were behind him, he told the *Reader's Digest* reporter: "I'd rather be in jail in America than free anywhere else." On a 1976 episode of *The 700 Club*, the former Black radical told host Pat Robertson that he no longer wanted to talk about race; Jesus Christ did not worry about skin color, and neither did he. Such comments did not deter Black evangelicals from reaching out to Cleaver for help with such groups as the Voice of Calvary Ministries, "a black Christian missionary organization," and the National Black Evangelical Association.[42]

A bevy of wealthy white evangelicals promoted the sincerity of Cleaver's conversion. Pat Matrisciana and Pat Boone (the born-again country singer) chaired Cleaver's West Coast legal defense fund. (Bayard Rustin, that stalwart of the mainstream civil rights movement, coordinated an East Coast defense committee.) The fact that Cleaver's former colleagues in the Black Panther Party now rejected him may have made him even more appealing to these right-leaning evangelicals. "Many of Mr. Cleaver's former associates have turned against him, blasting him with their hate," Boone and Matrisciana wrote in their appeal letter. Anticipating legal costs of $250,000, they aggressively solicited donations.[43]

Colson in particular became a mentor to Cleaver. Colson's *Born Again* was published while Cleaver was still in prison; perhaps one of the Christians who visited Cleaver brought him a copy. Cleaver and Colson appeared together often in print, on television, and in person. The universality of Christ's redeeming love was a point they could convey simply by sharing the same stage. On an episode of *The 700 Club* in 1977, Colson told host Pat Robertson that Eldridge Cleaver now prayed with him and former senator Harold Hughes. Colson and Cleaver hit the evangelical lecture circuit in 1977 as notorious ex-con evangelical converts whose redemption in Christ seemed to justify the politics of economic "choice" over social justice demands for government intervention.[44]

Cleaver toured the centers of white evangelical power describing his thefts and rapes, prison terms, sojourn with the Black Panthers, and redemption through Christ during his exile and return to the United States. He dined at the home of Pat Boone in Beverly Hills, praying together with Boone's four daughters. He went to Lynchburg, Virginia, where the Reverend Jerry Falwell invited him to the pulpit of his Thomas Road Baptist Church in a nationally televised service. Before the month was out, he was a guest at the televised services at Robert Schuller's megachurch, Garden Grove Community Church, in Orange County. Cleaver told the Christians gathered before him, "Since that time [of conversion] I haven't met anyone that I don't love." Schuller's *Hour of Power* television program attracted a weekly audience estimated at 1.2 million viewers, and Cleaver was on the show at least twice. Cleaver made appearances on *The PTL Club* with Jim and Tammy Faye Bakker and delivered his testimony on *High Adventure Ministries*, hosted by George Otis. These appearances inspired some viewers to mail Eldridge donations of anywhere from $50 to $500 for his defense fund, while others offered him advice about Bible reading, faith, and the blessings of the Holy Spirit.[45]

Susan Atkins's *Child of Satan, Child of God* went on sale amid this swirl of media attention to born-again conversions by people who lived on the edges of social or political respectability. Editors at Logos International, an evangelical Protestant publishing house, hired journalist Bob Slosser to ghostwrite the book. Slosser built a career at the *New York Times* and other papers before he shifted to writing full-time for Christian audiences. In 1977, he wrangled the abject and objectionable life story of Susan Atkins into a narrative of redemption. The book featured semipornographic details of her sexual exploits and her immersion into the disreputable gang that surrounding Manson, including the murders the group undertook at Manson's direction. Atkins and Slosser concluded her book with her dramatic story of religious conversion and new commitment to Christ. Soon after her conversion, Atkins began a prison ministry to save the souls of her fellow inmates, of whom, she/Slosser wrote, "fifteen prayed the sinner's prayer, accepting Jesus as the Lord of their lives." Among the miracles of healing that she performed, she was especially proud that a lesbian turned straight thanks to her interventions.[46]

The intimacies of Atkins's ministry required careful management of the erotic possibilities among imprisoned women. Writing in Atkins's voice, Slosser presented Atkins as vigilantly heterosexual as she counseled a lesbian prisoner: "She wept softly and put her arm around me. But I didn't feel threatened. It was not a lesbian advance, I was sure." Slosser/Atkins likewise described her sexual relationship with a prison guard as a temporary relapse from her newfound Christian morality. Jack Adams was married when he came on to Atkins repeatedly, and "the old Susan" wanted to give in to his advances. The inclusion of the story seems intended to dispel rumors of her sexual involvement with men who worked at the prison. *Child of Satan, Child of God* portrayed Atkins's life as a story of Christian rescue from the sexual sins of the counterculture. She left behind the depravity of an amoral cult and embraced the heterosexual values of her new faith.[47]

Child of Satan, Child of God was not the only story of a Satanist turned Christian either. Comedian Mike Warnke's *The Satan-Seller* (1972) detailed his involvement with illegal drugs, free love, and "Satan worship" in California, followed by a dramatic experience of being saved by love for Jesus Christ. Like Atkins's book, *The Satan-Seller* teased the reader with soft-core sex scenes, including descriptions of how female Satanists, like women in the Children of God, seduced young men as part of the recruitment process. Warnke's description of his own recruitment into evangelicalism featured similarly exploitative erotic dynamics. He kidnapped off the streets a young woman named Mary and orchestrated her beating and gang rape as part of a "fertility ritual." In the weeks that followed, Warnke overdosed on heroin and went through withdrawal. He saw Mary again when she approached him on a college campus and told him that she loved him: "I've accepted Jesus as my Savior. And I love you." Overcome with awareness of his sin and a desire for redemption, he, too, was born again.[48]

Warnke turned out to be a profoundly unreliable narrator. He achieved some fame as a comedian among evangelicals, but journalists who looked into his background in the early 1990s discovered that his tale of Satanic association was fraudulent. Warnke initially called his critics Satanists, but he later confessed that he "overstated" his preconversion involvement with occult groups and practices. Here was another kind of false witness, a chronicle of a life's religious transformation premised on exaggerated or wholly invented facts.[49]

Explicit sexual violence against women filled Warnke's published conversion narrative. These descriptions of assault echoed Cleaver's references to raping women in his preconversion past. Along with the murder of Sharon Tate and scenes of sexual predation in Susan Atkins's book, Warnke's story narrated a Christian redemption that emerged through literal violations of women's bodies. Warnke and the other men who raped "Mary" faced no criminal penalties. As an author, Warnke did not dwell on the woman's experience of assault; the reader learned nothing of the physical (not to mention psychological) harm done to her aside from the fact that the men deposited her at a hospital after the attack. Women like Mary did not need to tell their stories because they served as plot devices, not subjects. The significance of Mary's story lies not in the experience of a woman subjected to such abuse but in the way that evangelical writers and editors transformed the figure of the violated woman into an instrument of salvation. Violence against women, and crimes against the state, served as catalysts for the protagonist's conversion. To be born again was to find not only eternal love but the protective reassurance that virile men could channel their violent impulses toward an intense passion for Christ.

The born-again stories that Colson, Cleaver, and Atkins told additionally emphasized that prison ministries could convert even the most miserable or objectionable person into a spirit-filled evangelist. It was an argument that targeted radical politics and the counterculture for mistakenly seeking to overthrow "the system." Evangelicals instead stressed that only individual conversions could bring about true social transformation. When Cleaver launched the Eldridge Cleaver Crusades in the summer of 1977, telling Colson that he hoped to start a prison ministry as well, he used the story of his born-again conversion as an argument for his legal innocence. Colson, Pat Matrisciana, Bob Schuller, and other white evangelical leaders organized a letter-writing campaign to Governor Jerry

Brown to grant Cleaver a pardon so that he could focus on his ministry. Many of the letters to Brown mentioned Colson as well. One man wrote, "I think [Cleaver] and Colson are doing more for old-fashioned Americanism than anybody I know of in America today." That so many of these evangelical converts spent time in prison accentuated the dramatic tension of their story arcs. Advocates for prison ministries promised spiritual liberation from the captivity of brainwashing.[50]

The more improbable or outrageous the born-again conversion, the bigger the headlines in the secular press and the more valuable the story for evangelical Christians. The conversion of pornographer Larry Flynt during a cross-country flight on his pink private jet, seated beside Ruth Carter Stapleton (Jimmy Carter's sister), made national news in November 1977. Flynt was best known for his magazine *Hustler*, the third-most-popular skin magazine of the era (behind *Playboy* and *Penthouse*), and for his insistence on his free speech rights to publish sexually explicit images and text. Flynt gave conflicting answers about the status of his faith. He told a reporter for the *Los Angeles Times*, "I just think this whole trip of being born again has been misinterpreted. I believe in God, Buddha, Muhammad. Man has created God in his image and everything else has gone to hell. That's why I'm opposed to organized religion." A week later he told George Vecsey of the *New York Times* that he was "a born-again Christian" and that he intended to "continue publishing pornography," adding, "And anybody who doesn't like it can go kiss a rope." Not everyone was convinced: "Cynics are saying that Mr. Flynt's 'conversion' … is a ploy to avoid jail on his pornography conviction." Using language similar to what Senator Hughes used to defend Colson, Ruth Stapleton urged critics to give Flynt time to transform into his Christian form: "Mrs. Stapleton told one audience not to expect Mr. Flynt to be a different person because, she said, 'he's a baby Christian.'" When a man shot Flynt in March 1978 outside the Georgia courthouse where Flynt stood trial on obscenity and pornography charges, Stapleton took the first available flight from her home in North Carolina to be at his bedside. Flynt was not the only pornographer to discover Jesus Christ. The *Los Angeles Times* reported, "Alleged Smut Dealer Turns Over New Leaf" when Tim Connor, the proprietor of an "adults-only" bookstore in southern California that recently closed, took a job running the bookstore for Trinity Christian Fellowship. "Connor told a reporter he has become a 'born-again Christian' although, he added, he does not compare himself to Larry Flynt."[51]

The "evangelical turn" of the musician Bob Dylan shocked many of his fans at the time and has continued to fascinate his critics and admirers. In the late 1970s, Dylan began to study evangelical ideas about the end times—eschatology—as taught by Hal Lindsey, the influential author of the book and film of premillennial apocalyptic prophesy, *The Late Great Planet Earth*. Between 1979 and 1981 Dylan released three Christian rock albums, only one of which approached the commercial success of his secular records. As religion scholar Kathryn Lofton notes, Dylan "was supposedly born-again." A minister at the Vineyard Fellowship in Southern California told reporters that Dylan, who was born to Jewish parents, now accepted Christ. Dylan's public relations team denied the pastor's claims. In a November 1980 interview in the *Los Angeles Times*, Dylan told a reporter that he "truly had a born-again experience, if you want to call it that." By 1984 he appeared to reverse course, saying, "I've never said I'm born again. That's just a media term." Perhaps Dylan was a sincere convert, or perhaps, instead, he remained a charlatan or seeker/artist without any firm religious identification. Like Sammy Davis Jr., Dylan posed for a photograph at the Western Wall in Jerusalem in the early 1970s, but unlike Davis, Dylan later said it was a publicity stunt. Dylan toyed with public expectations about revelations of the "real" person behind the celebrity image, only to undermine any certainty about his beliefs.[52]

Evangelicals' portrayals of spiritual self-transformation dominated how Americans spoke about religious authenticity in the 1970s. In books, magazines, television ministries, films, and media of all kinds, evangelicals linked conversion to several political projects, including prison ministries and ex-gay "conversion" or "reparative" therapy." From their beginnings in the early 1970s, the leaders of so-called ex-gay programs promised gay men, bisexuals, and lesbians a simultaneous conversion to heterosexuality and to Christianity. Anyone who disputed their arguments about Christian truth or claimed self-knowledge at odds with their biblical interpretations related to sexuality must have been brainwashed. Cults provided an apt metaphor for sexual captivity. Children and young people might be "recruited" (by a cult leader or by a gay teacher) into a corrupt spiritual or sexual lifestyle. In both scenarios, many parents forced their children to be "deprogrammed" and returned to Christianity. This worldview compared being gay to being in a cult: the result of hanging out with the wrong crowd, it required that your Christian elders rescue you and return you to an authentic Christian lifestyle.[53]

Atkins's fame among evangelicals was short-lived, perhaps because her conduct in prison fell short of any ideal of evangelical moral purity. She married twice during her decades of incarceration, first to Donald Lee Lai$ure, a Texan who used a dollar sign in place of the *s* in his last name. By the time Lai$ure married Atkins in 1981, he had been married thirty-five times already; his thirty-sixth marriage lasted a few months. She remarried in 1987, after forming a relationship with James W. Whitehouse, an attorney seeking her release. *Child of Satan, Child of God* asserted that Susan Atkins was born anew when she committed her life to Jesus Christ. The parole board apparently witnessed no such transformation and denied her petitions for release on seventeen occasions. She was sixty-one years old when she died in prison in 2009.[54]

Cleaver's ongoing religious quest took him out of evangelical Protestantism by the late 1970s, even as his ties to conservative American politics deepened. The Church of Jesus Christ of Latter-day Saints and the Unification Church of Rev. Sun Myung Moon were two of the groups that evangelical Protestants described as "cults" in the late 1970s and 1980s, not least because of their effective, aggressive proselytizing. Cleaver affiliated with both of them. In late 1980 or early 1981, Cleaver enrolled in a course—a "constitutional seminar"—hosted by a far-right organization called the Freemen Institute (some news outlets located those courses in Salt Lake City and others in San Jose). There he imbibed political lessons of the Freemen Institute's founder, Dr. Cleon Skousen, a political scientist on the faculty at Brigham Young University and a former member of the radically anti-Communist John Birch Society. Skousen promulgated right-wing conspiracy theories and free-market absolutism. He inspired far-right radio and television show host Glenn Beck, who hawked Skousen's books on his programs. Eldridge Cleaver was also impressed. In April 1981 Cleaver announced that he and his family were joining the Church of Jesus Christ of Latter-day Saints because it provided the spiritual home he sought. He was baptized into the faith in December 1983 at the Oakland Temple. From 1981 to 1984 he also toured extensively as a paid lecturer for the Collegiate Association for the Research of Principles, the Unification Church's missionary arm on college campuses. Aligned with Reverend Moon's staunch anti-Communism, globalism, and gender traditionalism, Cleaver lectured against socialism and in favor of American military interventions to oust democratically elected leftists in Central America.[55]

Like so many of the ex-Communists of the 1940s and 1950s, Cleaver converted both to Christianity and to conservatism. As the religious Right grew more capacious in the 1980s, Cleaver likely found a degree of political consistency among his different faiths. Leaders of the religious Right, including Jerry Falwell, rallied in defense of the Unification Church in 1982 when Reverend Moon was convicted of tax fraud. Moon claimed nonprofit status for his church as a religious institution, a request the federal government denied. Despite their considerable theological differences, evangelicals, Latter-day Saints members, and Moon's followers united in their defense of religious freedom, a principle they attached to freedom from government regulation.[56]

The language of choice provided ideological common ground for the emerging political alliance between evangelicals and free-market Republicans. For evangelical Protestants, and for the Roman Catholics with whom they increasingly made common cause, the choice of a faith was meant to be a choice that determined all aspects of an individual's identity. A man could make a decision for Christ, and it would lead him to embrace neoliberal economics, heterosexuality, and the GOP's promilitary funding priorities. Aspects of identity that did not conform to those values, such as a gay, lesbian, or transgender identity or a civil rights agenda that demanded an expansive welfare state, were corrupt "choices" and therefore illegitimate. As Republicans embraced free markets and born-again religion, among other priorities, they commended the choices of individual economic actors and the decisions of freely believing spiritual agents. They denigrated collectivist arguments for rights and disparaged expressions of personal identity that defied evangelical Christian interpretations of the Bible. Aided by dramatic stories of religious conversion in the 1970s, leaders of the emerging religious Right made the case for Christianity as a freedom-loving faith necessary for American democracy's survival.

Epilogue Authentic Politics, Passing Faiths

Clare Boothe Luce wanted to be remembered. During the final six years of her life, she shared her personal recollections and private papers with the writer Sylvia Jukes Morris. It took Morris another twenty-five years to complete a monumental, two-volume biography of Luce. The Library of Congress now holds the entirety of Luce's paper trail—diaries, congressional correspondence, speeches, drafts of plays, family letters, and more. Nearly 800 boxes document her remarkable life, one she considered, as her memories and records shared with Morris reveal, marked more by loss than accomplishment. In October 1987 her body ascended the steps of St. Patrick's Cathedral for a final time, carried in a pine coffin to one of two funeral masses. The mourners at St. Patrick's and at a second mass at the Church of St. Stephen Martyr in Washington attested to her long career of political importance. The attendees included former president Richard Nixon, CIA director William Webster, Senator Strom Thurmond, and the paleoconservative commentator Patrick Buchanan, some of the most hardline conservatives in American politics. In New York, Cardinal John O'Connor and William F. Buckley delivered eulogies. Luce had once belonged to a moderate, pro–civil rights faction of the Republican Party, but in her later years she aligned with Buckley's far-right (and white supremacist) conservatism.[1]

The relationship between religion and political authenticity had changed in the course of Luce's lifetime to a degree that would have been unimaginable when hate mail poured into her congressional office in 1946. Sectarian divisions that once made religious conversions controversial were subsumed into a bifurcated political landscape that sorted beliefs according to "liberal" and "conservative" above all other distinctions. Had Luce risen to political prominence in 1988 or 2012 she might have found herself warmly embraced by the descendants of the same evangelical Protestants who maligned her for "papism" when she converted. A conservative Christian ecumenism within the Republican Party embraced not only Roman Catholics and evangelicals, a realignment that began with men such as Chuck Colson in the 1970s, but also members of the Church of Jesus Christ of Latter-day Saints, such as presidential candidate and senator Mitt Romney, and Eastern Orthodox Christians, united under the combined banners of "family values" and fiscal conservatism.[2]

Chuck Colson was at the center of these political shifts within the Republican Party and the broader Christian conservative movement. In the 1980s and 1990s, he worked with Protestant and Catholic activists eager to resurrect the contrast between Christian democratic freedom and the totalitarian terrors of "Marxist-Leninism" that Luce, Whittaker Chambers, and others had highlighted in the early years of the Cold War. Foremost among those allies was Richard John Neuhaus. Since the early 1980s, Neuhaus had been writing and speaking in defense of "Christianity and Democracy." Fearful of Soviet domination and nuclear war, Neuhaus, who was a Lutheran minister, called on American churches to organize in defense of free markets, civil liberties, and free elections. He founded the journal *First Things* to give voice to political and religious conservatism. In 1990 he converted to Roman Catholicism, and he became a priest a year later. Neuhaus and Colson found common cause as two converts committed to conservative politics. Together they envisioned a broader Christian coalition, one that would unite Protestants and Catholics around shared political aims. They coedited *Evangelicals and Catholics Together: Toward a Common Mission* (1995), in which they made the case for a conservative movement that elevated a capacious Christian mission to promote "religious freedom." Colson and Neuhaus decried "abortion on demand," the exclusion of "our cultural heritage" from public school curricula, and tolerance for "sexual depravity." They defended free markets and an interventionist U.S. foreign policy. Their ecumenical vision represented one piece of a dramatic transformation of American religious conservatism.[3]

Time dulled the edges of midcentury accusations of religious imposture and racial threat. Muhammad Ali, who was vilified by mainstream Americans in the 1960s and 1970s for being unpatriotic, became a symbol of interfaith peace. Slowed by debilitating Parkinson's disease, Ali represented the greatness of American athleticism and the strength of American religious freedom when he lit the Olympic torch in 1996 in Atlanta.

In the fall of 2001 he appeared in *America: A Tribute to Heroes*, a star-studded televised fundraiser for the victims of the September 11 attacks on the World Trade Center and the Pentagon. Once derided for insisting that his name be announced as Muhammad Ali rather than Cassius Clay, Ali was introduced by the actor Will Smith (who had recently portrayed Ali in a biopic) as "one of the greatest heroes of our time, and he is a Muslim." No longer a threat or a joke because of his chosen Muslim faith, Ali now epitomized the endurance of American democracy and its ethos of religious toleration. In 2005, President George W. Bush, a Republican and an evangelical Protestant, presented Ali with the Medal of Freedom. These honors recognized Ali, once castigated for refusing the military draft, for his humanitarian work and his persistent pacifism.[4]

Sammy Davis Jr. even became symbol of religious authenticity because of his Blackness, not in spite of it. A 1991 episode of *The Simpsons*, "Like Father, Like Clown," invoked Davis to explain Jewishness. The episode spoofed *The Jazz Singer*, the first "talking" film, which starred the famed Jewish entertainer Al Jolson. In the most famous scene in *The Jazz Singer*, Jolson's character applies blackface as he bemoans the ways he has disappointed his Jewish mother by refusing to become a cantor, preferring the lights of the theater instead. He then sings "My Mammy," a minstrel song, as his Jewish mother kvells from the audience. *The Simpsons* parodied that plotline. On this episode, the main character, Bart, an ill-behaved ten-year-old, tries to mend fences between his TV hero Krusty the Clown and Krusty's father, who is an Orthodox rabbi. Like the Al Jolson character who ran from a life as a cantor, Krusty regrets that he abandoned his heritage in exchange for a career as a sadistic TV host. Krusty applies clown paint in a sequence that corresponds to Jolson's dramatic application of blackface in *The Jazz Singer*. *The Simpsons* episode concludes on a different note, resolving the tension between a Black face and a Jewish soul that Jolson's character embodied. Bart convinces Krusty's estranged father to give his son a second chance. "The Jews are a swinging bunch of people," Bart tells the father over a game of chess. Awestruck, the rabbi asks, "Who said that? Rabbi Hillel?" No, Bart, explains, it was the great entertainer Sammy Davis Jr. himself. Aired slightly more than a year after Davis's death, the episode honored Davis as an authority on Jewish pride and identity.[5]

The politics of authenticity lived on. Mass movements at the end of the twentieth century captured the persistent drive for authentic self-discovery and of belonging within a community of believers. As historian Deborah Gray White explains, many Americans were "searching for identity," confronting the age's uncertainties by trying and often failing to find common ground. Black men gathered for the Million Man March in 1997, and Promise Keepers marched by the hundreds of thousands in celebration of "men's rights." White Christian nationalism promised another kind of politics grounded in claims of religious authenticity, one in which race is real, gender is fixed, and the nation's Christian origins are assured. These and other movements coalesced around race, gender, and sexuality as sources of authentic identity, even as the nation—and identity itself—appeared more fractured and fragmented than ever.[6]

The possibility of discovering the elusive essence of the authentic person, meanwhile, drove entire industries of self-help guides, healers, fitness regimens, TED talks, life coaches, talk shows, reality television makeovers, and cosmetics brands. Therapeutic language infused a cultural fascination with introspection and the pursuit of authentic self-understanding in the early twenty-first century. This "therapeutic ethos" did not displace religious confessions so much as merge with them, making the one increasingly indistinguishable from the other. Conversion, like the self-help ethos, suggested the possibility of choosing to live according to a better and more sincere inner compass. Ostensibly secular media such as television and magazines translated religious language about contrition, self-examination, and self-transformation—the elements of a Protestant conversion narrative—into the consumerist idioms of the "total makeover." In the 2010s, the business of self-help—renamed the "personal development industry"—generated about $10 billion in annual revenue from books, workshops, websites, motivational speakers, coaching, retreats, apps, gizmos, meal plans, facials, and more. Perhaps no American mastered this language of public confession in the service of self-transformation so adroitly as Oprah Winfrey. As religion scholar Kathryn Lofton shows, when the television talk shows of the 1980s made room for reality television programs in the 1990s, The Oprah Winfrey Show (1986–2011) increasingly featured a "public ritual" of confession that allowed both guests and viewers to "be made whole again." The overworked nanny gets a minivan; the exhausted middle-aged homemaker finds the perfect hairstyle and acquires a closet of designer clothes. American consumerism and American religion celebrated the freedom to choose an authentic self. Practices outside the bounds of organized religion offered seekers resources for spiritual connection. Pathways to self-discovery that once motivated public confessions of religious conversion no longer required either religion or a public.[7]

If one person's spiritual truth is another person's brainwashing, a politics invested in authentic faith must find ways to distinguish artifice from reality. For forty years after the end of World War II, religious conversions played out on the national stage as contests over revealed truth, personal sincerity, and American freedoms. The opposite of freedom was enslavement and captivity, of a life enchained to false dogmas within the prison of totalitarian mind control. With so much at stake, notable religious conversions sparked national conversations about which aspects of identity a person might choose, and which they could not choose, or could not choose credibly. Debates about religious authenticity raised questions about the fitness of certain faiths for democracy, the security of the nation's government, and the role of religion in shaping public life. This history highlights the struggle at the heart of the American experiment not only over religion's role in public life but also over the ways in which race, gender, and sexuality shape lived experiences of democracy and freedom.

Acknowledgments

I am the daughter of a religious convert, with clear memories of well-meaning childhood friends asking me, "Well, what *are* you?" and of classmates at religious school observing, "But you don't *look* Jewish!" If those formative experiences piqued my curiosity about the subject of conversion, this project swept those interests in wholly unanticipated directions. During the years that I spent investigating conversion's history, many friends and colleagues told me stories about the religious conversions that animated their own family histories. Some wondered why I did not include the histories of other prominent converts. The fact that this topic calls to mind so many potential research subjects reinforces my conclusion that conversion is one of the most central, if underexamined, aspects of American religious life.

Researching and writing this book brought me into a network of extraordinary scholars and reminded me of the indispensability of kindhearted friends. Darren Dochuk, Alison Greene, Christine Heyrman, Randall Stephens, Matthew Avery Sutton, and anonymous readers for the press read and critiqued the complete manuscript, some of them more than once. I am at a loss for how to acknowledge my debts to Serena Mayeri, Bethany Moreton, and Julia Ott, brilliant scholars and dear friends. Thank you all for your encouragement at times when I lost the thread of hope that binds an author to her book and for friendship that sweetens the deal. For reading chapters and offering advice, I am additionally indebted to Anne Boylan, Gillian Frank, Jim McCartin, Samira Mehta, Brendan Pietsch, and Daniel Rodgers. Jim also took me on a tour of St. Patrick's Cathedral and opened my eyes to the rituals of Catholic conversion. Judith Weisenfeld is the most generous scholar I have ever met; she turned me on to Mary Lou Williams and the connections between religious and racial identities. Jon Butler and Joanne Meyerowitz continue to counsel and encourage me; I will always think of myself as their student. Conversations with Susan Strasser inspired broader reading and deeper thinking when this project was in its earliest stages. Hours spent writing in the company of friends Lila Corwin Berman, Kimberly Blockett, Eve Buckley, Gillian Frank, Alison Greene, Samira Mehta, and Dael Norwood eased the loneliness of an often solitary pursuit. Kim cheered this book's progress during weekly phone calls from the summer of 2012 until its completion, providing not only support and accountability but unfaltering friendship. I am grateful for the additional suggestions and support I received from Michael Scott Alexander, Adam Arenson, James Brophy, Matthew Cressler, Cornelia Dayton, K. Healan Gaston, Sarah Barringer Gordon, Bruce Haynes, Matthew Hedstrom, Randal Maurice Jelks, Stephanie Kerschbaum, Rachel Kranson, Kevin Kruse, Jenny Wiley Legath, Amanda Littauer, Kathryn Lofton, Elaine Tyler May, Linda McClain, Debra Hess Norris, Catherine Osborne, Rebecca Ann Rix, Leigh Eric Schmidt, Will Schultz, David Shearer, Josef Sorett, Sharon Ullman, and an anonymous reviewer for *American Jewish History*. My intellectual debt to all of these scholars is boundless, and my gratitude for their kindness is equally so. Any remaining errors or shortcomings in this book are my own.

Lectures and conference presentations encouraged me to refine my argument and press on with the research. I especially thank Philip Nord and the faculty and students who provided feedback during my presentation to the Shelby Cullom Davis Center at Princeton University in 2012. For other conference and lecture opportunities, I thank Bethany Moreton, Axel Schäfer, Heather White, and audience members at the 2013 annual meeting of the American Historical Association; the attendees of a 2013 talk for the University of Delaware's Program in Jewish Studies; Michael Scott Alexander, fellow panelists, and audience members at a panel about "The Color Issue" at the 2016 meeting of the American Jewish Historical Society's biennial conference; Owen Williams and audience members at Transylvania University; the participants in the 2016–17 Religion and Public Life seminar at Princeton's Center for the Study of Religion; Stephen Wittek, Paul Yachnin, and Lia Markey for the Politics of Conversion conference hosted by the Newberry Library in the fall of 2017; organizers of and audience members at the Swarthmore Discussion Group; and the Center for the Study of Religion, the Program in Gender and Sexuality Studies, Jenny Wiley Legath, Regina Kunzel, and audience members at a presentation about Muhammad Ali at Princeton University in the spring of 2019.

Librarians and archivists made this book possible. At the University of Delaware Library and Special Collections, I thank Megan Gaffney and the magnificent Interlibrary Loan department, Meghann Matwichuk,

Rebecca Johnson Melvin, Carol Rudisell, and Kaitlyn Tanis. I additionally thank Bruce Kirby, Elizabeth A. Novara, and many other archivists at the Library of Congress Manuscripts and Archives Division; David Sager at the Recorded Sound Research Center at the Library of Congress; Katherine Graber and Bob Shuster at the Billy Graham Center Archives and Keith Call in Special Collections at Wheaton College; David J. Stiver in Special Collections at the Graduate Theological Union; Shane T. MacDonald, Dustin Booher, and others at the American Catholic History Research Center at the Catholic University of America; staff at the Harvard Law School Library; Tal Nadan at the New York Public Library Manuscripts and Archives (Schwarzman Building); Iris Donvan at the Bancroft Library at the University of California, Berkeley; staff at the Columbia University Rare Book and Manuscript Library and David A. Olson at the Columbia University Center for Oral History; Phillip Runkel in the Department of Special Collections and University Archives at Marquette University; at the University of Notre Dame, Debra Dochuk in Special Collections and William Kevin Cawley, Joe Smith, and Elizabeth Hogan at the Archives; Dr. Paul Pearson at the Thomas Merton Center at Bellarmine University; Joe Peterson at the Institute of Jazz Studies at Rutgers University–Newark; Alexsandra M. Mitchell at the Schomburg Center for Research in Black Culture; Jerry Schwarzbard and Holly Farrar at the Jewish Theological Seminary library; Gary Zola, Dana Herman, Elisa Ho, Julianna Witt, and Joe Weber at the Jacob Rader Marcus Center of the American Jewish Archives in Cincinnati; Sister Connie Derby at the Department Archive for the Diocese of Rochester; Nancy Freeman at the Women and Leadership Archives of Loyola University Chicago; Jennifer M. Reibenspies and Leslie J. Winter at the Cushing Memorial Library and Archives at Texas A&M University; Kimberly Johnson and Megan Haase at Texas Women's University; Iris Afantchao in the Special Collections Department at Smith College; Doug Remley at the National Museum of African American History and Culture; Matthew Lutts at AP Images; and Holly Reed at the National Archives and Records Administration. Special thanks to Jeff Thompson at the Church History Library for the Church of Jesus Christ of Latter-day Saints, who tracked down Harvey Matusow's baptismal records.

Research and travel grants provided crucial support. My thanks to the University of Delaware for a General University Research Fellowship, summer research support from the Department of History, research funds from the College of Arts and Sciences, and a research grant from the Yetta and Frank Chaiken Center for Jewish Studies. For external research travel grants, my thanks to Gary Zola for a Director's Fellowship from the Jacob Rader Marcus Center at the American Jewish Archives; Kathleen Sprows Cummings and Pete Hlabse at the Cushwa Center for the Study of American Catholicism; and an Evangelism Research Grant from the Torrey M. Johnson Sr. Scholarship Fund at the Billy Graham Center Archives. A visiting affiliation with the Center for the Study of Religion at Princeton University during a 2016–17 sabbatical leave provided a lively community of scholars and access to crucial library resources; my thanks to Bob Wuthnow, Jennifer Wiley Legath, and Anita Kline for facilitating it.

My colleagues at the University of Delaware in the Department of History, the Program in Jewish Studies, and the Department of Women and Gender Studies supply friendship and a supportive community of scholars. In addition to those already mentioned, I thank especially Zara Anishanslin, Cheryl Hicks, Peter Kolchin, Patricia Sloane-White, David Suisman, and Owen White. Cathy Allison, Deborah Hartnett, Doug Tobias, and Katie Whitlock assisted me with expense reports and much else. For approving sabbatical leaves and providing other intangible forms of support, I thank department chairs Arwen Mohun, James Brophy, and Alison Parker; Polly Zavadivker, director of the Program in Jewish Studies; associate deans Debra Hess Norris and Lauren Petersen; and deans George Watson and John A. Pelesko.

Several research assistants further aided this project. My thanks to Maria Brandt, Alexander Callaway, Julia Click, Alison Kreitzer, Satomi Minowa, Will Schultz, Hillary Neben Trout, Natalie Walton, and Erika Weidemann.

Joyce Seltzer intervened at a crucial point in the writing process, helping me take apart and reassemble this book until it cohered. Roxanne Donovan showed me how to keep hold of myself in the midst of my work. Geri Thoma made the magic happen to bring this book to the University of North Carolina Press. I am grateful as well to Daniel Gerstle for aiding that process. Editor Debbie Gershenowitz "got" this book from our first conversation about it and improved it in countless ways. Mary Carley Caviness, Catherine Robin Hodorowicz, Jay Mazzocchi, Andrew Winters, and Iza Wojciechowska at UNC Press moved this book through production seamlessly. My thanks to all of the anonymous reviewers of this book, whose feedback deeply informed my revisions.

Friendships near and far kept me going, especially when a global pandemic upended many plans. My deepest gratitude goes to Natalie Tronson, who always understands. My love and thanks also to Dilruba Ahmed, Judy Golden Becker, Diana Boghosian, Patricio Boyer, Sara Bressi, Janet Chen, Jayatri Das, Sarina Elmariah, K. Healan Gaston, Ronni Hayon, Heather Hanson, Deborah Kahn, Sabrina Koogler, Beth Linker, Margaret Schotte, Rachel Sandler Stern, Leah Hart Tennen, and Sarah Tuttle.

Members of my family shared joy and generosity throughout this journey. My thanks especially to my parents, Nancy and Charles Davis, who keep the faith in more ways than one. Mom's keen ear for language and eye for typos improved this book in countless ways. My sister, Sarah Davis, encourages me to keep writing, offers the best parenting advice, and always makes time for a chat. Richard Price, Allison and Greg Wasserman, Vayu O'Donnell, and Paloma Castro, along with my nieces and nephews, remind me of joys not found between the pages of books. I am so fortunate to have Sandra Hoffman as my mother-in-law and friend. I wish I could share this book as well with Roy Hoffman, but mostly I wish I could introduce him to the granddaughter who so often reminds us of him.

My greatest debt is, as always, to Mark Hoffman. Mark, you are my rock. I love you and the life we make together. Jon and Hannah, I promised you years ago that I would dedicate this book to you. Thank you for gently asking if I thought I might ever finish it. This book is for you, from a heart bursting with gratitude.

Notes

ABBREVIATIONS

AJA   Jacob Rader Marcus Center of the American Jewish Archives, Cincinnati, Ohio

CBLP   Clare Boothe Luce Papers, Library of Congress, Manuscripts and Archives Division, Washington, D.C.

CWCP   Papers of Charles W. Colson, Wheaton College Billy Graham Center Archives, Wheaton, Illinois

HLS   Harvard Law School Library, Cambridge, Massachusetts

ECP   Papers of Eldridge Cleaver, Bancroft Library, University of California, Berkeley

WC   Wheaton College Billy Graham Center Archives, Wheaton, Illinois

PROLOGUE

1. Reeves, *America's Bishop*, 135–36, 170–81.

2. Scholars of religion tend to write about the "terrors" of conversion in terms of the believer's experiences of overwhelm in the presence of divine truths (or neurosis), of men and women collapsing in paroxysms of unearned grace or weeping in the presence of God's light, or of personal journeys from doubt to conviction, but many conversions also shocked the system of an anxious public. Among the many useful social histories of religious conversion, see Mullen, *Chance of Salvation*; Ariel, *Evangelizing the Chosen People*; Jacoby, *Strange Gods*; and John Owen King, *Iron of Melancholy*, 1–12. On twentieth-century self-fashioning and authenticity in relationship to celebrities (what scholar Chris Rojek calls the "peculiarly powerful affirmations of belonging" that people find in celebrities), see Ponce de Leon, *Self-Exposure*; Dyer, *Stars*, 23–24; and Rojek, *Celebrity*, 52.

3. Some readers will question the extent to which the individuals this book discusses are celebrities, embodying a kind of fame that occupies the intersection of public renown, media sensationalism, and personal fascination. Leo Braudy distinguishes between an ancient and early modern emphasis on renown earned for noble deeds, compared to the modern celebrity, who is famous for being famous. Much like Braudy, Joshua Gamson traces a shift from a pre-1950s celebrity culture premised on "greatness" to a late twentieth-century process of celebrity production that created an artificial and commodified kind of fame. More recently, Sharon Marcus has described celebrity as a drama that has circulated since the

early nineteenth century in Europe and the United States. This cultural drama engages media producers, publics, and celebrities, all of whom have power and without any one of whom celebrity could not be meaningful. According to this definition, neither Clare Boothe Luce nor Whittaker Chambers attracted the far-reaching "publics" for celebrity status, while Marilyn Monroe, Elizabeth Taylor, Sammy Davis Jr., and Muhammad Ali all attained celebrity status. That said, the history of celebrity is not a central concern of this book. See Braudy, *Frenzy of Renown*; Gamson, *Claims to Fame*; Marcus, *Drama of Celebrity*; and Marshall, *Celebrity and Power*.

4. Neil J. Young, *We Gather Together*; Moreton, "Knute Gingrich, All American?," 134; Goodstein, "Gingrich Represents," A12, 17; Jeremy W. Peters, "As Marco Rubio Speaks," A18. Since the 1990s, the Christian nationalism associated with a major faction of the Republican Party has welcomed token racial minorities but otherwise embraced a presumptively white (and often white supremacist) vision of muscular, militarist assertions of American power. On racial and ethnic tokenism within modern American conservatism, see Dillard, *Guess Who's Coming*. On hypermasculine white supremacist ideology within American evangelical Christianity, see Du Mez, *Jesus and John Wayne*.

5. On the development of and distinctions between pluralist and exceptionalist notions of a Judeo-Christian American ideal, and on the ideal's significance more broadly, see Gaston, *Imagining Judeo-Christian America*, 11–18, chaps. 4–5; Gaston, "Cold War Romance," 1133–58; Bowman, *Christian*, 122–29; Moore, *GI Jews*, 118–26; Stahl, *Enlisting Faith*, esp. chap. 3; Schultz, *Tri-faith America*; Dollinger, *Quest for Inclusion*, chap. 3; and Svonkin, *Jews Against Prejudice*, chap. 1. For liberal Protestant concern, see Fey, "Can Catholicism Win America?," 1378–80. A subsequent article series questioned the strength of mainline Protestantism to maintain the nation's moral center; see Morrison, "Can Protestantism Win America?" See also Carpenter, *Revive Us Again*, 187–89.

6. Wall, *Inventing the "American Way,"* 77–87; Stevens, *God-Fearing and Free*, esp. intro. and chap. 1; Herzog, *Spiritual-Industrial Complex*, chaps. 2–3; Preston, *Sword of the Spirit*, chaps. 22–24; Sehat, *Myth*, chap. 11.

7. Hammond, *God's Businessmen*, esp. chap. 5; Kruse, *One Nation under God*, chaps. 1, 4; Brownell, *Showbiz Politics*, chap. 4; Wall, *Inventing the "American Way,"* 4–10; Bowman, *Christian*, chap. 5.

8. According to the Roman Catholic Church's own records, between 1926 and 1945, over 1.1 million Americans converted to Catholicism, the number of conversions nearly tripling from 35,751 in 1926 to a record 115,214 in 1947. O'Brien, *Winning Converts*, 137; "How to Win," 60. See also Ellis, *American Catholicism*, 128–29. For a discussion of parish-level and laity-directed conversion efforts earlier in the twentieth century, see O'Brien, *White Harvest*. See also Hedstrom, *Rise of Liberal Religion*, 174; Butler, *God in Gotham*, chap. 5; Ribuffo, "God and Contemporary Politics," 1517–19; and Price, *Temples*.

9. Weisenfeld, *New World A-coming*, chaps. 1–2; Bowman, *Christian*, chap. 6; Von Eschen, *Race against Empire*, chap. 7; Dudziak, *Cold War Civil Rights*, chap. 4; Biondi, *To Stand and Fight*, chap. 8.

10. Ellen Herman, *Romance of American Psychology*, 58–59, chap. 5; Meyerowitz, "'How Common Culture,'" 1057–85; Charles King, *Gods of the Upper Air*, chap. 13.

11. Lane, *Surge of Piety*, 11–14; Rebecca L. Davis, "'My Homosexuality,'" 349–50; Blair, "How Norman Vincent Peale"; George, *God's Salesman*, chap. 5; Bowler, *Blessed*, chap. 3.

12. Hawkins, *Archetypes of Conversion*, chaps. 1–3; Harpham, "Conversion and the Language," 42–50; Harline, *Conversions*, 72; Hindmarsh, *Evangelical Conversion Narrative*, 4–5, 22–23; Augustine, *Confessions*, Book X:16, 222–23.

13. The anthropological, sociological, and literary literature on conversion is vast. For a few salient examples not already cited, see Rambo, *Understanding Religious Conversion*; and Gooren, *Religious Conversion and Disaffiliation*. On conversion as an awakening, see DeGloma, "Awakenings," 519–40. On converts' "rhetoric of continuity," see Johnston, "I Was Always," 550. Newman cited in O'Malley, "Church's Closet," 250. On Davis, see Conaway, "Instead of Fighting," 114; and Davis, Boyar, and Boyar, *Yes I Can*, 319. In a classic work from 1933, religion scholar A. D. Nock distinguished between conversion, or the full reorientation of the individual's belief system, and adhesion, when the individual shifts religious affiliation for cultural or political reasons without radically altering his or her belief system. See Nock, *Conversion*, 7, 134. Too often, scholars discuss "conversion" to mean only sanctification or spiritual rebirth, the narrative from sin to salvation.

14. See Anderson, *Identity's Strategy*, intro. and chap. 2. On choice, authenticity, gender, and the "self," see esp. Najmabadi, *Professing Selves*, chap. 8.

15. Dorsey, *Sacred Estrangement*, intro.; Hobson, *But Now I See*; Esther Newton and Shirley Walton, "The Personal Is Political: Consciousness-Raising and Personal Change in the Women's Liberation Movement" (paper presented at Symposium: Anthropologists Look at the Study of Women, location unknown, November 19, 1971), 1–2, 16–47, in box 33, folder 562, Birkby Papers, Smith College Archives, Northampton, Massachusetts; Brereton, *From Sin to Salvation*, 106–9; Dawkins, *God Delusion*; Hitchens, *God Is Not Great*; Lawrence Wright, *Going Clear*.

16. Butler, *Awash in a Sea*, chap. 2; Heyrman, *Southern Cross*, chap. 1; Hatch, *Democratization of American Christianity*, chap. 4; O'Toole, *Faithful*, 73–84. On missions and conversions, see Heyrman, *American Apostles*, 3–16; Mullen, *Chance of Salvation*; Conroy-Krutz, *Christian Imperialism*, chaps. 3, 5; Dolan, *Catholic Revivalism*, chap. 2; and Ariel, *Evangelizing the Chosen People*, 38–39.

17. Mullen, *Chance of Salvation*, esp. intro.; Wenger, *Religious Freedom*, chap. 2. For an interpretation that emphasizes persistent forms of coercion within American religious conversions, see Jacoby, *Strange Gods*, chap. 15.

18. Stephens, *Fire Spreads*; Wacker, *Heaven Below*, intro.; Numbers, *Prophetess of Health*, chap. 2; Hammond, *God's Businessmen*, chap. 3; Sutton, *Aimee Semple McPherson*, chaps. 2–3; Dochuk, *From Bible Belt*, chaps. 3, 8.

19. On religious writing as intellectual production, linking stories of the self to the pursuit of freedom, see Jelks, *Faith and Struggle*, 3–5.

20. Isabel Hill to Gretta Palmer, July 25, 1946, box 120, folder 11, CBLP.

CHAPTER 1

1. This description of the ritual of conversion and baptism draws from McGrail, *Rite of Christian Initiation*, chap. 2. Sheen's preparation would have begun before Luce arrived, as he knelt at the altar in the cathedral's sanctuary and recited psalms and prayers according to the prescribed priestly rituals. The *Ordo baptismi adultorum* was a series of exorcisms and prayers codified during the Counter-Reformation in sixteenth- and seventeenth-century Europe to emphasize the boundaries between Catholics and their Protestant challengers. Sheen had the option of leading Luce through an abbreviated conversion ritual, originally designed for children and increasingly used by American priests for all converts. Sheen and Luce were sticklers for formality; they might have wanted to avoid shortcuts on Luce's road to Catholicism. Or perhaps Sheen deferred to Luce's busy schedule and modern sensibility and performed the shorter series of rites, which had fewer exorcisms. (The rite was revised and abbreviated during the Second Vatican Council in the 1960s.) See also Sylvia Jukes Morris, *Price of Fame*, 162–66.

2. Mrs. Kenneth L. (Ethel Dom) Martin to Luce, February 20, 1946, box 123, folder 7, CBLP; Josephine Leddy to Luce, February 17, 1946, box 123, folder 5, CBLP ("I would like you to know you were held as an example in our church at Sunday Mass."); "Clare Boothe Luce Becomes a Catholic," 1; "Joins Catholics," 5B; "Mrs. Luce Receives First Communion," 1. See also "Mrs. Luce Becomes a Catholic," 1, 29.

3. On the contrast between secularism/Communism/materialism and Christianity/democracy/spirituality in Cold War American political discourse, see Gaston, *Imagining Judeo-Christian America*, 129–31, 154–60; and Bowman, *Christian*, 120–29.

4. Henry R. Luce, "American Century."

5. Sheed, "Clare Boothe Luce," 24; Sylvia Jukes Morris, *Rage for Fame*, 153–55.

6. Sylvia Jukes Morris, *Rage for Fame*, 240–44; Sheed, "Clare Boothe Luce," 36.

7. Brinkley, *Publisher*, 195, 306; Morris, *Rage for Fame*, 357–64; Sheed, "Clare Boothe Luce," 35.

8. Sheed, "Clare Boothe Luce," 27; Clare Boothe Luce, transcript of "An Answer to Dorothy Thompson," speech given at the Work with Willkie rally, New York City, October 15, 1940, in box 668, folder 9, CBLP.

9. TRB, "New Republicanism," 575; See also Harriman, "Candor Kid," 32; and "New Face," 20.

10. *New York Daily News* quoted in "New Face," 20; Shadegg, *Clare Boothe Luce*, 166–69; Gervasi, "Globaloney Girl," 20, 47–48; Henle, *Au Clare de Luce*, 1–2. See also Sheed, *Clare Boothe Luce*, 92–93.

11. Clare Boothe Luce, "'Real' Reason," pt. 1, 125–31; Harriman, "Candor Kid," 21. Luce describes these deaths briefly in the first part of her *McCall's* article. In the March issue of *McCall's* she explained why Freudian psychoanalysis, Marxism, and liberalism all failed to address the great questions of "Life and Death" she presented in part 1.

12. Shadegg, *Clare Boothe Luce*, 187–89; Brinkley, *Publisher*, 308–9, 320; Clare Boothe Luce, "'Real' Reason," pt. 1, 130; Henry Luce to Dr. Douglas Gordon Campbell, February 8, 1944, box 3, folder 7, CBLP.

13. "Wallace Confident," 24.

14. Wiatrak to Luce, June 30, 1944, 1, 2, box 758, folder 2, CBLP; Wiatrak to Luce, ca. July 1944, 1–2, box 758, folder 2, CBLP; Gretta Palmer to Luce, February 10, March 7, and undated, 1947, box 759, folder 12, CLBP; Luce to Palmer, January 31, 1947, box 760, folder 2, CBLP; Wiatrak to Luce, ca. August 1944, 10, box 758, folder 2, CBLP; Vanda Wiatrak Schiff to Luce, June 30, 1944, back of p. 1, box 758, folder 4, CBLP. Wiatrak's first letter to Luce was a response to an article she had written about Madame Chiang Kai-shek, the wife of the leader of the National-ist Party in China, which appeared in the September 28, 1942, issue of *Scholastic*. Wiatrak's obituary states that he first wrote to Luce in 1940; see Crimmins, "Rev. Edward Wiatrak."

15. Hedstrom, *Rise of Liberal Religion*, 155; Clare Boothe Luce, "'Real' Reason," pt. 1, 123; Smith, *Look of Catholics*, intro. and chap. 4.

16. Clare Boothe Luce, "'Real' Reason," pt. 3, 76, 78, 85; Wiatrak to Luce, January 19, April 8, 1946, 2, box 759, folder 3, CBLP. The spontaneous recitation of the Our Father occurs in other Catholic conversion memoirs; see Dulles, *Testimonial to Grace*, 54.

17. Sheen, *Treasure in Clay*, 264; Clare Boothe Luce, "'Real' Reason," pt. 3, 85; Sheen to Luce, [1946], 3–4, box 759, folder 1, CBLP. On Sheen's celebrity converts, see Riley, *Fulton J. Sheen*, chap. 3; Reeves, *America's Bishop*, 135–36; Sheen, *Treasure in Clay*, 255–66; and Olmsted, *Red Spy Queen*, 146–48.

18. Luce to R. E. Anderson, June 27, 1946, box 21, folder 1, CBLP.

19. Palmer, "New Clare Luce," 22.

20. Gleason, "American Catholics," 26–27; "Convert Specialist," 48. Many of these testimonies mentioned his conversion of Luce as especially newsworthy; *Beatificationis et canonizationis*, 344, 401, 504, 558, 913.

21. Reeves, *America's Bishop*, 234; Crosby, *God, Church, and Flag*, chap. 10; Herzog, *Spiritual-Industrial Complex*, 55–60, 65. See also Spellman, "Communism is Un-American," 25–28, 124–26.

22. Dochuk, *From Bible Belt*, 146–47, 150–52, 160.

23. Clare Boothe Luce, *The Communist Challenge to a Christian World*, pam-

phlet, reprint of November 17, 1946, letter in *New York Herald Tribune*, 5, in box 299, folder 14, CBLP; Clare Boothe Luce, "The Journey's End, Notes for speech: St. Paul's Guild - Hotel Plaza," March 30, 1948, card 8, in box 682, folder 10, CBLP. See also "The American Way and Christianity," address given at St. Joseph's College Alumnae Assoc., Bushnell Memorial, Hartford, Conn., April 6, 1948, 26, in box 682, folder 12; Clare Boothe Luce, "Christianity in the Atomic Age," [1948], in box 683, folder 1; and Clare Boothe Luce, "Christianity and the Red Religion," [November 20, 1947], in box 682, folder 1, all in CBLP.

24. *Christopher News Notes* had a circulation of 800,000 by 1954. On Keller's anti-Communism, see Chinnici, *Living Stones*, 195–96; and Armstrong, *Out to Change*, 101–11. On the Convert Makers of America, see Odou, "Convert Makers of America," 40; and Convert Makers of America pamphlets, in box 22, folder 2, National Council of Catholic Men Records; and in box 13, folder 71, National Catholic News Service Records, both in American Catholic History Research Center and University Archives, Washington, D.C. *Time* highlighted much of this information about Catholic conversion in the United States in "How to Win," 60–61; Katharine O. Athey to Luce, May 10, 1947, box 127, folder 7, CBLP. On the Converts' League, see McAvoy, *Roman Catholicism*, 85.

Two other groups, both directed by laity, had very modest success in reaching new converts: the Catholic Truth Guild, founded in 1919 and led by David Goldstein, who had converted from Judaism, and by Martha Moore Avery, a convert from Unitarianism; and the Catholic Evidence Guild, transplanted to the United States from England during the 1920s by Frank Sheed, who went on to become a publisher of Catholic books and a confidant of Clare Boothe Luce. See Campbell, "Rise of the Lay," 429–34; Mnsgr. Cummings [Epiphany Rectory, Chicago] to John A. O'Brien, August 2, 1947, 2, box 4, folder 43, O'Brien Papers, University of Notre Dame Archives, South Bend, Indiana.

25. Holden, "The Information Center," 188, 191; Donovan, "Pauline Alertness Wins 1300 Converts," 127. The Paulist congregation of priests was established in the 1850s by an American convert and was devoted to supporting Catholic missions; see William J. Quinlan, "Into the Highways and Byways," in O'Brien, *Winning Converts*, 162. On advertising and religion, see Susan Curtis, *Consuming Faith*, 234–36, 240–42; and Hammond, *God's Businessmen*, 63. This religious reliance on well-known spokespeople mirrored similar efforts by state and national political campaigns, which increasingly sought Hollywood actors as candidate surrogates and fundraising attractions; see Brownell, *Showbiz Politics*, chap. 3.

26. Fessenden, "Convent, the Brothel," 451–78. For discussions of anti-Catholicism in the nineteenth-century United States, see Franchot, *Roads to Rome*; Fessenden, *Culture and Redemption*; and O'Toole, *Faithful*, 89–93. Both Franchot and Fessenden emphasize the importance of gender to American anti-Catholicism. See also K. Anderson to Luce, [1946], box 121, folder 1, CBLP; Gretta

Palmer to Luce [probably January 26, 1947, a Monday], 1, box 759, folder 12, CBLP; and Luce to Gretta Palmer, January 31, 1947, 4, box 760, folder 2, CBLP.

27. Kertzer, *Pope and Mussolini*; Riebling, *Church of Spies*; McGreevy, *Catholicism and American Freedom*, 166–68, 213.

28. Florence Hall to Luce, [1947], box 135, folder 2, CBLP; John Howard Toynbee Falk to Luce, April 2, 1947, box 133, folder 4, CBLP.

29. V. E. Johnson to Luce, March 14, 1946, box 123, folder 1, CBLP. Luce's papers at the Library of Congress contain dozens and dozens of examples of these criticisms. From a single folder of correspondence from 1946, see Marion DeLashmott to Luce, July 30, 1946 (menopause); Wales S. Dement to Luce, June 24, 1946 (only followers of the Gospels find salvation); and Elizabeth Dickinson to Luce, March 3, 1946 (no Roman Catholic should be permitted to hold public office), all in box 122, folder 1, CBLP.

30. Page to Luce, February 18, 1946, box 124, folder 2, CBLP; "4th draft" and "5th draft" of part 1 of the "'Real' Reason" article, dated November 27 and November 28, 1946, respectively, in box 309, folder 3, CBLP.

31. Allitt, *Catholic Converts*, chaps. 5–7; Allitt, "American Women Converts," 57–79; Newman, *Apologia pro vita sua*, xviii–xix, chap. 3; Dulles, *Testimonial to Grace*, 50–55, 87–91, 114–18. On the Dulles family's religious and political affiliations, see Preston, *Sword of the Spirit*, 385–86, 450–64. Avery Dulles went on to have a storied career. He became a Jesuit, authored dozens of theological books and articles, and was eventually anointed a cardinal in 2001. After his death in 2008, the conservative journal *First Things* eulogized the passing of the Catholic Church's "most distinguished American theologian"; Guarino, "Why Avery Dulles Matters," 40.

32. George T. Bye to Luce, September 13, 1946, box 278, folder 7, CBLP; Ida G. Henley [secretary for George Bye] to Luce, December 9, 1946, box 278, folder 7, CBLP; Curtis Publishing Company Research Department, *Some Important Facts*, 1–2; Association of National Advertisers, *Magazine Circulation*, 85; Crossley, Inc., *National Study*, 6, 10; Peterson, *Magazines*, 60. Luce donated the money to one of Monsignor Sheen's pet charities, a maternity hospital in Alabama for "colored" women and their infants; Luce to Joseph A. Breig, November 30, 1946, box 121, folder 5, CBLP; "Clare Luce Gives 10 G's," 4. See Peterson for *McCall's* circulation figures from 1900 to 1963. As scholar Dianne Harris explained, magazines such as *McCall's* "created an imaginary world of idealized Americans—especially of American women—who all happened to be white, heterosexual, beautiful, clean, well organized, and financially comfortable"; Harris, *Little White Houses*, 62.

33. "Converts of Color," 29; McKay, "Why I Became," 32; McKay to Father Cantwell, October 7, 1944, box 1, folder 1, McKay Papers, New York Public Library, New York; Cyprian Davis, *History of Black Catholics*, chap. 9; Cressler, *Authentically Black*, chap. 2; Jelks, *Faith and Struggle*, chap. 2; Sorett, *Spirit in the Dark*, 84–93;

Wayne F. Cooper, *Claude McKay*, chap. 12; Booker, *Lift Every Voice*, chap. 7; Kernodle, *Soul on Soul*, chaps. 9–11; Dahl, *Morning Glory*, 288–98, 295; Jelks, *Faith and Struggle*, 84–88; Williams to Cardinal Cooke, September 28, 1969, box 19, folder 6, Williams Papers, Institute of Jazz Studies, Newark, New Jersey.

34. Ponce de Leon, *Self-Exposure*, chap. 4.

35. Katharine O. Athey to Luce, May 10, 1947, box 127, folder 7, CBLP. On the magazine's original plan to print only two installments, see Ida G. Henley [secretary to George Bye] to Luce, December 9, 1946, box 278, folder 7, CBLP; Shadegg, *Clare Boothe Luce*, 210.

36. Clare Boothe Luce, "'Real' Reason," pt. 1, 118, 124.

37. Luce, 16.

38. Luce, pt. 2, 16, 154, 156; Hedstrom, *Rise of Liberal Religion*, 94; Heinze, "Jews and American Popular Psychology," 950–77; Heinze, *Jews and the American Soul*, chap. 11.

39. Clare Boothe Luce, "'Real' Reason," pt. 2, 171. Among myriad examples of the comparison between Communism and religion, see Crossman, *God That Failed*.

40. Clare Boothe Luce, "'Real' Reason," pt. 3, 27, 76.

41. Wenger, *Religious Freedom*, 18–19; Neil J. Young, *We Gather Together*, chap. 1; V. Dowell to Luce, April 20, 1947, 3, 4, box 132, folder 5, CBLP. See also Hannah Pageler to Luce, April 13, 1947, box 142, folder 3, CBLP.

42. Elmer E. Dimmerman to Luce, March 12, 1947, box 132, folder 1, CBLP. See, e.g., C. L. Miller to Luce, January 30, 1947, box 140, folder 8; Daniel E. Moran to Luce, January 13, 1947, box 140, folder 11; and Matt R. Sawyer to Luce, March 20, 1947, box 143, folder 8, all in CBLP; W. T. Townshend to Luce, April 17, 1947, box 145, folder 6, CBLP.

43. Phebe M. Harrison to Luce, April 4, 1947, box 135, folder 5, CBLP; Neil J. Young, *We Gather Together*, 93–96; McGreevy, *Catholicism and American Freedom*, 166–80.

44. Schwager to Luce, [1947], box 143, folder 11, CBLP.

45. Joseph Alberts to Luce, April 7, 1947, 2, 7; Luce to Joseph Alberts, May 13, 1947, both in box 127, folder 4, CBLP.

46. Luce to Elmer E. Dimmerman, June 10, 1947, 1, box 132, folder 1, CBLP; Luce to Walter A. Hanson, September 26, 1947, box 135, folder 4, CBLP.

47. Copy of Otis L. Wiese to George T. Bye, September 16, 1946, box 278, folder 7, CBLP; secretary of Clare Boothe Luce to Beatrice B. Brown, July 8, 1947, box 128, folder 11, CBLP; Bye to Luce, March 21, 25, 1947, box 278, folder 10, CBLP. Clare Boothe Luce's papers contain dozens of such letters. For three, see William A. Ashe to editor, April 23, 1947, box 127, folder 7; and Joseph E. Murphy [New York] to *McCall's* magazine, May 15, 1947, box 141, folder 3, both in CBLP; and Ellen T. Allen to Wiese, September 20, 1947, box 127, folder 4, CBLP.

48. Clare Boothe Luce, "Under the Fig Tree," 214, 226–27.

49. Clare Boothe Luce, "Converts," pt. 1, 655; and pt. 2, 715–20; Orsi, *History and Presence*, chap. 1.

50. Luce to Frater Louis [Thomas Merton], September 7, 1948; Frater Louis to Dorothy Farmer, October 15, 1948; Farmer to Frater Louis, Feast of the Immaculate Conception 1948, all in box 147, folder 11, CBLP; Barbara Ward to Luce, December 19, 1948, box 761, folder 2, CBLP. See also Frater Louis to Luce, September 15, 1948; and Frater Louis to Luce, August 23, 1948, 2, both in box 761, folder 1, CBLP.

51. Lewis, *Screwtape Letters*, 31; Zanuck to Luce, telegram, [1947], box 147, folder 3, CBLP; Luce to Lewis, draft letter, April 1948, box 156, folder 1, CBLP; Sylvia Jukes Morris, *Price of Fame*, 191–92, 202–7, 233, 242–43, 286, 290–92, 242–43, 481–82; *Christopher Awards to Twenty-Five Individuals*, pamphlet, in Keller to Luce, January 15, 1953, box 290, folder 11, CBLP. The play *Child of the Morning* (1951) told the story of a Catholic girl in Brooklyn who dies while fighting off a rapist. It closed less than two weeks after it opened at the Shubert Theatre in Boston. Her article in *Sports Illustrated* was the cover story for the issue and then continued for an additional issue. See Clare Boothe Luce, "Heaven Below," 25–38; and Clare Boothe Luce, "Adventures on the Reef," 52–61.

52. Morris, 554–56, 576–81, 591.

CHAPTER 2

1. Chambers to D. M. Ladd and J. Edgar Hoover, memo, February 18, 1949, 14, document 2152, reel 44, box 46, folder 10, Hiss Defense Collection, HLS.

2. Historian Andrea Friedman provides an excellent discussion of these memoirs as examples of "psychological citizenship," in which the authors dramatized their emotional pain and loneliness as a way to build sympathy for their political decisions; see Andrea Friedman, *Citizenship*, 18–30. See also Bowman, *Christian*, chap. 5.

3. Crossman, *God That Failed*, 2–3; Donner, "Informer," 298–309. Michael Kimmage describes Lionel and Diana Trilling's "conversion" to Communism in 1931, even though they did not join the Communist Party; Kimmage, *Conservative Turn*, 58.

4. Gitlow, *I Confess*, 580–90; Bloom, *Prodigal Sons*, esp. chap. 11.

5. Hyde, *I Believed*, 312; Herzog, *Spiritual-Industrial Complex*, 39–45; Rebecca L. Davis, "'Not Marriage at All,'" 1146–48.

6. Grant, "Louis Francis Budenz," 299–300, 303–4, 345.

7. Rebecca L. Davis, *More Perfect Unions*, 53–54, 60–62; Grant, "Louis Francis Budenz," 369–70; Lichtman, "Louis Budenz," 26–27; Grant, "Louis Francis Budenz," 335, 358–77; Sheen, *Treasure in Clay*, 260–61, 265–66; Reeves, *America's Bishop*, 170–72. Budenz describes his decision to break with the Communist Party and return to the "faith of [his] fathers" in his autobiography; Budenz, *This Is My Story*, chap. 10, 347–51.

8. Budenz had his first interview with the FBI on December 7, 1945; Grant, "Louis Francis Budenz," 382; Ross, "Budenz Book," 15; Lichtman and Cohen, *Deadly Farce*, 9–11. Sheen was proud of his close ties to the FBI, boasting in his autobiography that he had been an intermediary between a Communist Party defector and the bureau; Sheen, *Treasure in Clay*, 86–87. The historian Steven Rosswurm claims that "the Bureau provided a good deal of help when it came to [Sheen's] renowned convert-making, especially for his work with Louis Budenz"; see Rosswurm, *FBI*, 4–5. Rosswurm's evidence for FBI involvement in Budenz's relationship with Sheen prior to his conversion is shaky. Stronger evidence demonstrates that Sheen served as an intermediary between Budenz and the FBI *after* his conversion; Rosswurm, *FBI*, 83–86.

9. "Third Member of House," 17; "Budenz Asserts Russia Plans," 7; "Budenz to Tour Nation," 16; Grant, "Louis Francis Budenz," 396; Louis F. Budenz, "The Communist Conspiracy" (lecture presented at the Paulist Forum's 1948 fall lecture series, "Can the American Way Survive?," September 13, 1948), in box 703, folder 13, CBLP; Crosby, *God, Church, and Flag*, 58–61. Shannon, "Strange Case," 9–10; Lichtman, "Louis Budenz," 25–54; Grant, "Louis Francis Budenz," 402, 405; Donner, "Informer," 302–4, 307. The lecture tour was extensive; see Steyskal, "Chicago Cubs," F1, 8.

10. Bentley, *Out of Bondage*, 258–69.

11. Reumann, *American Sexual Character*, chap. 2; Rebecca L. Davis, *More Perfect Unions*, 167–68; Griffith, "Religious Encounters," 349–77; Igo, *Averaged American*, chap. 5.

12. "Miss Bentley, Former Red Spy," 17; "In Retreat," 1; "Elizabeth Bentley," 16; "Miss Bentley, Ex-Spy," 31; May, *Un-American Activities*, chaps. 18–19. By 1950 Bentley sought relief from the relentless inquiries of the FBI, even though at times she was equally persistent in asking agents for help, especially when she was in debt; see Kessler, *Clever Girl*, 191–95.

13. Bentley, *Out of Bondage*, 284–85.

14. Kessler, *Clever Girl*, 110; Olmsted, *Red Spy Queen*, 94–95; "Faculty Greets 15 New Members," *Skyscraper*, October 10, 1949, 3; and "Miss Bentley to be Guest Speaker at Homecoming," *Skyscraper*, November 7, 1949, 3, both in Women and Leadership Archives, Chicago, Illinois.

15. The Hiss trials, and the involvement of Whittaker Chambers in them, have occasioned vast scholarly attention. For the most comprehensive and richly documented explanations of the case, see Weinstein, *Perjury*; and Tanenhaus, *Whittaker Chambers*, chaps. 17–24.

16. Jacoby, *Alger Hiss*; Cooke, *Generation on Trial*.

17. David K. Johnson, *Lavender Scare*, 76; Tanenhaus, *Whittaker Chambers*, 61; Weinstein, *Perjury*, 59–61, 89, 146.

18. Weinstein, *Perjury*, 343–45; Helen Duggan, "Memorandum re Laurence

Duggan," interview by Edward McLean, December 27, 1948, cited in Tanenhaus, *Whittaker Chambers*, 579n20; Dean, *Imperial Brotherhood*, 74–75. Duggan said in 1948 that her brother, who worked at *Time*, Chambers's former employer, had told her that his colleagues at *Time* viewed the case this way.

19. Tanenhaus, *Whittaker Chambers*, 154, 165, 171; Weinstein, *Perjury*, 296; Chambers, *Witness*, 129–30, 482–85.

20. Binger testified that the only psychopathic symptoms Chambers did *not* exhibit were alcoholism and drug addiction. Weinstein, *Perjury*, 432–33, 438, 578n30; Canaday, *Straight State*, 219–21, 227–47.

21. Weinstein, *Perjury*, 503; Kimmage, *Conservative Turn*, 205. On the 60,000 initial run, see Hutchens, "On the Books," E3; and Lee, *Hidden Public*, 186.

22. Chambers, *Witness*, 16.

23. Chambers feared that he had aligned with the Christian God but also with the losing side in the battle for history; Chambers, 25. See also Bowman, *Christian*, 108–10.

24. Gaston, *Imagining Judeo-Christian America*, 123–25.

25. Herberg, "From Marxism to Judaism," 25 (Herberg quote in Diggins, *Up from Communism*, 280); Herberg, "Biblical Basis," 37; Gaston, "Cold War Romance," 1154.

26. Diggins, *Up from Communism*, 245, 280–83, 345, 433; Dos Passos, "Mr. Chambers's Descent," 11; Eastman, *Reflections on the Failure*, 84.

27. Diggins, *Up from Communism*, 404–6. See also Oppenheimer, *Exit Right*, chaps. 1–2.

28. Chambers, *Witness*, 113, 119–22, 129; Tanenhaus, *Whittaker Chambers*, 7, 41.

29. Chambers, *Witness*, 115, 117.

30. Chambers, 150–66.

31. Chambers, 168–285, quotes on 184, 185.

32. Chambers, 65, 164, 196, 502; Tanenhaus, *Whittaker Chambers*, 65, 502. As Sam Tanenhaus writes in his biography of Chambers, faculty and students at Columbia called for Chambers's expulsion after he published poems that mocked Jesus in the literary journal he also edited. See Tanenhaus, *Whittaker Chambers*, 31–33. On his work in the Communist Party, see Chambers, *Witness*, chap. 4.

33. Edwards, "Memorable, Merciless, and Masterful," C3; Jordan-Smith, "Whittaker Chambers," E5; Hansen, "Meet the 'Witness,'" I10; Duffield, "Amazing Autobiography," E1; Babcock, "Among the Authors," I12; Nixon, "Plea," 12.

34. McCarraher, *Christian Critics*, 98; Schlesinger, "Whittaker Chambers," 41; Thomas O'Neill, "Reporter," 1–2; Howe, "God, Man, and Stalin," 502; Diggins, *Up from Communism*, 279–80; Howe, "Answer to Critics," 115–52.

35. Richard Morris, "Chambers's Litmus Paper Test," 13; Charles Alan Wright, "Long Work of Fiction," 11.

36. "Witness," *Newsday*, 43; Hutchens, "On the Books," E3; Chambers, "I Was the Witness"; Chambers, "Witness," 150–316; Dora K. Bent, letter to the editor, *Chicago Daily Tribune*, May 25, 1952, C6.

37. Weinstein, *Perjury*, appendix.

38. Weinstein and Vassiliev, *Haunted Wood*, chap. 2; G. Edward White, *Alger Hiss's Looking-Glass Wars*. On the persistent ambiguity surrounding the innocence or guilt of Alger Hiss, see "Alger Hiss Spy Case." For an argument assessing Hiss's guilt, see Kutler, "Rethinking the Story."

39. Zeligs, *Friendship and Fratricide*, 211, 325–26, 328, 331. See also Robert Cantwell to Zeligs, March 23, 1963, box 2, folder 2; Zeligs to Cantwell, March 20, 1963, box 2, folder 2; and Rev. Canon Robert Cromey to Zeligs, January 23, 1964, box 2, folder 6, all in Zeligs Papers, HLS.

40. Herald to Zeligs, February 7, 1963; and Leon Herald, interview with Zeligs, May 10, 1963, transcript, both in box 3, folder 22, Zeligs Papers, HLS.

41. Barron, "Online, the Hiss Defense," G1; Hiss, *Laughing Last*. The website Tony Hiss maintained, at https://files.nyu.edu/th15/public, is no longer active.

CHAPTER 3

1. Marder, "The Man Who 'Knew,'" E1, 7; Lichtman and Cohen, *Deadly Farce*, 9–10.

2. Streatfeild, *Brainwash*, 1–4; Bowman, *Christian*, 116–17.

3. "Fruits of Brainwashing," 26; "Twenty-Two," 320.

4. Adorno et al., *Authoritarian Personality*.

5. Warren I. Susman, *Culture as History*, chap. 14; Gleason, "Identifying Identity," 910–31; Fromm, *Escape from Freedom*, 141, 206, 254–55.

6. Natalie Zemon Davis, *Trickster Travels*, chap. 6; Mihm, *Nation of Counterfeiters*, 13–19; Halttunen, *Confidence Men*, chap. 2; Kevin Young, *Bunk*, chap. 1; Snorton, *Black on Both Sides*, chap. 2.

7. Fessenden, "Convent, the Brothel," 453–60; Dunfey, "'Living the Principle,'" 523; O'Malley, "Church's Closet," 228–59.

8. Leavitt, *From Catharine Beecher*, chap. 1; Moskowitz, *In Therapy*.

9. Gleason, "Identifying Identity," 914–15; Lawrence Jacob Friedman, *Identity's Architect*, 159, 161, 283–86; Erikson, *Childhood and Society*, chap. 7; Erikson, *Young Man Luther*, 93–97.

10. Meyerowitz, "'How Common Culture Shapes,'" 1057; Wall, *Inventing the "American Way*," 87–95.

11. Cohen-Cole, *Open Mind*, chap. 2; Riesman, *Lonely Crowd*, xiii, chap. 1, quote on 9. See also Melley, *Empire of Conspiracy*, 47–61.

12. Nisbet, *Quest for Community*, 3, 9.

13. Hedstrom, *Rise of Liberal Religion*, 115, 118, 180–94; Fosdick, *On Being*, intro. and chap. 3. On the importance of religious writers for spreading social sci-

entific ideas of identity and psychology, see Hedstrom, *Rise of Liberal Religion*, 71–79; and Heather White, *Reforming Sodom*, chap. 2.

14. Heinze, *"Peace of Mind,"* 32; Liebman, *Peace of Mind*, 12; emphasis in the original; Sheen, *Peace of Soul*, chap. 7; Heinze, "Clare Boothe Luce," 361–76.

15. Massa, *Catholics and American Culture*, 39–42; Hedstrom, *Rise of Liberal Religion*, 194–96.

16. Mott, *Seven Mountains*, 205–17; Furlong, *Merton*, chap. 8; Merton, *Seven Storey Mountain*, part 2.

17. Gardiner, "Poetry, Criticism, Memoirs," xxx; Robert Giroux to Merton, January 11, 1950, in Giroux, *Letters*, 57–58; Robert Giroux to Merton, July 9, 1951, in Giroux, 98–99; Giroux, 193n1.

18. Fisher, *Catholic Counterculture in America*, 205–6; "Best Sellers," January 9, 1949, B7; "Best Sellers," January 23, 1949, B7; O'Brien, *Road to Damascus*.

19. Gregory, "Life and Poems," 4.

20. Peale, *Guide to Confident Living*; Massa, *Catholics and American Culture*, 41; Butler, *God in Gotham*, 193–99; Rebecca L. Davis, "'My Homosexuality,'" 347–48.

21. Fromm to Merton, December 8, 1954, 2, section A, Merton Papers, the Thomas Merton Center at Bellarmine University.

22. Coffman, "You Cannot Fool," 200, 204–7; Frankl, *Televangelism*, 73.

23. Douglas T. Miller, "Popular Religion," 68–71; Kruse, *One Nation under God*, 67–75; Hadden and Swann, *Prime Time Preachers*, 9.

24. Matusow, *False Witness*, 19–21.

25. Matusow, 27. On his unlikability, see also Schrecker, *Many Are the Crimes*, 312.

26. On the 1949 Smith Act trial, see Schrecker, *Many Are the Crimes*, 97–98, 104–5. See also Biondi, *To Stand and Fight*, chap. 7; Hornaday, "Matusow Stages Press Conference," 14; Matusow, *False Witness*, 27, 44–47.

27. Matusow, *False Witness*, 29, 33. Department of Justice quote in Schrecker, *Many Are the Crimes*, 349.

28. Hornaday, "Matusow Stages Press Conference," 14; "Matusow Termed 'Planted' Witness," 8.

29. Marder, "The Man Who 'Knew,'" E1; Lichtman and Cohen, *Deadly Farce*, 2.

30. Matusow, *False Witness*, chap. 6; Schrecker, *Many Are the Crimes*, 309–55, quote on 342.

31. FitzGerald, *Evangelicals*, 194–95; Lichtman and Cohen, *Deadly Farce*, 95–96; "Bishop Oxnam," 6. See also Herzog, *Spiritual-Industrial Complex*, 68.

32. Marder, "The Man Who 'Knew,'" E1; Lichtman and Cohen, *Deadly Farce*, 96, 99, 104–5.

33. According to records held by the Church History Library of the LDS Church, Matusow was baptized into the church on October 1, 1954, by Wilford R. Morris Jr.

in Dallas, Texas; "Dallas Ward, Form E for 1954," Record of Members Collection, CR 375 8, reel 1548, Church History Library, Church of Jesus Christ of Latter-day Saints, Salt Lake City, Utah. See also Lichtman and Cohen, *Deadly Farce*, 100.

The children of Israel occupy a special place in LDS theology that dates back to the interests of Joseph Smith, who admired Jewish covenantal theology; Epperson, "Jews in the Columns," 135–42. Smith and his successors preached the need to restore the ancient church among the descendants of Abraham. Their theology initially defined Israelites as Lamanites (Native Americans, believed by Mormons to be descendants of one of the lost tribes of Israel) and Anglo-Israelites (Mormons) but soon expanded to include any and all potential converts. While many Christians saw themselves as symbolic Israelites, nineteenth-century Mormons often spoke of themselves as literal descendants of the biblical Joseph; Mauss, "Mormonism's Worldwide Aspirations," 103–4, 107. Both Mormons and Jews esteem a return to a sacred land of biblical Zion, and while Mormons built their Zion in Utah, their leaders sojourned in Palestine as early as the 1840s to "dedicate" the land and pray for Jerusalem's rebuilding; VanDyke and Berrett, "In the Footsteps," 57–60.

34. Matusow more likely learned from Mormon instructors, who paraphrased the teaching of the apostle Paul, "that the ancient covenant with Abraham was fulfilled in the Christian gospel, to which the truly devout Jews must now turn, along with all of humankind." That said, the LDS Church attracted few if any Jewish converts despite some enthusiasm for missions to Jewish prospects in New York and elsewhere in the early twentieth century. A few "experimental" missions to Jews in American cities in the 1950s yielded little, and in 1960 the church decided to cease any special proselytizing among them; Mauss, "Mormonism's Worldwide Aspirations," 118; Mauss, "Mormon Semitism," 11–27; Charles L. Cohen, "Construction," 25–64. Members of the LDS Church would not find acceptance among evangelical Protestants or Roman Catholics, even in political coalitions, until much later in the twentieth and early twenty-first centuries; see Neil J. Young, *We Gather Together*, conclusion.

35. "Bishop Oxnam," 6; "Matusow Charge Repeated," 11; "Matusow Calls Oxnam Story," M24.

36. Schrecker, *Many Are the Crimes*, 349–50; Crist, "Matusow's Publisher Sentenced," 1; Alfred E. Kahn, "The Story behind this Book," in Matusow, *False Witness*, 7–13, quote on 10; Marder, "The Man Who 'Knew,'" E7; Leviero, "Role of Informers," E7.

37. Crist, "Red Trial Witness," 15; Lichtman and Cohen, *Deadly Farce*, 2; Schrecker, *Many Are the Crimes*, 351; Hornaday, "Matusow Stages Press Conference," 14; "Investigations," 21; Alsop, "Matter of Fact," 14.

38. Schrecker, *Many Are the Crimes*, 352; Lichtman and Cohen, *Deadly Farce*, 13–14; Crist, "Matusow's Publisher Sentenced," 1, 19.

39. McClure, "Richfield May Get," 1, 3; Lois M. Collins, "'Job' Turns His Trials"; "Eclectic Harvey Matusow Dies."

40. Melley, *Empire of Conspiracy*, 32.

41. Halle, *Cold War as History*, 202–3.

42. Halle, 202–25, 283–84; Carruthers, *Cold War Captives*, 180–85.

43. Whitfield, *Culture*, 214; Heller interview, 61, 64; Melley, *Empire of Conspiracy*, 73–78; Cuordileone, *Manhood*, chap. 3; Costigliola, "'Unceasing Pressure for Penetration,'" 1309–39; Dean, *Imperial Brotherhood*, 66–70, chap. 7.

44. Carruthers, *Cold War Captives*, 180–81, 205.

45. Carruthers, 186; Carruthers, "'Manchurian Candidate,'" 78–79, 90n34.

46. "Prisoners of Pavlov," 26; Dunne, *Cold War State*, 119–22; Carruthers, *Cold War Captives*, 193.

47. Zweiback, "21 'Turncoat GIs,'" 350–51; Carruthers, *Cold War Captives*, 176–77, 205–8, 228 ("rapes of justice"); Plant, *Mom*, 39–45, 100–103; Dunne, *Cold War State*, 124–25, 127; Cuordileone, *Manhood*, chap. 2.

48. Lizabeth Cohen, *Consumers' Republic*, 306; Mills, *White Collar*, xii; Whyte, *Organization Man*, 5.

49. Carruthers, *Cold War Captives*, 15.

50. Frankenheimer, *Manchurian Candidate*; Dunne, *Cold War State*, 138–41; Carruthers, "'Manchurian Candidate,'" 75–94; Jacobson and González, *What Have They Built*.

51. Melley, *Empire of Conspiracy*, 3, 36.

52. Lifton, *Thought Reform*, xi, 420–32.

53. L'Engle, *Wrinkle in Time*; Urban, *New Age, Neopagan*, 8.

CHAPTER 4

1. Davis, Boyar, and Boyar, *Yes I Can*, 204–11, quotes 210–11. Davis repeated this story in an interview with Alex Haley, published in *Playboy* in 1966. Referring then to the mark on his hand after surgery, he said, "It was kind of like a stigmata"; Sammy Davis Jr. interview, 492.

2. Conaway, "Instead of Fighting," 114; Berman, *Speaking of Jews*, 161–62.

3. Moore, *At Home in America*, chap. 9; Itzkovitz, "Passing Like Me," 40–46; Kaufman, *Jewhooing the Sixties*, intro.

4. Gordun, "Glamor Gals," 7.

5. Prell, *Fighting to Become Americans*, 72–77; Merwin, *In Their Own Image*, 102–9.

6. Ariel, *Evangelizing the Chosen People*, 38–39, 165; Rischin, *Promised City*, 199.

7. Dyer, *Stars*, 36; Robert E. Goldburg to Dr. Jacob Marcus, August 24, 1962, 1–2, Goldburg Letters, AJA; Marilyn Monroe certificate of conversion, July 1, 1956, Rare Documents File RD-522, AJA; "Goldburg, Robert (Meeting of Jewish

Historical Society of New Haven, June 6, 1982)," cassette C-3337, Goldburg Letters, AJA; Berman, *Speaking of Jews*, 145–51.

8. Weatherby, "Bewildered Goddess," 156; Prell, *Fighting to Become Americans*, 146–49; Antler, *You Never Call!*, 110–12, 139–43; Maxwell, "Dilemma of Marilyn Monroe," AW8. On the typecasting of Monroe as a "pin-up 'starlet'" in "'dumb blonde' roles," see Dyer, *Stars*, 69–70. These sexualized stereotypes fill scholarship on Monroe as well; for an example of a scholar describing Monroe as a "pneumatic starlet," see Schickel, *Intimate Strangers*, 111.

9. "Beauties Talk Fish," A24; Gordun, "Glamor Gals," 7; Segal, "Plain Talk," *Jewish Advocate*, A3; Segal, "Plain Talk," *American Israelite*, 1.

10. "Goldburg, Robert (Meeting of Jewish Historical Society of New Haven, June 6, 1982)," cassette C-3337; Robert E. Goldburg to Dr. Jacob Marcus, August 24, 1962; Goldburg to Dr. Bertram W. Korn, September 7, 1962; William Rosenwald to Goldburg, March 6, 1957; photograph of Monroe, Miller, and Goldburg at the Bellevue Stanford Hotel Dinner with handwritten caption, September 25, 1959, all in Goldburg Letters, AJA.

11. "Few Relatives," 1, 3; Laro, "Joe DiMaggio Weeps," 1.

12. Taylor Conversion Ceremony, AJA; Moore, *To the Golden Cities*, 60; Ivry, "Jew by Choice," 16; "Eddie and Liz Wed," 3.

13. The *Indian Express* quoted in "Indians Angered," 11.

14. "News Picture," March 5, 1959, 11; "Arabs Ban Liz," 1; "Marilyn Is Security Risk," 1; Glenn, "In the Blood?," 143–48; "News Picture," April 16, 1959, 7; "Liz Taking Burton," 2. The boycott likely bothered American Jews more than Israelis; see Eidlin, "Two Views," A2.

15. "Sammy Davis Takes Over Ciro's," 60; Haygood, *In Black and White*, 130–31.

16. Haygood, *In Black and White*, 130–31; "Davis to Frost," 15.

17. Melnick, *Right to Sing*, 37; Sammy Davis Jr., "Why I Became a Jew," 68; Davis, Boyar, and Boyar, *Yes I Can*, 153–54.

18. Davis, Boyar, and Boyar, *Yes I Can*, 200, 222; "Davis to Frost,'" 15; Sammy Davis Jr., "Why I Became a Jew," 68; Sammy Davis Jr. interview, 491–92. Biographer Wil Haygood conflates the gifts from Cantor and Curtis, writing that Cantor had given Davis a Star of David (rather than a mezuzah) that Davis wore around his neck; see Haygood, *In Black and White*, 184.

19. Haygood, *In Black and White*, 159; Davis, Boyar, and Boyar, *Yes I Can*, 216.

20. Davis, Boyar, and Boyar, *Yes I Can*, 216.

21. Davis, Boyar, and Boyar, 238, 244.

22. Davis, Boyar, and Boyar, 291.

23. Davis, Boyar, and Boyar, 287, 322; Pete Martin, "I Call," 45; Sammy Davis Jr., "Why I Became a Jew," 69.

24. Davis, Boyar, and Boyar, *Yes I Can*, 444–45.

25. Haygood, *In Black and White*, 186; Sammy Davis Jr., "Why I Became a Jew," 63; Davis, Boyar, and Boyar, *Yes I Can*, 390. Davis identifies the interview as

occurring on *Night Beat*. Wil Haygood identifies the program as *In the Spotlight*; Haygood, *In Black and White*, 232–33. The interview may have been in 1955 or 1956.

26. Davis, Boyar, and Boyar, *Why Me?*, 195.

27. Davis, Boyar, and Boyar, *Yes I Can*, 252; emphasis in the original.

28. Davis, Boyar, and Boyar, 285.

29. Raboteau, *Slave Religion*, 312; Dorman, *Chosen People*, 4, chap. 5; Weisenfeld, *New World A-coming*, 29–42; Haynes, *Soul of Judaism*, 77–85; Horowitz, *Kosher USA*, 137–39.

30. Goldstein, *Price of Whiteness*, 174–75; Berman, *Speaking of Jews*, 143–44.

31. "Certificate of Conversion: Sammy Davis, Jr.," October 11, 1960; and affirmation of faith/*Sh'ma* by Davis, officiated by Rabbi Harry Sherer, Temple Beth Sholom, Las Vegas, Nevada, both in Davis Papers, AJA; Berman, *Speaking of Jews*, 161. Kramer writes that Rabbi Harry Sherer of Las Vegas supervised Davis's formal instruction and ceremony; Kramer, "How I Got," 189.

32. Davis, Boyar, and Boyar, *Yes I Can*, 476–77; Sammy Davis Jr., "Why I Became a Jew," 69; "Davis' Son Celebrates," 2. Mark Davis's bar mitzvah ceremony was held at Temple Sinai in Reno, followed by a luncheon for 300 guests at Harrah's.

33. Marcin Williams, letter to the editor, *Ebony*, April 1960, 15; Gayle McQuinn, letter to the editor, *Ebony*, April 1960, 15–16; Schreig, "Inside Report," 14.

34. Haygood, *In Black and White*, 183; Davis, Boyar, and Boyar, *Yes I Can*, 134. For a variation on this joke ("Because he didn't have trouble enough before?"), told by a Jewish writer, see Milton K. Susman, "As I See It," 13. Comedian Nipsey Russell, who was African American and not Jewish, also called him "Samele"; see Conaway, "Instead of Fighting," 32.

35. Brownell, *Showbiz Politics*, 173–74; Raymond, *Stars for Freedom*, chaps. 2, 6.

36. J. Randy Taraborrelli, *Sinatra: Behind the Legend* (Seacaucus, N.J.: Carol Publishing Group, 1997), excerpted in Early, *Sammy Davis, Jr. Reader*, 185. Robinson, "Behind the Scene," 58–59; "Friars 'Roast,'" 60. Video of part of their performance at the Sands in 1960 is available at "Frank Sinatra Sammy Davis Dean Martin at the 1960 Sands Summit 2nd Night 2," YouTube video, 8:37, October 19, 2011, https://www.youtube.com/watch?v=85tZEEUGoX4.

37. "Why They Wait," 16; Sammy Davis Jr., "Is My Mixed Marriage Mixing Up My Kids?" 124. This performance appears to be from the mid-1960s; "Sammy Davis Jr.—I've Got You Under My Skin (Medley) RARE," YouTube video, 9:15, January 4, 2011, https://www.youtube.com/watch?v=HueEyusETJI. Davis did impressions of many of his idols and peers when singing "One for My Baby." Davis told a version of this joke to Alex Haley; see Sammy Davis Jr. interview, 476. On "acting Jewish" since 1947, see Bial, *Acting Jewish*, 1–29.

38. Berman, *Speaking of Jews*, 2–3.

39. Berman, "Jewish Urban Politics"; Greenberg, *Troubling the Waters*, 104–13, 209, 223–25; Webb, *Fight against Fear*, chap. 5; Dollinger, *Black Power*, chap. 6; Jacobson, *Roots Too*, chap. 4.

40. Melnick, *Right to Sing*, 12–13; Rogin, *Blackface, White Noise*, chap. 5; Sammy Davis Jr., "Why I Became a Jew," 68.

41. Zeitz, "'If I Am Not,'" 253–86; Staub, *Torn at the Roots*, 128–32.

42. Davis, Boyar, and Boyar, *Why Me?*, 195; "Sammy Davis Jr. Pays Homage," 56. The *New York Times* similarly reported that Davis described his visit to Israel as "just like coming home"; "Sammy Davis in Tel Aviv," 39.

43. "Sammy Davis Jr. Pays Homage," 56. A 1980 cover story about Davis in *Ebony* included a photograph of him praying at the Western Wall in Jerusalem; see "Sammy Davis Jr. on Sammy Davis Jr.," 130.

44. Davis, Boyar, and Boyar, *Why Me?*, 195; Dollinger, *Black Power*, 160–61; Joseph, *Waiting*, 194–95.

45. Davis, Boyar, and Boyar, *Why Me?*, 249–51, 263–64; Conaway, "Instead of Fighting," 110–11; Brownell, *Showbiz Politics*, 207–9, 213; Peters, "Afraid of Critics?," 10; "We Love You," 4; Saunders, "A 'Stab,'" 8; "McGovern Steps Up," 20.

46. Sammy Davis Jr., interview by Burt Boyar, March 1, 1986, Reno, Nevada, interview 11, RYL 4371, Boyar Collection, Library of Congress, Washington, D.C. For the version of this event that appeared in print, see Davis, Boyar, and Boyar, *Why Me?*, 269–73. See also Brownell, *Showbiz Politics*, 184, 197; Raymond, *Stars for Freedom*, 227–31; Critchlow, *When Hollywood was Right*, chap. 4.

47. "Allies No More?," 1, 10; Sundquist, *Strangers in the Land*, chap. 5; Carson, "Politics of Relations," 131–43; Jacobson, *Roots Too*, chap. 5; Zeitz, *White Ethnic New York*, chap. 6.

48. Haygood, *In Black and White*, 183–86.

49. Eig, *Ali*, 120–21; Wood, "Henry Cooper v Cassius Clay."

CHAPTER 5

1. Lipsyte, "Clay Discusses His Future," 34; Lipsyte, *Accidental Sportswriter*, 68–69; Hauser, *Muhammad Ali*, 81–84; Eig, *Ali*, 153; Bud Collins, "Clay Admits Belief," 39.

2. Eig, *Ali*, chap. 13; Remnick, *King of the World*, chap. 10; Lipsyte, *Accidental Sportswriter*, 62.

3. For a description of the program and its impact, see Marable, *Malcolm X*, 160–62; Balk and Haley, "Black Merchants of Hate," 68.

4. "Cassius Dubbed Muhammad Ali," 6M; "Now Hear the Message," 98.

5. Heyrman, *American Apostles*; GhaneaBassiri, *History of Islam*, chaps. 1–2; Marr, *Cultural Roots*, 1, chap. 4; Pearsall, *Polygamy*, 174–78, quote on 176.

6. GhaneaBassiri, *History of Islam*, chap. 4, 209–18; Clegg, *Original Man*, 18–19.

7. Weisenfeld, *New World A-coming*, 43–55, 110–15; Clegg, *Original Man*, 19; GhaneaBassiri, *History of Islam*, 206, 218–23; Gomez, *Black Crescent*, chap. 6.

8. Clegg, *Original Man*, 20–22; Edward E. Curtis, *Black Muslim Religion*, 2, 10–11; Gomez, *Black Crescent*, chap. 7.

9. Clegg, *Original Man*, 17–37, chap. 3; Weisenfeld, *New World A-coming*, 56–73; GhaneaBassiri, *History of Islam*, 223–24.

10. Marable, *Malcolm X*, 68–79, 96.

11. "I Like the Word Black," 27; "Negro Racists," 278; "Enter Muhammad?," 520.

12. Muhammad Cassius Clay, interview with Alex Haley, *Playboy*, October 1964, reprint in Haley Papers, New York Public Library, New York; Eig, *Ali*, chap. 9, quote on 87; Roberts and Smith, *Blood Brothers*, 15–16, 55–56; Cosgrove, *Cassius X*, 10–12, 76. African American–owned record companies often recorded popular ministers' sermons, and those records sold well. Farrakhan's song was a Nation of Islam sermon put to music; see Lerone A. Martin, *Preaching on Wax*.

13. "Cassius Clay Says," 1; "Clay Says He's for," A14; "Cassius Clay Almost Says," 1; Malcolm X interview, 19; Brady, "Clay Defends Muslims," H2; "Sonny, Clay Stage Near-Fight," B5; "Out of His Class," 4; McLeod, *Miami Times*, 6–17; Michaeli, *Defender*; Carroll, *Race News*, chap. 6.

14. Taylor, *Promise of Patriarchy*, 4; Edward E. Curtis, *Black Muslim Religion*, 118–27; Edward E. Curtis, "Embodying the Nation," 425–27.

15. Mildred O'Neill, "Cassius Clay Flies," 13; Perry, "Cassius Clay Shakes Up," 7; "Clay Addresses Muslims," 24; "Cassius Clay Speaks," B1; Brockenbury, "Tying the Score," B4; Jackson, "Sports of the World," 5.

16. "'Sweetest Thing,'" 1–2; "Cassius Clay Denies," 5; "Clay in Rap," A2; article by Bruce Hills in *Chicago Sun-Times*, July 3, 1963, retold in Roberts and Smith, *Blood Brothers*, 126; "Cassius Clay Almost Says," 1; Ahern, "Liston," 20.

17. Ziff, "Lowdown on Cassius," B3; Poinsett, "Look at Cassius Clay," 36; "Guess Who," 2C.

18. Putnam, "Dad Says," A1–2; "Cassius Joined Black Muslims," B1.

19. "Clay Ducks Muslim Charge," 29; "Father Calls Clay Muslim," 78. Many articles note the allegations of brainwashing and Clay's refusal to answer questions about it; see, e.g., "Police Prevent a Noisy Clay," 18. "'Brainwashing,'" B1; "Father Claims," 12; "Muslim Cassius Brainwashed," 17; "Clay, Liston, Swap Barbs," S17.

20. See Remnick, *King of the World*, 8–25, 150–51, 207, 226–29, 277–78.

21. Remnick, 230.

22. Taylor, *Promise of Patriarchy*, 107–12; Eig, *Ali*, 170–74, 272–74; Remnick, *King of the World*, 231.

23. Brown and Delsohn, *Out of Bounds*, 288; Cosgrove, *Cassius X*, 207–9; Eig, *Ali*, 152–53; Marable, *Malcolm X*, 88–89.

24. Lipsyte, "Clay Discusses His Future," 34; Lipsyte, *Accidental Sportswriter*, 68–69; Hauser, *Muhammad Ali*, 81–82.

25. Bud Collins, "Clay Admits Belief," 39; "I Believe in Islam," 1; Hauser, *Muhammad Ali*, 82–83; "Clay Says He Wants," 3.

26. Clegg, *Original Man*, 210–11.

27. Murray, "Sheik of Araby," B1.

28. Art Peters, "Cassius Clay's Upset Victory," 1.

29. "Army Keeps Clay in Dark," 54C; "Clay Flunks Test Again," 16; "Clay Plans Summer Bout," S17; "Clay Confused by Criticism," A9.

30. Phares, "Army Problem," 4; "Cassius to Join Malcolm?," 2; "US Army, Fans Reject Him," 4; "When 2 Plus 2," 2; "Ho Hum," 18; "Letters Demand," 47.

31. "Liston-Clay Fight Promotion Inquiry," 11; Eig, *Ali*, 162.

32. "Muhammad Ali (Cassius Clay)," 65; Jelks, *Faith and Struggle*, 98–105; Eig, *Ali*, 202–4.

33. Marable, *Malcolm X*, 181–83, 233.

34. "Champ Cassius Clay," 1, 4; Art Peters, "Cassius Clay's Upset Victory," 4; "Report Clay, Malcolm X," 10; Roberts and Smith, *Blood Brothers*, 251–55; Clegg, *Original Man*, 211–13; Eig, *Ali*, 166–69, 179–81; Marable, *Malcolm X*, chap. 15; Payne and Payne, *Dead Are Arising*, chap. 18.

35. Wu, *Radicals on the Road*; McAlister, *Epic Encounters*, chap. 2, esp. 91–93, 110–15; Fischbach, *Black Power and Palestine*, intro.; Staub, *Torn at the Roots*, chap. 4.

36. Weisenfeld, *New World A-coming*, intro.; Eig, *Ali*, 259–63; Clegg, *Original Man*, 246–48.

37. Eig, *Ali*, 266–71; Marqusee, *Redemption Song*, 1–3.

CHAPTER 6

1. Bugliosi and Gentry, *Helter Skelter*, pt. 2, quote on 106.

2. Atkins, *Child of Satan* (2005), 230; "People in the News," A2; Chandler, "Inmates 'Reborn.'"

3. Jenkins, *Mystics and Messiahs*, 16–17, 175–81, chap. 9; Robbins, *Cults, Converts*, 5–7, 72–74.

4. Smith and Kernochan, *Marjoe*; Coffman, "You Cannot Fool," 199; Hayward, *Age of Reagan*, 487–88; Flint and Porter, "Jimmy Carter," 48.

5. Conway and Siegelman, *Snapping*, 12, 40–41; Killen, *1973*, 113–14; Forbes, "Noel Paul Stookey," 12–17; Powell, "Sound of the Furay."

6. Vaca, *Evangelicals Incorporated*, 98, 116–22, 152–58; Frankl, *Televangelism*, 3; Oliver, "How to Be," 888; Steven P. Miller, *Age of Evangelicalism*, 9; Swartz, *Moral Minority*, chap. 1; Kucharsky, "Year of the Evangelical," 12–13; Woodward, Barnes, and Lisle, "Born Again!," 68–78; Graham, *How to Be*, 7; Rebecca L. Davis, *More Perfect Unions*, 204–12; Schäfer, *Countercultural Conservatives*, 154.

7. Quoted in Urban, *New Age*, 201–6, 214–15; Streatfeild, *Brainwash*, chap. 8;

Robbins, *Cults, Converts*, 39–40; Singer and Lalich, *Cults in Our Midst*, xix, 61–62; Langone, *Recovery from Cults*, preface.

8. Keegan, "At 12, He 'Disappears,'" 17.

9. Hassan, *Combatting Cult Mind Control*, chap. 7; Langone, *Recovery from Cults*, chaps. 7–8; Killen, *1973 Nervous Breakdown*, 114–24; Jenkins, *Mystics and Messiahs*, 192–93; Egelhof, "Ed Shapiro," N5; Matza, "Battle for Krishna Minds," 103–6; Schumach, "Judge Rejects Charges," 24; Janis Johnson, "Hare Krishna Cleared," A24.

10. Stewart, "'Brainwashed' by Cult," A4.

11. Graebner, *Patty's Got a Gun*, 69–79, 159–61. On Hearst and brainwashing, see also Toobin, *American Heiress*, 352–57.

12. Eskridge, *God's Forever Family*, chap. 7; Steven P. Miller, *Age of Evangelicalism*, 10, 16–19. For an example of evangelical criticism of the group, see Jacks, "Children of God," 18–23. By 1984, David Berg would claim that the Children of God had outposts in eighty countries with upward of 9,000 members. On the history of the Children of God, see Van Zandt, *Living*, chap. 2; Chancellor, *Life in The Family*, chap. 1; and Wangerin, *Children of God*, chap. 2.

13. "N.Y. Cites Sex Abuses," 5; "News in Religion," C13; Chancellor, *Life in The Family*, xvii.

14. Buursma, "Religion," 6.

15. Sugrue and Skrentny, "White Ethnic Strategy," 189–91; Colson to [White House] Staff, memorandum, August 28, 1972, 2, box 5, folder 17, CWCP; Colson, *Born Again* (2008), 102; "Politics Unchanged," 38.

16. Kutler, *Wars of Watergate*, 104, 106–7, quote on 107; Perlstein, *Nixonland*, 598; Colson, *Born Again* (2008), 70–71, 201–3.

17. Kutler, *Wars of Watergate*, 109–14, 216, 251–52, 277–78, quotes on 111, 114.

18. Kutler, 465, 576.

19. Sharlet, *Family*, chap. 4; Kruse, *One Nation under God*, 39–49.

20. Chuck Colson, interview by Mike Wallace, *60 Minutes*, vol. 6, no. 19, CBS News, May 26, 1974, transcript, 1, in box 11, folder 5, CWCP.

21. Colson, 3; Greider, "Colson, 'Mr. Tough Guy,'" A1; Sharlet, *Family*, 230.

22. Chuck Colson, interview by Mike Wallace, *60 Minutes*, vol. 6, no. 19, CBS News, May 26, 1974, transcript, 4, 6–7, in box 11, folder 5, CWCP.

23. Dochuk, *From Bible Belt*, chap. 6; Wacker, *America's Pastor*, 32–33; Sutton, *American Apocalypse*, 326–30.

24. Stephens, *Fire Spreads*, 26–30; Paul E. Johnson, *Shopkeeper's Millennium*, 95–102; Frankl, *Televangelism*, 4; Bendroth, "Why Women Loved," 254; Hankins, *Jesus and Gin*, chap. 3; Sutton, *Aimee Semple McPherson*, chap. 3; Dochuk, *Anointed with Oil*, 353–56. On Christian radio's origins, see Carpenter, *Revive Us Again*, 126–40; and Hangen, *Redeeming the Dial*, chaps. 1, 2.

25. Bruce, *Pray TV*; Rolsky, *Rise and Fall*; Shawn David Young, *Gray Sabbath*; Stephens, *Devil's Music*, chap. 4; Woods, *Evangelical Christians*.

26. Douglas L. Hallett to Colson, February 2, 18, 1974; and Colson to Hallett, February 20, 1974, 1 ("I wish you weren't so goddamned sensitive! You and I will have trouble working together, we always do."); to Irving Paul Lazer, July 1, 1974; and to Kenneth L. Adams, memorandum from prison, September 22, 1974, all in box 88, folder 1, CWCP. Peter Schwed to Harold Matson, January 16, 1975; and Matson to Adams, January 17, 1975, both in box 88, folder 2, CWCP. Contract for *The Charles Colson Story* between Charles W. Colson and Chosen Books, signed and dated June 10, 1975, box 102, folder 1, CWCP; Oliver, "How to Be," 887, 901. See also Hugh R. Barbour [executive vice president, Fleming H. Revell Company] to Colson, August 18, 1978, box 102, folder 2, CWCP; Gallagher, "Dean Jones," B19; Robert L. Munger to "Born Again Partner," April 25, 1979, box 2, folder 1, Records of Prison Fellowship Ministries, WC.

27. Colson, *Born Again* (2008), 102–3.

28. Colson, 123, 125. Kendrick Oliver describes the scene on Phillips's porch as "part seduction, part prosecution." See Oliver, "How to Be," 892.

29. Colson, *Born Again* (2008), 129. On the role of pride in shaping Colson's narrative of sin and salvation, see Griffin, "Rhetoric of Form," 152–63.

30. Colson, *Born Again* (2008), 133, 142.

31. Colson, 146–47.

32. Colson, 177–78.

33. Erzen, "Testimonial Politics," 991–92, 996.

34. Spence, *Knocking the Hustle*, quote on xxiv, see also chap. 1; Melinda Cooper, *Family Values*, chap. 2; Swinth, "Post-Family Wage," 311–35.

35. Rodgers, *Age of Fracture*.

36. Promotional poster for *Born Again* (1978), box 52, folder 8, Records of Prison Fellowship Ministries, WC; Colson, *Born Again* [1978 or 1979], [29, 31].

37. Chandler, "Inmates 'Reborn,'" 1, 3.

38. Cleaver, *Soul on Ice*.

39. Joseph, *Waiting*, 212; Murch, *Living*, 151–54, 162–68.

40. Fredrica [Teer?] to Cleaver, February 16, 1975, box 2, folder 4, Cleaver Collection, Cushing Memorial Library and Archives, Texas A&M University, College Station, Texas; Joseph, *Waiting*, 238; Hilliard and Cole, *This Side of Glory*, 210–11; Cleaver, "Why I Left," 37; Cleaver, *Soul on Fire*, 220–21.

41. Chandler, "Tells of Spiritual Rebirth," C3. On the DeMoss family's philanthropy, see correspondence in box 33, folder 12, Wilson Papers, WC. Ames et al., "Hymn to Adoption," 52; Hoffman, "Picture Is Jumbled," A18. See also Wells, "Born Again Black Panther," 368–72.

42. Barlett, "Education of Eldridge Cleaver," 65; Steadman, "Lord's Touch," A1; John M. Perkins to Cleaver, March 25, 1977, box 17, folder 16, Records of Voice of Calvary Ministries, WC.

43. Boone and Matrisciana to Art DeMoss, November 15, 1976, carton 6, folder 2, ECP. See also Sharlet, *Family*, 240.

44. Program of the Thirty-Fourth Annual Convention, National Religious Broadcasters, January 23–26, 1977, box 57, folder 11, Records of National Religious Broadcasters, WC. See also Ritter, "Cleaver and Colson," 24. At an event in January 1977, Colson introduced Cleaver to Tom Phillips, who promised to send "checks"; see Colson to Cleaver, January 31, 1977. On connecting Cleaver to the Billy Graham Evangelical Association, see Colson to Cleaver, May 12, June 12, 1977. See also W. Stanley Mooneyham [World Vision International] to Colson, June 8, 1977; all in carton 7, folder 41, ECP.

45. Cleaver, "Prodigal Returns Home," 5–6; Rout, *Eldridge Cleaver*, 228–29; "Eldridge Cleaver Guests Today," *Community Church News* 6, no. 44 (October 31, 1976), 1, copy in carton 9, folder 39, ECP; Robert H. Schuller, *But—God Can!* (Garden City, Calif.: 1976), 16–17, in carton 8, folder 24, ECP; Ralph C. Osborn to Cleaver, December 2, 1976, carton 7, folder 39, ECP; Vecsey, "Preacher Who Pioneered," 26. On Schuller's support of Cleaver, see correspondence in box 2, folders 8–17, Cleaver Collection. Cleaver saved many of these letters; see, e.g., Denise Kasper-Whaley to Cleaver, October 20, 1976; Hilda K. Maynard to George Otis, December 16, 1976; and Mrs. Charles Curtis to [Otis], December 9, 1976, all in carton 6, folder 32, ECP. See additional correspondence in carton 6, folders 32–40, ECP.

46. FitzGerald, *Evangelicals*, 376; Kruse, *One Nation*, 280; Atkins, *Child of Satan* (2005), 281–86, quoted at 285. Logos International, a Christian press based in Plainfield, New Jersey, first published *Child of Satan, Child of God*. Within a year, Logos had sold the book rights to Bantam, a major secular publisher in New York. A small publisher of esoteric books put out a 2005 edition. See Atkins, *Child of Satan* (2005); and Atkins, *Child of Satan* (1977).

47. Atkins, *Child of Satan* (2005), 284, chap. 25.

48. Warnke, *Satan-Seller*, 109–12, 121–22.

49. Ferraiuolo, "Warnke Calls Critics Satanists," 49; Ferraiuolo, "Warnke Admits 'Failure,'" 88–89.

50. Jack Wyrtzen [director, Word of Life International] to Brown, March 3, 1977; see also Graham Gilmer Jr. to Brown, March 2, 1977, both in carton 6, folder 41, ECP.

51. Liddick, "Flynt's Hustler Arrives," E6; Vecsey, "Self-Styled Pornographer," A16; "Alleged Smut Dealer," A3.

52. Lofton, "I Don't Want," 156–59; Hilburn, "Dylan," 8; Maxa, "Front Page People," SM4; Loder, "Rolling Stone Interview," 17; Wilentz, *Bob Dylan in America*, 176–83; Steven P. Miller, *Age of Evangelicalism*, 21; "Bob Dylan Gives Rare Interview."

53. Erzen, *Straight to Jesus*, chap. 4; Fetner, "Ex-gay Rhetoric," 75–77.

54. Fox, "Susan Atkins," A20.

55. Neil J. Young, *We Gather Together*, 190–91; Maust, "Cleaver," 23; Zaitchik, "Meet the Man"; "Cleaver Says He Will"; Speer, "Eldridge Cleaver Affirms," 3;

Bringhurst, "Eldridge Cleaver's Passage," 82–83, 88–92; Lavelle, "From 'Soul on Ice,'" 68.

56. Curry, "Clerics Urge," 3.

EPILOGUE

1. Sylvia Jukes Morris, "In Search," 33; Sylvia Jukes Morris, *Price of Fame*, 601–2. See also Buckley, "Clare Boothe Luce," 20–22; Krebs, "Clare Boothe Luce," 1, 41.

2. Neil J. Young, *We Gather Together*, 264–97.

3. Neuhaus, "Christianity and Democracy," 30–37; Young, *We Gather Together*, 251–52.

4. Marqusee, *Redemption Song*; Gallen and McCarthy-Miller, *America*.

5. Lynch and Bird, *The Simpsons*; Davis, Boyar, and Boyar, *Why Me?*, 193–94.

6. Deborah G. White, *Lost in the USA*, 1–3, chap. 1, 183–88; Rodgers, *Age of Fracture*; Whitehead and Perry, *Taking America Back*.

7. Lofton, *Consuming Religion*; Simonds, *Women and Self-Help*, chap. 2; Illouz, *Saving the Modern Soul*, intro., chap. 5; Roof, *Spiritual Marketplace*, 46–76. In 2008 *Forbes* estimated the worth of the self-help industry at $11 billion; see Linder, "What People Are Still Willing to Pay For." Several marketing websites estimated the worth of the self-help industry in 2016 as approximately $10 billion; see, e.g., "$9.9 Billion Self-Improvement Market." On Oprah Winfrey, see Lofton, *Oprah*, 95, 97, 109–10.

Bibliography

MANUSCRIPT COLLECTIONS
Berkeley, California
    Bancroft Library, University of California
        Papers of Eldridge Cleaver
Cambridge, Massachusetts
    Harvard Law School Library
        Hiss Defense Collection (microfilm)
        Meyer A. Zeligs Papers
Chicago, Illinois
    Women and Leadership Archives, Loyola University Chicago
        Skyscraper (Mundelein College student paper)
Cincinnati, Ohio
    The Jacob Rader Marcus Center of the American Jewish Archives
        Sammy Davis Jr. Papers
        Robert E. Goldburg Letters
        Rare Documents File RD-522
        Elizabeth Taylor Conversion Ceremony, March 26, 1959, CD-1357
            (audio)
College Station, Texas
    Cushing Memorial Library and Archives, Texas A&M University
        Eldridge Cleaver Collection
Denton, Texas
    Special Collections and University Archives, Texas Woman's University,
        the Woman's Collection
        Choice Foundation Collection
Lansing, Michigan
    Archives of Michigan
        Gospel Films Collection
Louisville, Kentucky
    The Thomas Merton Center at Bellarmine University
        Merton Collection
New York, New York
    Columbia Center for Oral History, Columbia University
        Thomas Merton Papers

New York Public Library, Schomburg Center for Research in Black Culture,
Manuscripts, Archives, and Rare Books Division
Alex Haley Papers
Claude McKay Papers
Newark, New Jersey
Institute of Jazz Studies
Mary Lou Williams Papers
Northampton, Massachusetts
Smith College Archives
Phyllis Birkby Papers
Salt Lake City, Utah
Church History Library, Church of Jesus Christ of Latter-day Saints
Record of Members Collection
University of Utah Libraries, Special Collections
Freeman Institute Records
South Bend, Indiana
University of Notre Dame Archives
Papers of John A. O'Brien
Washington, D.C.
American Catholic History Research Center and University Archives,
Catholic University of America
National Catholic News Service Records
National Council of Catholic Men Records
Library of Congress, Manuscripts and Archives Division
Clare Boothe Luce Papers
Library of Congress, Recorded Sound Division
Burt Boyar Collection of Sammy Davis Jr. Biographical Materials
Wheaton, Illinois
Wheaton College Billy Graham Center Archives
Papers of Charles W. Colson
Papers of Grady Baxter Wilson
Records of National Religious Broadcasters
Records of Prison Fellowship Ministries
Records of Voice of Calvary Ministries

ARTICLES IN NEWSPAPERS AND POPULAR PERIODICALS
Adelson, Alan. "Allies No More?" *Wall Street Journal*, December 31, 1968, 1, 10.
Ahern, John. "Liston: Winner Take All?" *Boston Globe*, February 14, 1964, 20.
"The Alger Hiss Spy Case." *American History Magazine*, June 12, 2006.
"Alleged Smut Dealer Turns Over New Leaf." *Los Angeles Times*, September 20,
1978, A3.

Alsop, Stewart. "Matter of Fact: Legal Lying." *New York Herald Tribune*, January 28, 1955, 14.

Ames, Katrine, Elizabeth Ann Leonard, Shawn D. Lewis, and Peter Annin. "A Hymn to Adoption—or Is It?" *Newsweek*, April 6, 1992, 52.

"Arabs Ban Liz." *Jewish Advocate*, March 19, 1959, 1.

"Army Keeps Clay in Dark." *Newsday*, March 19, 1964, 54C.

Babcock, Frederic. "Among the Authors." *Chicago Daily Tribune*, May 11, 1952, I12.

Balk, Alfred, and Alex Haley. "Black Merchants of Hate." *Saturday Evening Post*, January 26, 1963, 68–75.

Barlett, Laile E. "The Education of Eldridge Cleaver." *Reader's Digest*, September 1976, 65–72.

Barron, James. "Online, the Hiss Defense Doesn't Rest." *New York Times*, August 16, 2001, G1.

"Beauties Talk Fish." *Jewish Advocate*, April 23, 1959, A24.

"Best Sellers." *Washington Post*, January 9, 1949, B7.

"Best Sellers." *Washington Post*, January 23, 1949, B7.

"Bishop Oxnam Says Red Quiz Accuser Retracts." *Los Angeles Times*, October 19, 1954, 6.

Blair, Gwenda. "How Norman Vincent Peale Taught Trump to Worship Himself." *Politico*, October 6, 2015. https://www.politico.com/magazine/story/2015/10/donald-trump-2016-norman-vincent-peale-213220.

Brady, Dave. "Clay Defends Muslims, Hits Integration." *Los Angeles Times*, February 2, 1964, H2.

"'Brainwashing': Father Says Clay Joined Muslims at 18." *Washington Post and Times Herald*, February 7, 1964, B1.

Brockenbury, L. I. "Tying the Score: Clay Wants Answer." *Los Angeles Sentinel*, February 20, 1964, B4.

Buckley, William F. "Clare Boothe Luce, RIP." *National Review*, November 6, 1987, 20–22.

"Budenz Asserts Russia Plans to Destroy US." *New York Herald Tribune*, October 14, 1946, 7.

"Budenz to Tour Nation Assailing Communism." *New York Herald Tribune*, October 13, 1945, 16.

Buursma, Bruce. "Religion: Sex Cult Was 'Hell,' Insider Says in Book." *Chicago Tribune*, August 11, 1984, 6.

"Cassius Clay Almost Says He's a Muslim." *New York Amsterdam News*, January 25, 1964, 1.

"Cassius Clay Denies Joining Black Muslims." *Atlanta Daily World*, July 6, 1963, 5.

"Cassius Clay Says He's Not a Muslim Member." *Afro-American*, July 20, 1963, 1.

"Cassius Clay Speaks at Muslim's Meeting." *Washington Post*, January 24, 1964, B1.

"Cassius Dubbed Muhammad Ali." *Oregonian*, March 8, 1964, 6M.

"Cassius Joined Black Muslims at 18, Father Says." *Los Angeles Times*, February 7, 1964, B1.

"Cassius to Join Malcolm? 'Black Nationalist Party' Planned for 'Self-Defense.'" *New Journal and Guide*, March 14, 1964, 1–2.

Chambers, Whittaker. "I Was the Witness." *Saturday Evening Post*, weekly from February 9 to April 12, 1952.

"Champ Cassius Clay at Home in Harlem's Hotel Theresa Suite." *Philadelphia Tribune*, March 3, 1964, 1, 4.

Chandler, Russell. "Inmates 'Reborn': Conversions to Christ—a Prison Revival." *Los Angeles Times*, March 15, 1976, 1, 3, 20.

———. "Tells of Spiritual Rebirth." *Los Angeles Times*, September 14, 1976, C1–4.

"Clare Boothe Luce Becomes a Catholic." *New York Times*, February 17, 1946, 1.

"Clare Luce Gives 10 G's to Hospital." *New York Amsterdam News*, March 15, 1947, 4.

"Clay Addresses Muslims." *Boston Globe*, January 23, 1964, 24.

"Clay Confused by Criticism Following Army Rejection." *Baltimore Sun*, March 22, 1964, A9.

"Clay Ducks Muslim Charge: Sect Has 'Brain Washed' Him, Says Dad." *Boston Globe*, February 7, 1964, 29–30.

"Clay Flunks Test Again, Hopes for Fight, Tour." *Richmond Times*, March 21, 1964, 16.

"Clay in Rap at Negro Civil Rights Athlete." *Los Angeles Times*, July 6, 1963, A2.

"Clay, Liston, Swap Barbs: Boxers Talk on Closed Circuit to New York." *Baltimore Sun*, February 14, 1964, S17, S19.

"Clay Plans Summer Bout: Rejected by Army, Champ May Travel Overseas." *Baltimore Sun*, March 21, 1964, S17.

"Clay Says He's for the 'BM's.'" *Los Angeles Sentinel*, July 18, 1963, A14.

"Clay Says He Wants Peace; Finds It in Black Muslims." *Baltimore Sun*, February 28, 1964, 3.

"Clay to Feel a Draft—Army Style." *Miami Herald*, January 24, 1964, 3C.

Cleaver, Eldridge. "The Prodigal Returns Home." *Faith at Work*, June 1978, 5–6.

———. "Why I Left the U.S. and Why I Am Returning." *New York Times*, November 18, 1975, 37.

"Cleaver Says He Will Join Church." *Deseret News*, April 6–8, 1981.

Collins, Bud. "Clay Admits Belief in Black Muslim Credo." *Boston Globe*, February 27, 1964, 39.

Collins, Lois M. "'Job' Turns His Trials into Blessings." *Deseret News*, March 27, 1999. https://www.deseret.com/1999/3/27/19436597/job-turns-his-trials

-into-blessings-br-once-hated-informant-now-spends-his-time-cash
-helping-others.

Conaway, James. "Instead of Fighting for a Place on It, Sammy Davis Jr. Has Bought the Bus." *New York Times Magazine*, October 15, 1972, 32–33, 110–19.

"Converts of Color." *Ebony*, March 1946, 28–31.

"Convert Specialist." *Newsweek*, February 26, 1940, 48.

Crimmins, Jerry. "Rev. Edward Wiatrak: Had Luce Conversion Role." *Chicago Tribune*, November 1, 1989, 16S.

Crist, Judith. "Matusow's Publisher Sentenced to 6 Months." *New York Herald Tribune*, February 10, 1955, 1–2.

———. "Red Trial Witness Says Testimony Was False." *New York Herald Tribune*, February 1, 1955, 15.

Curry, George E. "Clerics Urge Pardon for Rev. Moon." *Chicago Tribune*, August 21, 1985, 3.

Davis, Sammy, Jr. Interview by Alex Haley. *Playboy*, December 1966. Reprinted in Early, *Sammy Davis, Jr. Reader*, 476–92.

———. "Is My Mixed Marriage Mixing Up My Kids?" *Ebony*, October 1966, 124–32.

———. "Why I Became a Jew." *Ebony*, February 1960, 62–69.

"Davis' Son Celebrates Bar Mitzvah." *Milwaukee Sentinel*, May 21, 1973, 2.

"Davis to Frost: 'I Am a Black Jew.'" *New Pittsburgh Courier*, November 13, 1971, 15.

Donner, Frank J. "The Informer." *Nation*, April 10, 1954, 298–309.

"Don't Call Me Cassius Clay: Army Rejects Muhammad Ali." *Seattle Daily Times*, March 20, 1964, 48.

Dos Passos, John. "Mr. Chambers's Descent into Hell." *Saturday Review*, May 24, 1952, 11.

Duffield, Marcus. "Amazing Autobiography of a Famous Ex-Communist." *New York Herald Tribune*, May 25, 1952, E1, E18.

"Eclectic Harvey Matusow Dies at 75 after Colorful Life." *Deseret News*, February 2, 2002. https://www.deseret.com/2002/2/2/19634886/eclectic-harvey-matusow-dies-at-75-after-colorful-life.

"Eddie and Liz Wed in Jewish Service." *Jerusalem Post*, May 14, 1959, 3.

Edwards, Willard. "Memorable, Merciless, and Masterful." *Chicago Daily Tribune*, May 25, 1952, C3.

Egelhof, Joseph. "Ed Shapiro, or Vasu Gopal? 4 Sides Fight over Fate of Hare Krishna Youth." *Chicago Tribune*, October 16, 1976, N5.

Eidlin, Harold. "Two Views of the State Department." *Jewish Advocate*, January 11, 1962, A2.

"Elizabeth Bentley, Former Soviet Spy, Becomes a Catholic." *Chicago Daily Tribune*, November 17, 1948, 16.

"Enter Muhammad?" *National Review*, July 2, 1963, 519–21.

"Father Calls Clay Muslim; He's Mum." *Newsday*, February 7, 1964, 78.

Ferraiuolo, Perucci. "Warnke Admits 'Failure': Comedian Says He Exaggerated Role as Satanist." *Christianity Today*, May 17, 1993, 88–89.

———. "Warnke Calls Critics Satanists." *Christianity Today*, November 9, 1992, 49.

"Few Relatives, Friends to Attend Marilyn Rites." *Los Angeles Times*, August 7, 1962, 1, 3.

Fey, Harold Edward. "Can Catholicism Win America?" *Christian Century*, November 29, 1944, 1378–80.

Forbes, Cheryl. "Noel Paul Stookey Down Home." *Christianity Today*, May 19, 1978, 12–17.

"For Bloodshed: Malcolm X Organizing Black Nationalist Party." *Jersey Journal and Jersey Observer*, March 9, 1964, 1.

Fox, Margalit. "Susan Atkins, 61, Is Dead; Charles Manson Follower." *New York Times*, September 26, 2009, A20.

Fraley, Oscar. "Father Claims Sect Dominates Son: Yon Cassius 'Brainwashed' by Black Muslims Says Pop." *New Journal and Guide*, February 15, 1964, 12.

"Friars 'Roast' Sammy Davis Jr." *Jet*, February 7, 1963, 60.

"Fruits of Brainwashing." *New York Times*, January 28, 1954, 26.

Gallagher, Mike. "Dean Jones, Disney Movie Star, Became a Born-Again Christian." *New York Times*, September 3, 2015, B19.

Gardiner, Harold C. "Poetry, Criticism, Memoirs and Shorter Fiction." *America*, November 13, 1948, xxx.

Gervasi, Frank. "Globaloney Girl." *Collier's*, March 27, 1943, 20, 47–48.

Goodstein, Laurie. "Gingrich Represents New Political Era for Catholics." *New York Times*, December 17, 2011, A12, 17.

Gordun, Jack H. "Glamor Gals as Jewish Wives." *Jewish Advocate*, May 9, 1957, 7.

Gregory, Horace. "Life and Poems of a Trappist Monk." Review of *The Seven Storey Mountain*, by Thomas Merton. *New York Times Book Review*, October 3, 1948, 4, 33.

Greider, William. "Colson, 'Mr. Tough Guy,' Finds Christ." *Washington Post and Times Herald*, December 17, 1973, A1.

"Guess Who." *Miami Herald*, January 25, 1964, 2C.

Hansen, Harry. "Meet the 'Witness'—a Modest Man—and Confident." *Chicago Daily Tribune Magazine of Books*, June 1, 1952, I10.

Harriman, Margaret Case. "The Candor Kid." Pt. 1. *New Yorker*, January 4, 1941, 21–29.

Heller, Joseph. Interview by Sam Merrill. *Playboy*, June 1975, 61, 64.

Herberg, Will. "From Marxism to Judaism." *Commentary*, January 1947, 25–32.

Hilburn, Robert. "Dylan: 'I Learned That Jesus Is Real and I Wanted That'; Dylan Confirms His Commitment." *Los Angeles Times*, November 23, 1980, X1, 8.

Hoffman, Jan. "Picture Is Jumbled on Which Abortion Messages Can Get on TV." *New York Times*, June 11, 1992, A12.

"Ho Hum." *Oregonian*, March 18, 1964, 18.

Hornaday, Mary. "Matusow Stages Press Conference: Born in Bronx 'Addicted to Headlines.'" *Christian Science Monitor*, February 4, 1955, 14.

Howe, Irving. "God, Man, and Stalin." *Nation*, May 24, 1952, 502–4.

"How to Win a Convert." *Time*, July 12, 1948, 60–61.

Hutchens, John K. "On the Books." *New York Herald Tribune*, February 17, 1952, E3.

"I Believe in Islam, Love, Says Non-Mixer Cassius." *Miami Herald*, February 28, 1964, 1.

"I Like the Word Black." *Newsweek*, May 6, 1963, 27–28.

"Indians Angered at Marriage Ban." *Jewish Advocate*, June 1, 1961, 1, 11.

"In Retreat: Ex–Red Spy Studies to be Catholic." *Los Angeles Times*, November 16, 1948, 1.

"Investigations: False Witness." *Time*, February 14, 1955, 21.

Ivry, Benjamin. "A Jew by Choice: Elizabeth Taylor, 1932–2011." *Forward*, March 23, 2011, 16.

Jacks, David. "Children of God: Disciples of Deception." *Christianity Today*, February 18, 1977, 18–23.

Jackson, Marion E. "Sports of the World." *Atlanta Daily World*, February 22, 1964, 5.

Johnson, Janis. "Hare Krishna Cleared of 'Mind Control.'" *Washington Post*, March 21, 1977, A24.

"Joins Catholics, Mrs. Luce Not Up for Re-election." *Cleveland Call and Post*, March 30, 1946, 5B.

Jordan-Smith, Paul. "Whittaker Chambers Tells His Awakening." *Los Angeles Times*, May 25, 1952, E5.

Keegan, Anne. "At 12, He 'Disappears' into Krishna." *Chicago Tribune*, December 7, 1975, 17.

Krebs, Albin. "Clare Boothe Luce Dies at 84." *New York Times*, October 10, 1987, 1, 41.

Kucharsky, David. "The Year of the Evangelical '76." *Christianity Today*, October 22, 1976, 12–13.

Kutler, Stanley I. "Rethinking the Story of Alger Hiss." Review of *Alger Hiss's Looking Glass Wars: The Covert Life of a Soviet Spy*, by G. Edward White. FindLaw, August 6, 2004. https://supreme.findlaw.com/legal-commentary /rethinking-the-story-of-alger-hiss.html.

Laro, Frank. "Joe DiMaggio Weeps at Marilyn's Funeral: Ex-husband Grief-Stricken in His Final Farewell." *Los Angeles Times*, August 9, 1962, 1, 13.

"Letters Demand: Put Clay in the Army." *San Francisco Chronicle*, April 3, 1964, 47.

Leviero, Anthony. "Role of Informers Now under Inquiry." *New York Times*, February 6, 1955, E7.

Liddick, Betty. "Flynt's Hustler Arrives in Los Angeles: 'Heretic' Paul Krassner Is the New Publisher." *Los Angeles Times*, January 25, 1978, E1, 6.

Linder, Melanie. "What People Are Still Willing to Pay For." *Forbes*, January 15, 2009. https://www.forbes.com/2009/01/15/self-help-industry-ent-sales-cx_ml_0115selfhelp.html?sh=39d9f03e6758.

Lipsyte, Robert. "Clay Discusses His Future, Liston and Black Muslims." *New York Times*, February 27, 1964, 34.

"Liston-Clay Fight Promotion Inquiry." *Irish Times*, February 28, 1964, 11.

"Liz Taking Burton under the Huppah." *Jerusalem Post*, December 25, 1963, 2.

Loder, Kurt. "The Rolling Stone Interview: Bob Dylan." *Rolling Stone*, June 21, 1984, 14–24, 28.

Luce, Clare Boothe. "Adventures on the Reef." *Sports Illustrated*, August 18, 1958, 52–61.

———. "Converts and the Blessed Sacrament." Pts. 1 and 2. *Sentinel*, November 1950, 651–55; December 1950, 715–20.

———. "The Heaven Below." *Sports Illustrated*, August 11, 1958, 25–38.

———. "The 'Real' Reason." Pts. 1–3. *McCall's*, February 1947, 16, 117–35; March 1947, 16–17, 153–56, 160–61, 167–68, 171–72, 175–76; April 1947, 26–27, 76–80, 85–88, 90.

Luce, Henry R. "The American Century." *Life*, February 17, 1941. Reprinted in Henry Luce, "The American Century," *Diplomatic History*, 23, no. 2 (1999): 159–71.

Malcolm X. Interview by Alex Haley. *Playboy*, May 1963, 18–24.

Marder, Murray. "The Man Who 'Knew 10,000 Commies by Sight': Harvey Matusow, Incredible Witness." *Washington Post*, February 6, 1955, E1, 7.

"Marilyn Is Security Risk in Egypt." *Jerusalem Post*, October 22, 1959, 1.

Martin, Pete. "I Call on Sammy Davis Jr." *Saturday Evening Post*, May 21, 1960, 44–45, 104, 106, 108.

"Matusow Calls Oxnam Story 'Half-Truths,'" *Washington Post and Times*, October 24, 1954, M24.

"Matusow Charge Repeated by Bishop Oxnam to Probe." *New York Herald Tribune*, October 19, 1954, 11.

"Matusow Termed 'Planted' Witness." *New York Times*, February 4, 1955, 8.

Matza, Michael. "The Battle for Krishna Minds: From Newton to Nirvana; Who Controls Ed Shapiro?" *Boston Phoenix*, November 16, 1976, 103–6.

Maust, John. "Cleaver: Gazing at a Different Moon." *Christianity Today*, December 7, 1979, 49–50.

Maxa, Rudy. "Front Page People: Bob Dylan Knocks on Heaven's Door." *Washington Post Magazine*, May 27, 1979.

Maxwell, Elsa. "The Dilemma of Marilyn Monroe." *Washington Post and Times Herald*, May 12, 1957, AW8, 10.

McClure, Bill. "Richfield May Get State's 1st Public Access TV Station." *Richfield (Utah) Reaper*, August 30, 1995, 1, 3.

"McGovern Steps Up Drive to Boost Black Turnout." *Afro-American*, November 4, 1972, 20.

McKay, Claude. "Why I Became a Catholic." *Ebony*, March 1946, 32.

"Miss Bentley, Ex-spy, Becomes a Catholic." *New York Times*, November 16, 1948, 31.

"Miss Bentley, Former Red Spy Ring Aid, in Catholic Retreat." *Chicago Daily Tribune*, November 16, 1948, 17.

Morris, Richard. "Chambers's Litmus Paper Test." *Saturday Review*, May 24, 1952, 13.

Morris, Sylvia Jukes. "In Search of Clare Boothe Luce." *New York Times*, January 31, 1988, SM22–27, 33.

Morrison, Charles Clayton. "Can Protestantism Win America?" *Christian Century*, April 3, 1946, 425–27; May 22, 1946, 650–53; and June 22, 1946, 746–50.

"Mrs. Luce Becomes a Catholic, Says She Is Quitting Public Life." *New York Herald Tribune*, February 17, 1946, 1, 29.

"Mrs. Luce Receives First Communion." *Catholic Courier Journal*, February 21, 1946, 1.

"Muhammad Ali (Cassius Clay) Meets with Muslim Leader." *Seattle Times*, March 15, 1964, 65.

Murray, Jim. "The Sheik of Araby." *Los Angeles Times*, March 12, 1964, B1, B3.

"Muslim Cassius Brainwashed, Confused, Says His Father." *Afro-American*, February 15, 1964, 17.

"The Negro Racists." *Nation*, April 6, 1963, 278.

"New Face." *Time*, September 21, 1942, 20.

"News in Religion: Children of God Deny Charges." *Chicago Tribune*, November 9, 1974, C13.

"The News Picture: People." *Jewish Advocate*, March 5, 1959, 11.

"The News Picture: People." *Jewish Advocate*, April 16, 1959, 7.

"$9.9 Billion Self-Improvement Market Challenged by Younger and More Demanding Millennials, Changing Technology." *WebWire*, August 2, 2017. https://www.webwire.com/ViewPressRel.asp?aId=211649.

Nixon, Richard. "Plea for an Anti-Communist Faith." *Saturday Review*, May 24, 1952, 12–13.

"Now Hear the Message of the Black Muslims from Their Leader." *Esquire*, April 1963, 97–101.

"N.Y. Cites Sex Abuses by Children of God Sect." *Chicago Tribune*, October 15, 1974, 5.

O'Neill, Mildred. "Cassius Clay Flies to Greet Elijah: Won't Say He's Turned Muslim." *Afro-American*, October 12, 1963, 13.

O'Neill, Thomas. "Reporter at Both Alger Hiss Trials Reviews Whittaker Chambers Book." *Baltimore Sun*, May 22, 1952, 1–2.

"Out of His Class." *Afro-American*, February 15, 1964, 4.

Palmer, Gretta. "The New Clare Luce." *Look*, April 15, 1947, 21–27.

"People in the News: 'Born Again.'" *Independent Press-Telegram* (Long Beach, Calif.), December 28, 1975, A2.

Perry, Harmon G. "Cassius Clay Shakes Up Game in Atlanta." *Atlanta Daily World*, November 29, 1963, 7.

Peters, Art. "Afraid of Critics? Not Sammy Davis." *Philadelphia Inquirer*, August 24, 1972, 10.

———. "Cassius Clay's Upset Victory over Sonny Liston Stirs Rumors of Split." *Philadelphia Tribune*, February 29, 1964, 1–2.

Peters, Jeremy W. "As Marco Rubio Speaks of Faith, Evangelicals Keep Options Open." *New York Times*, December 4, 2015, A18.

Phares, Don. "Army Problem for Muslim Members: Hint New Champ Signed GI Papers as Islamite." *Philadelphia Tribune*, March 3, 1964, 1, 4.

Poinsett, Alex. "A Look at Cassius Clay: Biggest Mouth in Boxing." *Ebony*, March 1963, 35–42.

"Police Prevent a Noisy Clay from Crashing Liston's Camp." *New York Times*, February 8, 1964, 18.

Powell, Mark Allan. "The Sound of the Furay." *Christianity Today*, December 27, 2005.

"The Prisoners of Pavlov." *Life*, October 5, 1953, 26.

"Program Guests Listed." *Times Recorder*, March 18, 1977, 7A.

Putnam, Pat. "Dad Says Cassius Muslim 'Prisoner.'" *Miami Herald*, February 7, 1964, A1–2.

"Report Clay, Malcolm X Plan New Organization." *Chicago Daily Defender*, March 2, 1964, 10.

Ritter, Bill. "Cleaver and Colson Praise the Lord." *In These Times*, April 13, 1977, 24.

Robinson, Louie. "Behind the Scene as Sammy Weds: Jewish Rites Were Preceded." *Jet*, December 1, 1960, 56–59.

Ross, Don. "Budenz Book Cites Spiritual Tussle as a Red: Ex-editor of 'Daily Worker' Says Soviet Secret Police Control Communist Party." *New York Herald Tribune*, March 14, 1947, 15.

"Sammy Davis in Tel Aviv; Rejoices in 'Homecoming.'" *New York Times*, July 21, 1969, 39.

"Sammy Davis Jr. on Sammy Davis Jr., Sex, Suicide, Success, Richard Nixon, Frank Sinatra, Black and White Women, Blacks and Jews." *Ebony*, March 1980, 125–35.

"Sammy Davis Jr. Pays Homage to Israeli Wall." *Jet*, August 7, 1969, 56.

"Sammy Davis Takes Over Ciro's." *Jet*, August 18, 1955, 60–61.

Saunders, Warner. "A 'Stab' at Soul Brother No. 1." *Chicago Daily Defender*, November 14, 1972, 8.

Schlesinger, Arthur, Jr. "Whittaker Chambers and his 'Witness.'" *Saturday Review*, May 24, 1953, 39–41.

Schreig, Samuel. "Inside Report." *Jewish Criterion* (Pittsburgh), January 5, 1962, 14.

Schumach, Murray. "Judge Rejects Charges of 'Brainwashing' against Hare Krishna Aides." *New York Times*, March 18, 1977, 24.

"Segal, Alfred. "Plain Talk: All about Gefilte Fish." *American Israelite*, August 29, 1957, 1–2.

———. "Plain Talk: All about Gefilte Fish." *Jewish Advocate*, August 22, 1957, A3.

Shannon, William V. "The Strange Case of Louis Budenz." *New Republic*, October 22, 1951, 9–10.

Sheed, Wilfrid. "Clare Boothe Luce: What a Woman Had to Do to Make It in the American Century." *Harper's*, February 1982, 21–38.

"Sonny, Clay Stage Near-Fight at Airport: Police 'Save' Champ." *Los Angeles Times*, January 27, 1964, B5.

Speer, John C. "Eldridge Cleaver Affirms Seriousness about Mormonism, Offers to Proselyte." *Herald* (Provo, Utah), April 10, 1981, 3.

Spellman, Francis. "Communism Is Un-American." *American Magazine*, July 1946, 124.

Steadman, Ethel A. "Lord's Touch Changed an Envoy of Hate." *Virginian-Pilot* (Norfolk), [1976], A1, A4.

Stewart, Barry. "'Brainwashed' by Cult." *Chicago Tribune*, November 9, 1975, A4.

Steyskal, Irene. "Chicago Cubs Plan to Study World Affairs." *Chicago Daily Tribune*, October 20, 1946, F1, 8.

Susman, Milton K. "As I See It." *Jewish Criterion* (Pittsburgh), May 10, 1957, 13.

"'The Sweetest Thing Next to God': Has Cassius Clay Gone Black Muslim?" *Afro-American*, July 13, 1963, 1–2.

"Third Member of House Quits 'Win the Peace.'" *New York Herald Tribune*, April 4, 1946, 17.

TRB. "The New Republicanism." *New Republic*, November 2, 1942, 575.

"The Twenty-Two." *Commonweal*, January 1, 1954, 320–21.

"US Army, Fans Reject Him: Cassius Can't Understand Recent Deluge of Criticism." *Augusta (Ga.) Chronicle*, March 22, 1964, 4.

Vecsey, George. "Preacher Who Pioneered Drive-In Religion Gains Followers with His Upbeat TV Show." *New York Times*, October 11, 1977, 26.

———. "Self-Styled Pornographer Says He Has Changed, but Not into a Traditional Christian: 'Turned Off by Pornography.'" *New York Times*, February 2, 1978, A16.

"Wallace Confident." *New York Sun*, November 1, 1944, 24.

Weatherby, W. J. "A Bewildered Goddess Analyzes Her Life." *Ladies' Home Journal*, April 1976, 91, 154, 156.

"We Love You, Sammy, But ..." *Milwaukee Star*, September 7, 1972, 4.

"When 2 plus 2 = 4F: Clay: Army's Decision, Not Mine." *Dallas Morning News*, March 22, 1964, 2.

"Why They Wait for Sammy Davis Jr." *New York Times*, May 9, 1964, 16.

"The Witness." *Newsday*, February 8, 1952, Nassau ed., 43.

Wood, Jack. "Henry Cooper v Cassius Clay: The Punch That (Almost) Changed the World." Reprinted in *Daily Mail*, May 3, 2011. https://www.dailymail .co.uk/sport/othersports/article-1382819/Henry-Cooper-v-Cassius-Clay -The-punch-changed-world.html.

Woodward, Kenneth L., John Barnes, and Laurie Lisle. "Born Again!" *Newsweek*, October 25, 1976, 68–78.

Wright, Charles Alan. "A Long Work of Fiction." *Saturday Review*, May 24, 1952, 11–12.

Zaitchik, Alexander. "Meet the Man Who Changed Glenn Beck's Life." *Salon*, September 16, 2009.

Ziff, Sid. "Lowdown on Cassius." *Los Angeles Times*, January 28, 1964, B3.

FILMS AND TELEVISION PROGRAMS

"Bob Dylan Gives Rare Interview." *60 Minutes*, December 5, 2004, https://www .cbsnews.com/news/60-minutes-bob-dylan-rare-interview-2004/.

Frankenheimer, John, dir. *The Manchurian Candidate*. 1962; Santa Monica, Calif.: MGM Home Entertainment, 1998. DVD.

Gallen, Joel, and Beth McCarthy-Miller, dirs. *America: A Tribute to Heroes*. Studio City, Calif.: Tenth Planet Productions, 2001. DVD.

Lynch, Jeffrey, and Brad Bird, dirs. *The Simpsons*. Season 3, episode 41, "Like Father, Like Clown." Aired October 24, 1991, on Fox.

Rapper, Irving, dir. *Born Again*, 20th anniversary edition. 1978; Edmonton, Alta.: Crown Video, 1998. VHS.

Smith, Howard, and Susan Kernochan, dirs. *Marjoe*. New York: Cinema 10, 1972.

JOURNAL ARTICLES, DISSERTATIONS, AND CHAPTERS OF EDITED BOOKS

Allitt, Patrick. "American Women Converts and Catholic Intellectual Life." *U. S. Catholic Historian* 13, no. 1 (1995): 57–79.

Bendroth, Margaret. "Why Women Loved Billy Sunday: Urban Revivalism and Popular Entertainment in Early Twentieth-Century American Culture." *Religion and American Culture* 14, no. 2 (2004): 251–71.

Berman, Lila Corwin. "Jewish Urban Politics in the City and Beyond." *Journal of American History* 99, no. 2 (2012): 492–519.

Bringhurst, Newell G. "Eldridge Cleaver's Passage through Mormonism." *Journal of Mormon History* 28, no. 1 (2002): 80–110.

Campbell, Debra. "The Rise of the Lay Catholic Evangelist in England and America." *Harvard Theological Review* 79, no. 4 (1986): 413–37.

Carruthers, Susan L. "'The Manchurian Candidate' (1962) and the Cold War Brainwashing Scare." *Historical Journal of Film, Radio and Television* 18, no. 1 (1998): 75–94.

Carson, Clayborne. "The Politics of Relations between African-Americans and Jews." In *Blacks and Jews: Alliances and Arguments*, edited by Paul Berman, 131–43. New York: Delacorte, 1994.

Chambers, Whittaker. "Witness." In *Reader's Digest Condensed Books*, 150–316. Pleasantville, N.Y.: Reader's Digest Association, 1952.

Coffman, Elesha. "You Cannot Fool the Electric Eye." In *Billy Graham: American Pilgrim*, edited by Andrew S. Finstuen, Anne Blue Wills, and Grant Wacker, 197–215. New York: Oxford University Press, 2017.

Cohen, Charles L. "The Construction of the Mormon People." *Journal of Mormon History* 32, no. 1 (2006): 25–64.

Costigliola, Frank. "'Unceasing Pressure for Penetration': Gender, Pathology, and Emotion in George Kennan's Formation of the Cold War." *Journal of American History* 83, no. 4 (1997): 1309–39.

Curtis, Edward E. "Embodying the Nation of Islam." *Modern American History* 1, no. 3 (2018): 425–29.

Davis, Rebecca L. "'My Homosexuality Is Getting Worse Every Day': Norman Vincent Peale, Psychiatry, and the Liberal Protestant Response to Same-Sex Desires in Mid-Twentieth Century America." In *American Christianities: A History of Dominance and Diversity*, edited by Catherine A. Brekus and W. Clark Gilpin, 347–65. Chapel Hill: University of North Carolina Press, 2011.

———. "'Not Marriage at All, but Simple Harlotry': The Companionate Marriage Controversy." *Journal of American History* 94, no. 4 (2008): 1137–63.

DeGloma, Thomas. "Awakenings: Autobiography, Memory, and the Social Logic of Personal Discovery." *Sociological Forum* 25, no. 3 (2010): 519–40.

Donovan, Joseph P. "Pauline Alertness Wins 1300 Converts." In O'Brien, *Winning Converts*, 113–30.

Dunfey, Julie. "'Living the Principle' of Plural Marriage: Mormon Women, Utopia, and Female Sexuality in the Nineteenth Century." *Feminist Studies* 10, no. 3 (1984): 523–36.

Epperson, Steven. "Jews in the Columns of Joseph's 'Times and Seasons.'" *Dialogue* 22, no. 4 (1989): 135–42.

Erzen, Tanya. "Testimonial Politics: The Christian Right's Faith-Based

Approach to Marriage and Imprisonment." *American Quarterly* 59, no. 3 (2007): 991–1015.

Fessenden, Tracy. "The Convent, the Brothel, and the Protestant Woman's Sphere." *Signs* 25, no. 2 (January 2000): 451–78.

Fetner, Tina. "Ex-gay Rhetoric and the Politics of Sexuality: The Christian Antigay/Pro-family Movement's 'Truth in Love' Ad Campaign." *Journal of Homosexuality* 50, no. 1 (2005): 71–95.

Flint, Andrew R., and Joy Porter. "Jimmy Carter: The Re-emergence of Faith-Based Politics and the Abortion Rights Issue." *Presidential Studies Quarterly* 35, no. 1 (2005): 28–51.

Gaston, K. Healan. "The Cold War Romance of Religious Authenticity: Will Herberg, William F. Buckley Jr., and the Rise of the New Right." *Journal of American History* 99, no. 4 (March 1, 2013): 1133–58.

Gleason, Philip. "American Catholics and the Mythic Middle Ages." In *Keeping the Faith: American Catholicism, Past and Present*, edited by Philip Gleason, 11–34. Notre Dame, Ind.: University of Notre Dame Press, 1987.

———. "Identifying Identity: A Semantic History." *Journal of American History* 69, no. 4 (1983): 910–31.

Glenn, Susan. "In the Blood? Consent, Descent, and the Ironies of Jewish Identity." *Jewish Social Studies* 8, no. 2/3 (2002): 139–52.

Grant, Jimmy Randall. "Louis Francis Budenz: The Origins of a Professional Ex-Communist." Ph.D. diss., University of South Carolina, 2006.

Griffin, Charles J. G. "The Rhetoric of Form in Conversion Narratives." *Quarterly Journal of Speech* 76, no. 2 (May 1990): 152–63.

Griffith, R. Marie. "The Religious Encounters of Alfred C. Kinsey." *Journal of American History* 95, no. 2 (September 2008): 349–77.

Guarino, Thomas G. "Why Avery Dulles Matters." *First Things*, no. 193 (May 2009): 40–46.

Harpham, Geoffrey Galt. "Conversion and the Language of Autobiography." In *Studies in Autobiography*, edited by James Olney, 42–50. New York: Oxford University Press, 1988.

Hedstrom, Matthew S. "Psychology and Mysticism in 1940s Religion: Reading the Readers of Fosdick, Liebman, and Merton." In *Religion and the Culture of Print in Modern America*, edited by Charles Lloyd Cohen and Paul S. Boyer, 243–67. Madison: University of Wisconsin Press, 2008.

Heinze, Andrew R. "Clare Boothe Luce and the Jews: A Chapter from the Catholic-Jewish Disputation of Postwar America." *American Jewish History* 88, no. 3 (2000): 361–76.

———. "Jews and American Popular Psychology: Reconsidering the Protestant Paradigm of Popular Thought." *Journal of American History* 88, no. 3 (2001): 950–77.

————. "*Peace of Mind* (1946): Judaism and the Therapeutic Polemics of Postwar America." *Religion and American Culture* 12 (2002): 31–58.

Herberg, Will. "The Biblical Basis of American Democracy." *Thought* 30, no. 1 (1955): 37–50.

Holden, Vincent F. "The Information Center." In O'Brien, *Winning Converts*, 187–97.

Howe, Irving. "An Answer to Critics of American Socialism." *New International* 18 (May–June 1952): 115–52.

Itzkovitz, Daniel. "Passing Like Me: Jewish Chameleonism and the Politics of Race." In *Passing: Identity and Interpretation in Sexuality, Race, and Religion*, edited by María Carla Sánchez and Linda Schlossberg, 38–63. New York: New York University Press, 2001.

Johnston, Erin F. "'I Was Always This Way …': Rhetorics of Continuity in Narratives of Conversion." *Sociological Forum* 28, no. 3 (2013): 549–73.

Kramer, William M. "How I Got to Officiate at the Wedding of Sammy Davis Jr. and May Britt." *Western States Jewish History* 42, no. 2/3 (Winter/Spring 2010): 188–91.

Lavelle, Ashley. "From 'Soul on Ice' to 'Soul for Hire'? The Political Transformation of Black Panther Eldridge Cleaver." *Race and Class* 54, no. 2 (2012): 55–74.

Lichtman, Robert M. "Louis Budenz, the FBI, and the 'List of 400 Concealed Communists': An Extended Tale of McCarthy-Era Informing." *American Communist History* 3, no. 1 (2004): 25–54.

Lofton, Kathryn. "I Don't Want to Fake You Out: Bob Dylan and the Search for Belief in History." In *Cultural Icons and Cultural Leadership*, edited by Peter Iver Kaufman and Kristin M. S. Bezio, 152–66. Cheltenham, UK: Edward Elgar, 2017.

Luce, Clare Boothe. "Under the Fig Tree." In O'Brien, *Road to Damascus*, 213–39.

Mauss, Armand L. "Mormonism's Worldwide Aspirations and Its Changing Conceptions of Race and Lineage." *Dialogue* 34, no. 3/4 (Fall 2001): 103–33.

————. "Mormon Semitism and Anti-Semitism." *Sociological Analysis* 29, no. 1 (Spring 1968): 11–27.

Meyerowitz, Joanne. "'How Common Culture Shapes the Separate Lives': Sexuality, Race, and Mid-Twentieth-Century Social Constructionist Thought." *Journal of American History* 96, no. 4 (2010): 1057–84.

Miller, Douglas T. "Popular Religion of the 1950's: Norman Vincent Peale and Billy Graham." *Journal of Popular Culture* 9, no. 1 (1975): 66–76.

Moreton, Bethany. "Knute Gingrich, All American? White Evangelicals, US Catholics, and the Religious Genealogy of Political Realignment." In *Faithful Republic: Religion and Politics in Modern America*, edited by Andrew

Preston, Bruce J. Schulman, and Julian E. Zelizer, 131–51. Philadelphia: University of Pennsylvania Press, 2015.

Moskowitz, Eva S. *In Therapy We Trust: America's Obsession with Self-Fulfillment*. Baltimore: Johns Hopkins University Press, 2001.

Neuhaus, Richard John. "Christianity and Democracy (Statement Adopted in 1981 by the Institute on Religion and Democracy)." *First Things*, no. 66 (October 1996): 30–37.

Odou, John E. "Convert Makers of America." In O'Brien, *Winning Converts*, 35–42.

Oliver, Kendrick. "How to Be (the Author of) Born Again: Charles Colson and the Writing of Conversion in the Age of Evangelicalism." *Religions* 5, no. 3 (2014): 886–911.

O'Malley, Patrick R. "The Church's Closet: Confessionals, Victorian Catholicism, and the Crisis of Identification." In *Passing: Identity and Interpretation in Sexuality, Race, and Religion*, edited by María Carla Sánchez and Linda Schlossburg, 228–59. New York: New York University Press, 2001.

Ribuffo, Leo P. "God and Contemporary Politics." *Journal of American History* 79, no. 4 (1993): 1515–33.

Sugrue, Thomas J., and John D. Skrentny. "The White Ethnic Strategy." In *Rightward Bound: Making America Conservative in the 1970s*, edited by Bruce J. Schulman and Julian E. Zelizer, 171–92. Cambridge, Mass.: Harvard University Press, 2008.

Swinth, Kirsten. "Post–Family Wage, Postindustrial Society: Reframing the Gender and Family Order through Working Mothers in Reagan's America." *Journal of American History* 105, no. 2 (2018): 311–35.

VanDyke, Blair G., and LaMar C. Berrett. "In the Footsteps of Orson Hyde: Subsequent Dedications of the Holy Land." *Brigham Young University Studies Quarterly* 47, no. 1 (January 2008): 57–93.

Wells, Dan. "Born Again Black Panther: Race, Christian Conservatism, and the Remaking of Eldridge Cleaver." *Religion and American Culture* 30, no. 3 (2020): 361–96.

Zeitz, Joshua. ""If I Am Not for Myself …'": The American Jewish Establishment in the Aftermath of the Six Day War." *American Jewish History* 88, no. 2 (2000): 253–86.

Zweiback, Adam J. "The 21 'Turncoat GIs': Nonrepatriations and the Political Culture of the Korean War." *Historian* 60, no. 2 (1998): 345–62.

BOOKS AND REPORTS

Adorno, Theodor W., Else Frankel-Brunswik, Daniel J. Levinson, and R. Nevitt Sanford. *The Authoritarian Personality*. Studies in Prejudice 3. New York: Harper, 1950.

Allitt, Patrick. *Catholic Converts: British and American Intellectuals Turn to Rome*. Ithaca, N.Y.: Cornell University Press, 1997.

Anderson, Dana. *Identity's Strategy: Rhetorical Selves in Conversion*. Studies in Rhetoric/Communication. Columbia: University of South Carolina Press, 2007.

Antler, Joyce. *You Never Call! You Never Write! A History of the Jewish Mother*. New York: Oxford University Press, 2007.

Ariel, Yaakov S. *Evangelizing the Chosen People: Missions to the Jews in America, 1880–2000*. Chapel Hill: University of North Carolina Press, 2000.

Armstrong, Richard. *Out to Change the World: A Life of Father James Keller of the Christophers*. New York: Crossroad, 1984.

Association of National Advertisers. *Magazine Circulation and Rate Trends, 1940–1959*. Association of National Advertisers: [New York], 1960.

Atkins, Susan. *Child of Satan, Child of God*. With Bob Slosser. Plainfield, N.J.: Logos International, 1977. Reprint, San Juan Capistrano, Calif.: Menelorelin Dorenay's, 2005.

Augustine. *Confessions*. Translated and with an introduction by R. S. Pine-Coffin. Harmondsworth, UK: Penguin Books, 1961.

Beatificationis et canonizationis servi dei Fultonii Ioannis Sheen archiepiscopi titularis neoportensis episcopi roffensis in America (1895–1979). Vol. 1. Rome: Nova Res, 2011. Copies located at Hesburgh Library Special Collections, University of Notre Dame, South Bend, Indiana.

Bentley, Elizabeth. *Out of Bondage: The Story of Elizabeth Bentley*. New York: Devin-Adair, 1951.

Berman, Lila Corwin. *Speaking of Jews: Rabbis, Intellectuals, and the Creation of an American Public Identity*. Berkeley: University of California Press, 2008.

Bial, Henry. *Acting Jewish: Negotiating Ethnicity on the American Stage and Screen*. Ann Arbor: University of Michigan Press, 2005.

Biondi, Martha. *To Stand and Fight: The Struggle for Civil Rights in Postwar New York City*. Cambridge, Mass.: Harvard University Press, 2003.

Bloom, Alexander. *Prodigal Sons: The New York Intellectuals and Their World*. New York: Oxford University Press, 1986.

Booker, Vaughn A. *Lift Every Voice and Swing: Black Musicians and Religious Culture in the Jazz Century*. New York: New York University Press, 2020.

Bowler, Kate. *Blessed: A History of the American Prosperity Gospel*. New York: Oxford University Press, 2013.

Bowman, Matthew Burton. *Christian: The Politics of a Word in America*. Cambridge, Mass.: Harvard University Press, 2018.

Braudy, Leo. *The Frenzy of Renown: Fame and Its History*. New York: Vintage Books, 1997.

Brereton, Virginia Lieson. *From Sin to Salvation: Stories of Women's Conversions, 1800 to the Present.* Bloomington: Indiana University Press, 1991.

Brinkley, Alan. *The Publisher: Henry Luce and His American Century.* New York: Knopf, 2010.

Brown, Jim, and Steve Delsohn. *Out of Bounds.* New York: Kensington, 1989.

Brownell, Kathryn Cramer. *Showbiz Politics: Hollywood in American Political Life.* Chapel Hill: The University of North Carolina Press, 2014.

Bruce, Steve. *Pray TV: Televangelism in America.* New York: Routledge, 1990.

Budenz, Louis F. *This Is My Story.* New York: Whittlesey House, 1947.

Bugliosi, Vincent, and Curt Gentry. *Helter Skelter: The True Story of the Manson Murders.* New York: Bantam Books, 1995.

Butler, Jon. *Awash in a Sea of Faith: Christianizing the American People.* Cambridge, Mass.: Harvard University Press, 1992.

———. *God in Gotham: The Miracle of Religion in Modern Manhattan.* Cambridge, Mass.: Harvard University Press, 2021.

Canaday, Margot. *The Straight State: Sexuality and Citizenship in Twentieth-Century America.* Princeton, N.J.: Princeton University Press, 2009.

Carpenter, Joel A. *Revive Us Again: The Reawakening of American Fundamentalism.* New York: Oxford University Press, 1997.

Carroll, Fred. *Race News: Black Journalists and the Fight for Racial Justice in the Twentieth Century.* Urbana: University of Illinois Press, 2017.

Carruthers, Susan L. *Cold War Captives: Imprisonment, Escape, and Brainwashing.* Berkeley: University of California Press, 2009.

Chambers, Whittaker. *Witness.* 1952. Reprint, Washington, D.C.: Regnery, 2001.

Chancellor, James D. *Life in The Family: An Oral History of the Children of God.* New York: Syracuse University Press, 2000.

Chinnici, Joseph P. *Living Stones: The History and Structure of Catholic Spiritual Life in the United States.* New York: Macmillan, 1989.

Cleaver, Eldridge. *Soul on Fire.* Waco, Tex.: Word Books, 1978.

———. *Soul on Ice.* 1968. Reprint, New York: Dell Publishing, 1991.

Clegg, Claude Andrew. *An Original Man: The Life and Times of Elijah Muhammad.* New York: St. Martin's, 1997.

Cohen, Lizabeth. *A Consumers' Republic: The Politics of Mass Consumption in Postwar America.* New York: Vintage Books, 2003.

Cohen-Cole, Jamie Nace. *The Open Mind: Cold War Politics and the Sciences of Human Nature.* Chicago: University of Chicago Press, 2014.

Colson, Charles W. *Born Again.* 1976. Reprint, Grand Rapids, Mich.: Chosen Books, 2008.

———. *Born Again.* Comic book. Ada, Mich.: Spire, [1978 or 1979].

Conroy-Krutz, Emily. *Christian Imperialism: Converting the World in the Early American Republic.* Ithaca, N.Y.: Cornell University Press, 2015.

Conway, Flo, and Jim Siegelman. *Snapping: America's Epidemic of Sudden Personality Change*. Philadelphia: Lippincott, 1978.

Cooke, Alistair. *A Generation on Trial: USA v. Alger Hiss*. New York: Knopf, 1952.

Cooper, Melinda. *Family Values: Between Neoliberalism and the New Social Conservatism*. New York: Zone Books, 2017.

Cooper, Wayne F. *Claude McKay: Rebel Sojourner in the Harlem Renaissance; A Biography*. Baton Rouge: Louisiana State University Press, 1987.

Cosgrove, Stuart. *Cassius X: The Transformation of Muhammad Ali*. Chicago: Lawrence Hill Books, 2020.

Cressler, Matthew J. *Authentically Black and Truly Catholic: The Rise of Black Catholicism in the Great Migration*. New York: New York University Press, 2017.

Critchlow, Donald. *When Hollywood Was Rights: How Movie Stars, Studio Moguls, and Big Business Remade American Politics*. New York: Cambridge University Press, 2013.

Crosby, Donald F. *God, Church, and Flag: Senator Joseph R. McCarthy and the Catholic Church, 1950–1957*. Chapel Hill: University of North Carolina Press, 1978.

Crossley, Inc. *National Study of Magazine Audiences, 1952: Nine Magazines, Conducted for Look Magazine; Working Manual*. [Cowles]: [New York], 1952.

Crossman, Richard, ed. *The God That Failed*. New York: Harper, 1950.

Cuordileone, K. A. *Manhood and American Political Culture in the Cold War*. New York: Routledge, 2005.

Curtis, Edward E. *Black Muslim Religion in the Nation of Islam, 1960–1975*. Chapel Hill: University of North Carolina Press, 2006.

Curtis Publishing Company Research Department. *Some Important Facts about Magazine Circulations*. Curtis: [Philadelphia], 1953.

Dahl, Linda. *Morning Glory: A Biography of Mary Lou Williams*. New York: Pantheon Books, 1999.

Davis, Cyprian. *The History of Black Catholics in the United States*. New York: Crossroad, 1990.

Davis, Natalie Zemon. *Trickster Travels: A Sixteenth-Century Muslim between Worlds*. New York: Hill and Wang, 2006.

Davis, Rebecca L. *More Perfect Unions: The American Search for Marital Bliss*. Cambridge, Mass.: Harvard University Press, 2010.

Davis, Sammy, Jr., Jane Boyar, and Burt Boyar. *Why Me? The Sammy Davis, Jr. Story*. New York: Farrar, Straus and Giroux, 1989.

———. *Yes I Can: The Story of Sammy Davis, Jr.* New York: Farrar, Straus and Giroux, 1965.

Dawkins, Richard. *The God Delusion*. Boston: Houghton Mifflin, 2006.

Dean, Robert D. *Imperial Brotherhood: Gender and the Making of Cold War Foreign Policy*. Amherst: University of Massachusetts Press, 2001.

Diggins, John P. *Up from Communism: Conservative Odysseys in American Intellectual History*. New York: Harper and Row, 1975.

Dillard, Angela D. *Guess Who's Coming to Dinner Now? Multicultural Conservatism in America*. New York: New York University Press, 2001.

Dochuk, Darren. *Anointed with Oil: How Christianity and Crude Made Modern America*. New York: Basic Books, 2019.

———. *From Bible Belt to Sunbelt: Plain-Folk Religion, Grassroots Politics, and the Rise of Evangelical Conservatism*. New York: W. W. Norton, 2011.

Dolan, Jay P. *Catholic Revivalism: The American Experience, 1830–1900*. Notre Dame, Ind.: University of Notre Dame Press, 1978.

Dollinger, Marc. *Black Power, Jewish Politics: Reinventing the Alliance in the 1960s*. Waltham, Mass.: Brandeis University Press, 2018.

———. *Quest for Inclusion: Jews and Liberalism in Modern America*. Princeton, N.J.: Princeton University Press, 2000.

Dorman, Jacob S. *Chosen People: The Rise of American Black Israelite Religions*. New York: Oxford University Press, 2013.

Dorsey, Peter A. *Sacred Estrangement: The Rhetoric of Conversion in Modern American Autobiography*. University Park: Pennsylvania State University Press, 1993.

Dudziak, Mary L. *Cold War Civil Rights: Race and the Image of American Democracy*. Princeton, N.J.: Princeton University Press, 2000.

Dulles, Avery. *A Testimonial to Grace*. New York: Sheed and Ward, 1946.

Du Mez, Kristin Kobes. *Jesus and John Wayne: How White Evangelicals Corrupted a Faith and Fractured a Nation*. New York: Liveright, 2020.

Dunne, Matthew W. *A Cold War State of Mind: Brainwashing and Postwar American Society*. Amherst: University of Massachusetts Press, 2013.

Dyer, Richard. *Stars*. London: Educational Advisory Service, British Film Institute, 1979.

Early, Gerald Lyn, ed. *The Sammy Davis, Jr. Reader*. New York: Farrar, Straus and Giroux, 2001.

Eastman, Max. *Reflections on the Failure of Socialism*. New York: Devin-Adair, 1955.

Eig, Jonathan. *Ali: A Life*. Boston: Houghton Mifflin Harcourt, 2017.

Ellis, John Tracy. *American Catholicism*. 2nd ed., rev. Chicago: University of Chicago Press, 1969.

Erikson, Erik. *Childhood and Society*. New York: W. W. Norton, 1950.

———. *Young Man Luther: A Study in Psychoanalysis and History*. New York: W. W. Norton, 1958.

Erzen, Tanya. *Straight to Jesus: Sexual and Christian Conversions in the Ex-gay Movement*. Berkeley: University of California Press, 2006.

Eskridge, Larry. *God's Forever Family: The Jesus People Movement in America.* Oxford: Oxford University Press, 2013.

Fessenden, Tracy. *Culture and Redemption: Religion, the Secular, and American Literature.* Princeton, N.J.: Princeton University Press, 2007.

Fischbach, Michael. *Black Power and Palestine: Transnational Countries of Color.* Stanford, Calif.: Stanford University Press, 2019.

Fisher, James Terence. *The Catholic Counterculture in America, 1933–1962.* Chapel Hill: University of North Carolina Press, 2001.

FitzGerald, Frances. *The Evangelicals: The Struggle to Shape America.* New York: Simon and Schuster, 2017.

Fleming, John V. *The Anti-Communist Manifestos: Four Books That Shaped the Cold War.* New York: W. W. Norton, 2009.

Fosdick, Harry Emerson. *On Being a Real Person.* New York: Harper and Brothers, 1943.

Franchot, Jenny. *Roads to Rome: The Antebellum Protestant Encounter with Catholicism.* Berkeley: University of California Press, 1994.

Frankl, Razelle. *Televangelism: The Marketing of Popular Religion.* Carbondale: Southern Illinois University Press, 1987.

Friedman, Andrea. *Citizenship in Cold War America: The National Security State and the Possibilities of Dissent.* Amherst: University of Massachusetts Press, 2014.

Friedman, Lawrence Jacob. *Identity's Architect: A Biography of Erik H. Erikson.* New York: Scribner, 1999.

Fromm, Erich. *Escape from Freedom.* New York: Farrar and Rinehart, 1941.

Furlong, Monica. *Merton: A Biography.* Rev. ed. Liguorni, Mo.: Liguorni, 1995.

Gamson, Joshua. *Claims to Fame: Celebrity in Contemporary America.* Berkeley: University of California Press, 1994.

Gaston, K. Healan. *Imagining Judeo-Christian America: Religion, Secularism, and the Redefinition of Democracy.* Chicago: University of Chicago Press, 2019.

George, Carol V. R. *God's Salesman: Norman Vincent Peale and the Power of Positive Thinking.* New York: Oxford University Press, 1993.

GhaneaBassiri, Kambiz. *A History of Islam in America: From the New World to the New World Order.* New York: Cambridge University Press, 2010.

Giroux, Robert. *The Letters of Robert Giroux and Thomas Merton.* Notre Dame, Ind.: University of Notre Dame Press, 2015.

Gitlow, Benjamin. *I Confess: The Truth about American Communism.* New York: E. P. Dutton, 1940.

Goldstein, Eric L. *The Price of Whiteness: Jews, Race, and American Identity.* Princeton, N.J.: Princeton University Press, 2006.

Gomez, Michael A. *Black Crescent: The Experience and Legacy of African Muslims in the Americas.* Cambridge: Cambridge University Press, 2005.

Gooren, Henri Paul Pierre. *Religious Conversion and Disaffiliation: Tracing Patterns of Change in Faith Practices*. New York: Palgrave Macmillan, 2010.

Graebner, William. *Patty's Got a Gun: Patricia Hearst in 1970s America*. Chicago: University of Chicago Press, 2008.

Graham, Billy. *How to Be Born Again*. Waco, Tex.: Word Books, 1977.

Greenberg, Cheryl Lynn. *Troubling the Waters: Black-Jewish Relations in the American Century*. Princeton, N.J.: Princeton University Press, 2006.

Griffith, R. Marie. *Moral Combat: How Sex Divided American Christians and Fractured American Politics*. New York: Basic Books, 2017.

Hadden, Jeffrey K., and Charles E. Swann. *Prime Time Preachers: The Rising Power of Televangelism*. Reading, Mass.: Addison-Wesley, 1981.

Halle, Louis J. *The Cold War as History*. New York: Harper and Row, 1967.

Halttunen, Karen. *Confidence Men and Painted Women: A Study of Middle-Class Culture in America, 1830–1870*. New Haven, Conn.: Yale University Press, 1982.

Hammond, Sarah Ruth. *God's Businessmen: Entrepreneurial Evangelicals in Depression and War*. Edited by Darren Dochuk. Chicago: University of Chicago Press, 2017.

Hangen, Tona J. *Redeeming the Dial: Radio, Religion and Popular Culture in America*. Chapel Hill: University of North Carolina Press, 2002.

Hankins, Barry. *Jesus and Gin: Evangelicalism, the Roaring Twenties, and Today's Culture Wars*. New York: Palgrave Macmillan, 2010.

Harline, Craig. *Conversions: Two Family Stories from the Reformation and Modern America*. New Haven, Conn.: Yale University Press, 2011.

Harris, Dianne Suzette. *Little White Houses: How the Postwar Home Constructed Race in America*. Minneapolis: University of Minnesota Press, 2013.

Hassan, Steven. *Combatting Cult Mind Control*. Rochester, N.Y.: Park Street, 1988.

Hatch, Nathan O. *The Democratization of American Christianity*. New Haven, Conn.: Yale University Press, 1989.

Hauser, Thomas. *Muhammad Ali: His Life and Times*. New York: Simon and Schuster, 2006.

Hawkins, Ann Hunsaker. *Archetypes of Conversion: The Autobiographies of Augustine, Bunyan, and Merton*. London: Associated University Presses, 1985.

Haygood, Wil. *In Black and White: The Life of Sammy Davis, Jr.* New York: Knopf, 2003.

Haynes, Bruce. *The Soul of Judaism: Jews of African Descent in America*. New York: New York University Press, 2018.

Hayward, Steven F. *The Age of Reagan: The Conservative Counterrevolution, 1980–1989*. New York: Crown Forum, 2009.

Hedstrom, Matthew S. *The Rise of Liberal Religion: Book Culture and American*

Spirituality in the Twentieth Century. New York: Oxford University Press, 2013.

Heinze, Andrew R. *Jews and the American Soul: Human Nature in the Twentieth Century*. Princeton, N.J.: Princeton University Press, 2004.

Henle, Faye. *Au Clare de Luce: Portrait of a Luminous Lady*. New York: S. Daye, 1943.

Herman, Ellen. *The Romance of American Psychology: Political Culture in the Age of Experts*. Berkeley: University of California Press, 1995.

Herzog, Jonathan P. *The Spiritual-Industrial Complex: America's Religious Battle against Communism in the Early Cold War*. New York: Oxford University Press, 2011.

Heyrman, Christine Leigh. *American Apostles: When Evangelicals Entered the World of Islam*. New York: Hill and Wang, 2015.

———. *Southern Cross: The Beginnings of the Bible Belt*. Chapel Hill: University of North Carolina Press, 1998.

Hilliard, David, and Lewis Cole. *This Side of Glory: The Autobiography of David Hilliard and the Story of the Black Panther Party*. Boston: Little, Brown, 1993.

Hindmarsh, D. Bruce. *The Evangelical Conversion Narrative: Spiritual Autobiography in Early Modern England*. Oxford: Oxford University Press, 2005.

Hiss, Tony. *Laughing Last: Alger Hiss*. Boston: Houghton Mifflin, 1977.

Hitchens, Christopher. *God Is Not Great: How Religion Poisons Everything*. New York: Twelve, 2007.

Hobson, Fred C. *But Now I See: The White Southern Racial Conversion Narrative*. Baton Rouge: Louisiana State University Press, 1999.

Horowitz, Roger. *Kosher USA: How Coke Became Kosher and Other Tales of Modern Food*. New York: Columbia University Press, 2016.

Hutchison, William R. *Religious Pluralism in America: The Contentious History of a Founding Ideal*. New Haven, Conn.: Yale University Press, 2003.

Hyde, Douglas. *I Believed*. New York: Putnam, 1950.

Igo, Sarah E. *The Averaged American: Surveys, Citizens, and the Making of a Mass Public*. Cambridge, Mass.: Harvard University Press, 2007.

Illouz, Eva. *Saving the Modern Soul: Therapy, Emotions, and the Culture of Self-Help*. Berkeley: University of California Press, 2008.

Jacobson, Matthew Frye. *Roots Too: White Ethnic Revival in Post–Civil Rights America*. Cambridge, Mass.: Harvard University Press, 2006.

Jacobson, Matthew Frye, and Gaspar González. *What Have They Built You to Do? The Manchurian Candidate and Cold War America*. Minneapolis: University of Minnesota Press, 2006.

Jacoby, Susan. *Alger Hiss and the Battle for History*. New Haven, Conn.: Yale University Press, 2009.

————. *Strange Gods: A Secular History of Conversion.* New York: Vintage Books, 2017.

Jelks, Randal Maurice. *Faith and Struggle in the Lives of Four African Americans: Ethel Waters, Mary Lou Williams, Eldridge Cleaver and Muhammad Ali.* New York: Bloomsbury Academic, 2019.

Jenkins, Philip. *Mystics and Messiahs: Cults and New Religions in American History.* Oxford: Oxford University Press, 2000.

Johnson, David K. *The Lavender Scare: The Cold War Persecution of Gays and Lesbians in the Federal Government.* Chicago: University of Chicago Press, 2004.

Johnson, Paul E. *A Shopkeeper's Millennium: Society and Revivals in Rochester.* New York: Hill and Wang, 1978.

Joseph, Peniel E. *Waiting 'til the Midnight Hour: A Narrative History of Black Power in America.* New York: Henry Holt, 2006.

Kaufman, David. *Jewhooing the Sixties: American Celebrity and Jewish Identity; Sandy Koufax, Lenny Bruce, Bob Dylan, and Barbra Streisand.* Waltham, Mass.: Brandeis University Press, 2012.

Kernodle, Tammy L. *Soul on Soul: The Life and Music of Mary Lou Williams.* Boston: Northeastern University Press, 2004.

Kertzer, David I. *The Pope and Mussolini: The Secret History of Pius XI and the Rise of Fascism in Europe.* New York: Random House, 2014.

Kessler, Lauren. *Clever Girl: Elizabeth Bentley, the Spy Who Ushered in the McCarthy Era.* New York: HarperCollins, 2003.

Killen, Andreas. *1973 Nervous Breakdown: Watergate, Warhol, and the Birth of Post-sixties America.* New York: Bloomsbury, 2006.

Kimmage, Michael. *The Conservative Turn: Lionel Trilling, Whittaker Chambers, and the Lessons of Anti-Communism.* Cambridge, Mass.: Harvard University Press, 2009.

King, Charles. *Gods of the Upper Air: How a Circle of Renegade Anthropologists Reinvented Race, Sex, and Gender in the Twentieth Century.* New York: Doubleday, 2019.

King, John Owen. *The Iron of Melancholy: Structures of Spiritual Conversion in America from the Puritan Conscience to Victorian Neurosis.* Middletown, Conn.: Wesleyan University Press, 1983.

Kruse, Kevin Michael. *One Nation under God: How Corporate America Invented Christian America.* New York: Basic Books, 2015.

Kutler, Stanley I. *The Wars of Watergate: The Last Crisis of Richard Nixon.* New York: Knopf, 1990.

Lane, Christopher. *Surge of Piety: Norman Vincent Peale and the Remaking of American Religious Life.* New Haven, Conn.: Yale University Press, 2016.

Langone, Michael D. *Recovery from Cults: Help for Victims of Psychological and Spiritual Abuse.* New York: W. W. Norton, 1993.

Leavitt, Sarah A. *From Catharine Beecher to Martha Stewart: A Cultural History of Domestic Advice*. Chapel Hill: University of North Carolina Press, 2002.

Lee, Charles. *The Hidden Public: The Story of the Book-of-the-Month Club*. Garden City, N.Y.: Doubleday, 1958.

L'Engle, Madeleine. *A Wrinkle in Time*. New York: Farrar, Straus and Giroux, 1963.

Lewis, C. S. *The Screwtape Letters*. 1942. Reprint, New York: HarperCollins, 2001.

Lichtman, Robert M., and Ronald Cohen. *Deadly Farce: Harvey Matusow and the Informer System in the McCarthy Era*. Urbana: University of Illinois Press, 2008.

Liebman, Joshua Loth. *Peace of Mind*. New York: Simon and Schuster, 1946.

Lifton, Robert Jay. *Thought Reform and the Psychology of Totalism: A Study of "Brainwashing" in China*. New York: W. W. Norton, 1961.

Lipsyte, Robert. *An Accidental Sportswriter: A Memoir*. New York: Ecco, 2011.

Lofton, Kathryn. *Consuming Religion*. Chicago: University of Chicago Press, 2017.

———. *Oprah: The Gospel of an Icon*. Berkeley: University of California Press, 2011.

Marable, Manning. *Malcolm X: A Life of Reinvention*. New York: Viking, 2011.

Marcus, Sharon. *The Drama of Celebrity*. Princeton, N.J.: Princeton University Press, 2019.

Marqusee, Mike. *Redemption Song: Muhammad Ali and the Spirit of the Sixties*. London: Verso, 1999.

Marr, Timothy. *The Cultural Roots of American Islamicism*. Cambridge: Cambridge University Press, 2006.

Marshall, P. David. *Celebrity and Power: Fame in Contemporary Culture*. Minneapolis: University of Minnesota Press, 1997.

Martin, Lerone A. *Preaching on Wax: The Phonograph and the Shaping of Modern African American Religion*. New York: New York University Press, 2014.

Massa, Mark Stephen. *Catholics and American Culture: Fulton Sheen, Dorothy Day, and the Notre Dame Football Team*. New York: Crossroad, 1999.

Matusow, Harvey. *False Witness*. New York: Cameron and Kahn, 1955.

May, Gary. *Un-American Activities: The Trials of William Remington*. New York: Oxford University Press, 1994.

McAlister, Melani. *Epic Encounters: Culture, Media, and US Interests in the Middle East, 1945–2000*. Berkeley: University of California Press, 2001.

McAvoy, Thomas Timothy. *Roman Catholicism and the American Way of Life*. Notre Dame, Ind.: University of Notre Dame Press, 1960.

McCarraher, Eugene. *Christian Critics: Religion and the Impasse in Modern American Social Thought*. Ithaca, N.Y.: Cornell University Press, 2000.

McGrail, Peter. *The Rite of Christian Initiation: Adult Rituals and Roman Catholic Ecclesiology*. Burlington, Vt.: Ashgate, 2013.

McGreevy, John T. *Catholicism and American Freedom: A History*. New York: W. W. Norton, 2003.

McLeod, Yanela G. *The Miami Times and the Fight for Equality: Race, Sport, and the Black Press, 1948–1958*. Lanham, Md.: Lexington Books, 2019.

Melley, Timothy. *Empire of Conspiracy: The Culture of Paranoia in Postwar America*. Ithaca, N.Y.: Cornell University Press, 2000.

Melnick, Jeffrey. *A Right to Sing the Blues: African Americans, Jews, and American Popular Song*. Cambridge, Mass.: Harvard University Press, 1999.

Merton, Thomas. *The Seven Storey Mountain*. New York: Harcourt Brace, 1948.

Merwin, Ted. *In Their Own Image: New York Jews in Jazz Age Popular Culture*. New Brunswick, N.J.: Rutgers University Press, 2006.

Michaeli, Ethan. *The Defender: How the Legendary Black Newspaper Changed America; From the Age of the Pullman Porters to the Age of Obama*. Boston: Houghton Mifflin Harcourt, 2016.

Mihm, Stephen. *A Nation of Counterfeiters: Capitalists, Con Men, and the Making of the United States*. Cambridge, Mass.: Harvard University Press, 2007.

Miller, Steven P. *The Age of Evangelicalism: America's Born-Again Years*. New York: Oxford University Press, 2014.

Mills, C. Wright. *White Collar: The American Middle Classes*. New York: Oxford University Press, 1951.

Moore, Deborah Dash. *At Home in America: Second Generation New York Jews*. New York: Columbia University Press, 1981.

———. *GI Jews: How World War II Changed a Generation*. Cambridge, Mass.: Belknap Press of Harvard University Press, 2004.

———. *To the Golden Cities: Pursuing the American Dream in Miami and L.A.* New York: Free Press, 1994.

Morris, Sylvia Jukes. *Price of Fame: The Honorable Clare Boothe Luce*. New York: Random House, 2014.

———. *Rage for Fame: The Ascent of Clare Boothe Luce*. New York: Random House, 1997.

Mott, Michael. *The Seven Mountains of Thomas Merton*. Boston: Houghton Mifflin, 1984.

Mullen, Lincoln A. *The Chance of Salvation: A History of Conversion in America*. Cambridge, Mass.: Harvard University Press, 2017.

Murch, Donna Jean. *Living for the City: Migration, Education, and the Rise of the Black Panther Party in Oakland, California*. Chapel Hill: University of North Carolina Press, 2010.

Najmabadi, Afsaneh. *Professing Selves: Transsexuality and Same-Sex Desire in Contemporary Iran*. Durham, N.C.: Duke University Press, 2014.

Newman, John Henry. *Apologia pro vita sua.* Edited and with an introduction by I. T. Ker. Penguin Classics. New York: Penguin Books, 1994.

Nisbet, Robert A. *The Quest for Community: A Study in the Ethics of Order and Freedom.* New York: Oxford University Press, 1953.

Nock, Arthur Darby. *Conversion: The Old and the New in Religion from Alexander the Great to Augustine of Hippo.* Baltimore: Johns Hopkins University Press, 1998.

Numbers, Ronald. *Prophetess of Health: Ellen G. White and the Origins of Seventh-Day Adventist Health Reform.* Rev. ed. Knoxville: University of Tennessee Press, 1992.

O'Brien, John A. *The Road to Damascus: The Spiritual Pilgrimage of Fifteen Converts to Catholicism.* Garden City, N.Y.: Doubleday, 1949.

———. *The White Harvest: A Symposium on Methods of Convert Making.* New York: Longmans, Green, 1927.

———. *Winning Converts: A Symposium on Methods of Convert Making for Priests and Lay People.* New York: P. J. Kenedy and Sons, 1948.

Olmsted, Kathryn S. *Red Spy Queen: A Biography of Elizabeth Bentley.* Chapel Hill: University of North Carolina Press, 2002.

Oppenheimer, Daniel. *Exit Right: The People Who Left the Left and Reshaped the American Century.* New York: Simon and Schuster, 2016.

Orsi, Robert A. *History and Presence.* Cambridge, Mass.: Belknap Press of Harvard University Press, 2016.

O'Toole, James M. *The Faithful: A History of Catholics in America.* Cambridge, Mass.: Belknap Press of Harvard University Press, 2010.

Payne, Les, and Tamara Payne. *The Dead Are Arising: The Life of Malcolm X.* New York: W. W. Norton, 2020.

Peale, Norman Vincent. *A Guide to Confident Living.* New York: Prentice-Hall, 1948.

Pearsall, Sarah M. S. *Polygamy: An Early American History.* New Haven, Conn.: Yale University Press, 2019.

Perlstein, Rick. *Nixonland: The Rise of a President and the Fracturing of America.* New York: Scribner, 2008.

Peterson, Theodore. *Magazines in the Twentieth Century.* 2nd ed. Urbana: University of Illinois Press, 1964.

Plant, Rebecca Jo. *Mom: The Transformation of Motherhood in Modern America.* Chicago: University of Chicago Press, 2010.

Ponce de Leon, Charles L. *Self-Exposure: Human-Interest Journalism and the Emergence of Celebrity in America, 1890–1940.* Chapel Hill: University of North Carolina Press, 2002.

Prell, Riv-Ellen. *Fighting to Become Americans: Jews, Gender, and the Anxiety of Assimilation.* Boston: Beacon, 1999.

Preston, Andrew. *Sword of the Spirit, Shield of Faith: Religion in American War and Diplomacy*. New York: Knopf, 2012.

Price, Jay M. *Temples for a Modern God: Religious Architecture in Postwar America*. New York: Oxford University Press, 2013.

Raboteau, Albert J. *Slave Religion: The "Invisible Institution" in the Antebellum South*. Oxford: Oxford University Press, 1978.

Rambo, Lewis R. *Understanding Religious Conversion*. New Haven, Conn.: Yale University Press, 1993.

Raymond, Emilie. *Stars for Freedom: Hollywood, Black Celebrities, and the Civil Rights Movement*. Seattle: University of Washington Press, 2015.

Reeves, Thomas C. *America's Bishop: The Life and Times of Fulton J. Sheen*. San Francisco: Encounter Books, 2001.

Remnick, David. *King of the World: Muhammad Ali and the Rise of an American Hero*. New York: Random House, 1998.

Reumann, Miriam G. *American Sexual Character: Sex, Gender, and National Identity in the Kinsey Reports*. Berkeley: University of California Press, 2005.

Riebling, Mark. *Church of Spies: The Pope's Secret War against Hitler*. New York: Basic Books, 2015.

Riesman, David. *The Lonely Crowd: A Study of the Changing American Character*. 1950. New Haven, Conn.: Yale University Press, 1967.

Riley, Kathleen L. *Fulton J. Sheen: An American Catholic Response to the Twentieth Century*. Staten Island, N.Y.: St. Pauls/Alba House, 2004.

Rischin, Moses. *The Promised City: New York's Jews 1870–1914*. Cambridge, Mass.: Harvard University Press, 1962.

Robbins, Thomas. *Cults, Converts, and Charisma: The Sociology of New Religious Movements*. London: Sage, 1988.

Roberts, Randy, and Johnny Smith. *Blood Brothers: The Fatal Friendship of Muhammad Ali and Malcolm X*. New York: Basic Books, 2016.

Rodgers, Daniel T. *Age of Fracture*. Cambridge, Mass.: Belknap Press of Harvard University Press, 2011.

Rogin, Michael. *Blackface, White Noise: Jewish Immigrants in the Hollywood Melting Pot*. Berkeley: University of California Press, 1996.

Rojek, Chris. *Celebrity*. London: Reaktion Books, 2001.

Rolsky, L. Benjamin. *The Rise and Fall of the Religious Left: Politics, Television, and Popular Culture in the 1970s and Beyond*. New York: Columbia University Press, 2019.

Roof, Wade Clark. *Spiritual Marketplace: Baby Boomers and the Remaking of American Religion*. Princeton, N.J.: Princeton University Press, 1999.

Rosswurm, Steven. *The FBI and the Catholic Church, 1935–1962*. Amherst: University of Massachusetts Press, 2009.

Rout, Kathleen. *Eldridge Cleaver*. Boston: Twayne, 1991.

Schäfer, Axel R. *Countercultural Conservatives: American Evangelism from the Postwar Revival to the New Christian Right*. Madison: University of Wisconsin Press, 2011.

Schickel, Richard. *Intimate Strangers: The Culture of Celebrity*. Garden City, N.Y.: Doubleday, 1985.

Schrecker, Ellen. *Many Are the Crimes: McCarthyism in America*. Boston: Little, Brown, 1998.

Schultz, Kevin Michael. *Tri-faith America: How Catholics and Jews Held Postwar America to Its Protestant Promise*. New York: Oxford University Press, 2011.

Sehat, David. *The Myth of American Religious Freedom*. New York: Oxford University Press, 2016.

Shadegg, Stephen C. *Clare Boothe Luce: A Biography*. New York: Simon and Schuster, 1970.

Sharlet, Jeff. *The Family: The Secret Fundamentalism at the Heart of American Power*. New York: HarperCollins, 2008.

Sheed, Wilfrid. *Clare Boothe Luce*. New York: Dutton, 1982.

Sheen, Fulton J. *Peace of Soul*. New York: Doubleday, 1949.

———. *Treasure in Clay: The Autobiography of Fulton J. Sheen*. San Francisco: Ignatius, 1993.

Simonds, Wendy. *Women and Self-Help Culture: Reading between the Lines*. New Brunswick, N.J.: Rutgers University Press, 1992.

Singer, Margaret Thaler, and Janja Lalich. *Cults in Our Midst*. San Francisco: Jossey-Bass, 1995.

Smith, Anthony Burke. *The Look of Catholics: Portrayals in Popular Culture from the Great Depression to the Cold War*. Lawrence: University Press of Kansas, 2010.

Snorton, C. Riley. *Black on Both Sides: A Racial History of Trans Identity*. Minneapolis: University of Minnesota Press, 2017.

Sorett, Josef. *Spirit in the Dark: A Religious History of Racial Aesthetics*. New York: Oxford University Press, 2016.

Spence, Lester K. *Knocking the Hustle: Against the Neoliberal Turn in Black Politics*. Brooklyn: Punctum Books, 2015.

Stahl, Ronit Y. *Enlisting Faith: How the Military Chaplaincy Shaped Religion and State in Modern America*. Cambridge, Mass.: Harvard University Press, 2017.

Staub, Michael E. *Torn at the Roots: The Crisis of Jewish Liberalism in Postwar America*. New York: Columbia University Press, 2002.

Stephens, Randall J. *The Devil's Music: How Christians Inspired, Condemned, and Embraced Rock 'n' Roll*. Cambridge, Mass.: Harvard University Press, 2018.

———. *The Fire Spreads: Holiness and Pentecostalism in the American South*. Cambridge, Mass.: Harvard University Press, 2010.

Stevens, Jason W. *God-Fearing and Free: A Spiritual History of America's Cold War*. Cambridge, Mass.: Harvard University Press, 2010.

Streatfeild, Dominic. *Brainwash: The Secret History of Mind Control*. London: Hodder and Stoughton, 2006.

Sundquist, Eric J. *Strangers in the Land: Blacks, Jews, Post-Holocaust America*. Cambridge, Mass.: Belknap Press of Harvard University Press, 2005.

Susman, Warren I. *Culture as History: The Transformation of American Society in the Twentieth Century*. New York: Pantheon, 1984.

Sutton, Matthew Avery. *Aimee Semple McPherson and the Resurrection of Christian America*. Cambridge, Mass.: Harvard University Press, 2007.

———. *American Apocalypse: A History of Modern Evangelicalism*. Cambridge, Mass.: Harvard University Press, 2014.

Svonkin, Stuart. *Jews against Prejudice: American Jews and the Fight for Civil Liberties*. New York: Columbia University Press, 1997.

Swartz, David R. *Moral Minority: The Evangelical Left in an Age of Conservatism*. Philadelphia: University of Pennsylvania Press, 2012.

Tanenhaus, Sam. *Whittaker Chambers: A Biography*. New York: Random House, 1997.

Taylor, Ula Y. *The Promise of Patriarchy: Women and the Nation of Islam*. Chapel Hill: University of North Carolina Press, 2017.

Toobin, Jeffrey. *American Heiress: The Wild Saga of the Kidnapping, Crimes and Trial of Patty Hearst*. New York: Anchor Books, 2017.

Urban, Hugh B. *New Age, Neopagan, and New Religious Movements: Alternative Spirituality in Contemporary America*. Berkeley: University of California Press, 2015.

U.S. Congress. House. Committee on Un-American Activities. *Hearings before a Subcommittee of the Committee on Un-American Activities on H.R. 4422 and H.R. 4581, Public Law 601 (Section 121, Subsection Q(2)), Proposed Legislation to Curb or Control the Communist Party of the United States*. 80th Cong., 2nd sess., 1948. Washington: Government Printing Office, 1948.

Vaca, Daniel. *Evangelicals Incorporated: Books and the Business of Religion in America*. Cambridge, Mass.: Harvard University Press, 2019.

Van Zandt, David E. *Living in the Children of God*. Princeton, N.J.: Princeton University Press, 1991.

Von Eschen, Penny M. *Race against Empire: Black Americans and Anticolonialism, 1937–1957*. Ithaca, N.Y.: Cornell University Press, 1997.

Wacker, Grant. *America's Pastor: Billy Graham and the Shaping of a Nation*. Cambridge, Mass.: Harvard University Press, 2014.

———. *Heaven Below: Early Pentecostals and American Culture*. Cambridge, Mass.: Harvard University Press, 2001.

Wall, Wendy. *Inventing the "American Way": The Politics of Consensus from the*

New Deal to the Civil Rights Movement. Oxford: Oxford University Press, 2008.

Wangerin, Ruth. *The Children of God: A Make-Believe Revolution?* Westport, Conn.: Bergin and Garvey, 1993.

Warnke, Mike. *The Satan-Seller.* Plainfield, N.J.: Logos International, 1972.

Webb, Clive. *Fight against Fear: Southern Jews and Black Civil Rights.* Athens: University of Georgia Press, 2001.

Weinstein, Allen. *Perjury: The Hiss-Chambers Case.* New York: Random House, 1997.

Weinstein, Allen, and Alexander Vassiliev. *The Haunted Wood: Soviet Espionage in America—the Stalin Era.* New York: Random House, 1999.

Weisenfeld, Judith. *New World A-coming: Black Religion and Racial Identity during the Great Migration.* New York: New York University Press, 2016.

Wenger, Tisa Joy. *Religious Freedom: The Contested History of an American Ideal.* Chapel Hill: University of North Carolina Press, 2017.

White, Deborah G. *Lost in the USA: American Identity from the Promise Keepers to the Million Mom March.* Urbana: University of Illinois Press, 2017.

White, G. Edward. *Alger Hiss's Looking-Glass Wars: The Covert Life of a Soviet Spy.* Oxford: Oxford University Press, 2004.

White, Heather. *Reforming Sodom: Protestants and the Rise of Gay Rights.* Chapel Hill: University of North Carolina Press, 2015.

Whitehead, Andrew L., and Samuel L. Perry. *Taking America Back for God: Christian Nationalism in the United States.* New York: Oxford University Press, 2020.

Whitfield, Stephen J. *The Culture of the Cold War.* 2nd ed. Baltimore: Johns Hopkins University Press, 1996.

Whyte, William H. *The Organization Man.* New York: Simon and Schuster, 1956.

Wilentz, Sean. *Bob Dylan in America.* New York: Doubleday, 2010.

Woods, Robert. *Evangelical Christians and Popular Culture: Pop Goes the Gospel.* Santa Barbara, Calif.: Praeger, 2013.

Wright, Lawrence. *Going Clear: Scientology, Hollywood, and the Prison of Belief.* New York: Knopf, 2013.

Wu, Judy Tzu-Chun. *Radicals on the Road: Internationalism, Orientalism, and Feminism during the Vietnam Era.* Ithaca, N.Y.: Cornell University Press, 2013.

Young, Kevin. *Bunk: The Rise of Hoaxes, Humbug, Plagiarists, Phonies, Post-Facts, and Fake News.* Minneapolis, Minn.: Graywolf, 2017.

Young, Neil J. *We Gather Together: The Religious Right and the Problem of Interfaith Politics.* New York: Oxford University Press, 2016.

Young, Shawn David. *Gray Sabbath: Jesus People USA, the Evangelical Left, and the Evolution of Christian Rock*. New York: Columbia University Press, 2015.

Zeitz, Joshua. *White Ethnic New York: Jews, Catholics, and the Shaping of Postwar Politics*. Chapel Hill: University of North Carolina Press, 2007.

Zeligs, Meyer A. *Friendship and Fratricide: An Analysis of Whittaker Chambers and Alger Hiss*. New York: Viking, 1967.

Index

Ahmadiyya movement, 125–26

Ali, Muhammad (Cassius Clay, Cassius X), 3, 11, 120, 121–42, 176–77; as brainwashed, 3, 121–22, 130–32, 141–42; and draft, 139–41; as heavyweight champion, 121, 140–41; name change to, 121, 123, 133–34. *See also* Nation of Islam

Ali, Noble Drew, 125–26

antiauthoritarianism, 167

Atkins, Susan, 143–45, 168–70, 172–73

authenticity, 11, 77; and conversion, 3–4, 7–8, 105; and democracy, 14, 68; and evangelicals, 146, 172–74; and ex-Communists, 57–58; and Jewish identity, 92–93, 102, 107, 116, 119, 177; lack of, 65, 91; and mass culture, 30–32; and mind control, 7, 151; and politics, 11, 44, 58, 119, 175–79; and popular advice, 71, 73, 76, 178; psychology of, 69–71; and race, 91, 92–93, 102, 126; and Roman Catholics, 13, 34, 38, 42; and Zionism, 115–16

authoritarianism, 89; and Communism, 5, 37; and government, 42, 67, 69; and religion, 2, 35–36, 143, 151; and *Thought Reform*, 90

"authoritarian personality," 7, 151

Authoritarian Personality, The (Adorno et al.), 69

Bentley, Elizabeth, 44, 47–51, 61, 196n12. *See also* informant system

bisexuality, 49, 60, 172. *See also* sexuality

Black freedom movement. *See* civil rights movement

Black Power, 93, 114, 117, 119, 138, 147

brainwashing: and Muhammad Ali, 121–22, 130–32, 141–42; and authentic faith, 179; and Communism, 3; and "cults," 143–45; and The Family, 151–52; and Patricia Hearst, 143, 150–51; and International Society for Krishna Consciousness, 148–50; and prisoners of war, 68–69, 87–90; and prison ministries, 171. *See also* captivity; mind control

Britt, May, 102, 108, 111, 113

Buckley, William F., 56, 58–59, 175

Budenz, Louis: and Elizabeth Bentley, 49, 51; and conversion, 25, 44–46, 67, 84–85, 196n8; as government informant, 46–47, 78; and marriage, 61; and self-transformation, 59. *See also* informant system

Budenz, Margaret, 46, 49

Burnham, James, 59

captivity, 9, 87–89, 131, 150, 171, 172, 179; and television, 67. *See also* mind control

Carter, Jimmy, 146, 181

celebrity, 187–88n3

Chambers, Whittaker: at Columbia, 197n32; as Communist, 61–62; and conversion, 11, 55, 57, 65,

Chambers, Whittaker (*continued*) 67–68, 84, 197n23; and depression, 63, 152; as ex-Communist, 43–44, 176; family background of, 59–61; and Alger Hiss, 2–3, 51–56; and sexuality, 54–56, 61–63, 65–66, 197n20; and *Witness*, 56–64

Children of God. *See* The Family

Christian Broadcasting Network, 158

Christian nationalism, 80, 178, 188n4

The Christophers, 24–25, 38

Church of Jesus Christ of Latter-day Saints (LDS), 70, 81, 199–200n33, 200n34

civil rights movement, 112–18, 122, 132–33, 139–42

Cleaver, Eldridge, 145–47, 165–68, 170–71, 173–74

Cohn, Roy, 79, 83

Colson, Charles "Chuck": and *Born Again* (book, film, and comic book), 146, 158–62, 165, 208n26; and Eldridge Cleaver, 168; and conversion, 3, 11, 145, 154–56, 161; and evangelical politics, 147, 163, 165, 176; as Nixon's "hatchet man," 152–56; and prison ministries, 162–63, 170–71

Communism, 2, 44–47, 52–54, 61–62, 77–79, 166–67; faith as antidote to, 14, 68; as false religion, 45, 62, 68–69; rejection of, 32–34, 43–44, 46–47, 173–74. *See also* Marxism

conversion: of Muhammad Ali, 121, 127–35; and anticolonialism, 138–40; and anti-Communism, 1–2, 24, 32–33, 43–47, 57; of Susan Atkins, 143, 168–69; of Elizabeth Bentley, 49–51; as "born again," 146–47, 156–57, 171; of Louis Budenz, 45–46; of Whittaker Chambers, 55, 60,

65–66; as choice, 9–10, 163–65; of Eldridge Cleaver, 166–68, 173–74; of Chuck Colson, 152–56, 158–62; to Communism, 44–45, 58–59; and "cults," 143–45; of Sammy Davis Jr., 92–93, 104–9, 111; definitions of, 8–9, 187n2, 189n13; of Avery Dulles, 28; of Bob Dylan, 171–72; and evangelicals, 145–47, 151–52, 157–58, 167–73; of Larry Flynt, 171; history of, 9–11; of Jews, 95–96; to Judaism, 94–96; of Clare Boothe Luce, 1–2, 12–13, 20–21, 29–34; of Harvey Matusow, 81; of Claude McKay, 29; and mind control, 70–71; of Marilyn Monroe, 94–96; to Nation of Islam, 122–27, 132–33; and Max Nussbaum, 99–101, 106–7; patriotism and, 67–68; and political truth, 62–63; popular representations of, 4; prison as a site of, 162–63, 165–66, 169–70; and racial politics of Israel, 100–102; and racial politics of United States, 91, 102–3, 111–15, 122–25, 133–34, 139–40, 167–68; to Roman Catholicism, 24–26, 28–29, 190n1, 192n24, 192n25; and self-help, 178–78; and Fulton Sheen, 1, 12–13, 20–23, 45–46, 49, 51, 99; suspicion of, 1–2, 34–40, 70–71, 130–31, 141, 172; of Elizabeth Taylor, 94–95, 99–102; of Mike Warnke, 169–70; of Mary Lou Williams, 29–30; and Zionism, 99–102, 115–17, 139. *See also* authenticity; brainwashing; missionaries

Crossman, Richard, 44–45

"cults," 91, 143–45; and "deprogramming," 149–50, 170, 172; and evangelicals, 3, 145–46, 151–52; and Nation of Islam, 123–24; and

Satanism, 169–70. *See also* brainwashing; captivity; The Family; International Society for Krishna Consciousness

Curtis, Tony, 92, 104

Davis, Sammy, Jr.: and authenticity, 8, 177; and May Britt, 102, 111; career of, 103–4, 203nn36–37; criticism of, 3, 111–12; and humor, 112–14; and Israel, 115–17, 204nn42–43; and Judaism, 11, 92–93, 104–10, 203nn31–32; and politics, 93, 112, 114–15, 117–19. *See also* Israel; Jim Crow laws; Nixon, Richard; *Simpsons, The*

democracy: and anti-Communism, 17–18, 43–45, 47–48, 57–59, 68; and anti-Islamic ideas, 124; and authentic faith, 68; and capitalism, 6, 16, 66, 174; and Christianity, 38, 42, 47, 64, 66, 67–68, 174, 176; and civil rights, 6; and Cold War, 5, 13, 58, 68, 87, 120; and cultural anthropology, 72; and Judeo-Christian ethos, 4–5; and Nation of Islam, 122; and progressive politics, 77; and religious conversion, 1–2, 119–20, 179; and Roman Catholicism, 13–14, 16, 20, 22–24, 26, 28, 30, 37–38; and sexuality, 47–48, 66

Dos Passos, John, 58–59

Dulles, Avery, 28–29, 193n31

Dylan, Bob, 94, 146, 171–72

Eastman, Max, 59

Ebony, 106, 108–9, 110, 130

ecumenism, 4–5, 14, 39, 58, 114, 176. *See also* "Judeo-Christian" ethos

Eisenhower, Dwight D., 28, 58, 76

Erikson, Erik, 7, 71–72. *See also* identity; psychology

evangelicalism, 145–48, 156–63, 167–68, 172–74, 176; and mass culture, 7, 37, 75–77, 146–47, 168, 172; and sexual violence, 159, 168–70; and television, 146–47, 156, 158, 167–68, 172–73

Falwell, Jerry, 158, 168, 174

The Family, 151–52, 154–56, 207n12

family magazines, 4, 28–31; and evangelicals, 158; and Kinsey Report, 48; and Nation of Islam, 123; and psychology, 71. *See also* *Ebony*; mass culture; *McCall's*

Farrakhan, Louis, 138

Federal Bureau of Investigation (FBI), 43–44, 46–47, 51, 55, 64–65, 78–80, 167, 196n8, 196n12; and COINTELPRO, 64. *See also* informant system

Fisher, Eddie, 95, 99–102, 106, 119

Flynt, Larry, 171–72

Fosdick, Harry Emerson, 73

freedom of conscience: and Muhammad Ali, 121–22, 136; and democracy, 5–6, 35, 68; and Roman Catholicism, 35

free will: and conversion, 9; and Patricia Hearst, 150; and mass culture, 88–89; and racism, 91

Fromm, Erich, 69, 73, 76, 90. *See also* social scientists

GI Joe, 15, 18–19

Graham, Billy, 7, 24, 37, 75–76, 146, 156–59

Hare Krishna. *See* International Society for Krishna Consciousness

Hearst, Patricia, 143, 148, 150–51, 152

Herberg, Will, 57–59, 63

heterosexuality: in *Born Again*, 159–60, 162; in *Child of Satan, Child of God*, 169; and Christianity, 44, 46–47, 174; and Cold War, 87; and ex-gay ministries, 172; and

heterosexuality (*continued*)
  respectability, 46–47, 49, 132,
  147; and sex appeal, 26, 49; in
  Soul on Ice, 166; and white Christian identity, 147–48; in *Witness*,
  61. *See also* sexuality
Hiss, Alger: defense of, 65–66; allegations against, 51–54, 64–65;
  sentencing of, 56; sexuality of,
  54–55, 65, 196–97n18; trials of, 2,
  44, 52–56, 198n38; and *Witness*,
  62–63
homophobia, 2, 55, 65–66, 88, 176.
  See also sexuality
homosexuality. *See* same-sex desire
House Un-American Activities
  Committee (HUAC), 43, 46–47,
  55, 62, 99. *See also* Chambers,
  Whittaker
Howe, Irving, 63

identity: and brainwashing, 139–40;
  and Jewishness, 93, 100–103, 107,
  110–19, 177; and mass culture,
  7; of Harvey Matusow, 77–85;
  and mistrust, 69–71, 77, 150; and
  politics, 138–39, 174, 177–78; and
  popular advice, 73–77; psychology of, 69, 71–72; and race, 70,
  91, 107, 111–19, 121–22; and religion, 2, 7–9, 66, 73–77, 130, 137,
  147–48; and sexuality, 3, 66, 70;
  social science of, 72–73
imposture, 3, 70, 176
informant system, 44–52, 67–68,
  77–79, 81–84. *See also* Bentley,
  Elizabeth; Budenz, Louis; Federal Bureau of Investigation;
  Matusow, Harvey
interfaith alliances. *See* ecumenism
interfaith marriage, 95–96, 102
International Society for Krishna
  Consciousness (ISKCON), 145,
  148–50
Israel: and Jewish identity, 100–

102, 115–17, 139; and Latter-day
  Saints, 81–82, 200nn33–34; and
  military actions, 93, 115–17, 138;
  and philanthropy, 102, 111

Jencks, Clifton, 79–80, 83
Jim Crow laws, 6, 85, 102–3, 113,
  115–17
Judaism, 2, 11, 81, 92–120; and
  anti-Black racism, 102–20; and
  Black Israelites, 110; depictions
  of, 95–96; efforts to hide identification with, 94; public fascination with, 94–95; and sexuality,
  96–103
"Judeo-Christian" ethos, 5–6, 14,
  93–94, 114, 188n5. *See also*
  democracy

Keller, James, 24–25, 41
Kinsey, Alfred, 48–49
Korean War, 85–87, 135; and pris-
  oners of war, 7, 67, 68, 87–89, 150

Leigh, Janet, 92, 104
Liebman, Joshua Loth, 73–75
Liston, Sonny, 121–23, 128, 131, 136
Luce, Clare Boothe, 1–2, 7, 12–42,
  74, 130, 152, 175, 195n51; article
  in *McCall's* by, 2, 20, 29–34,
  191n11; conversion of, 26–34;
  criticisms of, 35–40; death of, 42,
  175; depression of, 18; and Gerald
  Heard, 41–42; and LSD, 41–42;
  and Thomas Merton, 40–42
Luce, Henry, 2, 14–16, 30–31

Malloy, Father Joseph I., 13, 37–39
Manchurian Candidate (book and
  film), 89–90, 131, 141
"Manchurian candidates." *See*
  brainwashing
Marxism, 7, 33, 57–58, 166, 176,
  191n11
masculinity, 13, 54, 88, 105, 128–29,